Contents

WHERE THERE'S LIFE

Kathleen Dayus

Published by VIRAGO PRESS Limited 1985
20–23 Mandela Street, London NW1 0HQ

Reprinted 1986, 1989

British Library Cataloguing in Publication Data

Dayus, Kathleen
  Where there's life.
  1. Labour and labouring classes—England—
Birmingham (West Midlands)   2. Birmingham (West
Midlands, England)—Social life and customs
  I Title
  942.4'96083'0924   DA690.B6

ISBN 0–86068–623–X

Typeset by J & L Composition,
Filey, N Yorks
Printed in Finland by Werner Söderström Oy,
a member of Finnprint

Preface

One Christmas, in about 1970, I stayed with my daughter Jean and her family in Acocks Green, and we were sitting around the fire, each telling stories of what had happened in our lives, when all at once my youngest granddaughter, Christina, said, 'Tell us about your young days, Nan, when you were a little girl.'

'Well,' I replied, 'I didn't have such lovely presents as you today. Ours were an apple, an orange and a few nuts in our stocking, if we were lucky. I remember when we often had to beg for food outside factories with no boots on our feet in all kinds of weather, and sing outside the pub for a halfpenny or pennies to buy Christmas treats.'

'I can't believe that, our Nan,' she said.

Jean replied, 'It's quite true. Your Nan told us about the old days as soon as me and my sisters and brother came home from Dr Barnardo's homes. And why we were sent there.'

'I'll tell you more when you're older,' I said, 'but this is not the time or place.'

'You should write a book, our Nan.'

'I will one day,' I replied.

And when I got home, after that lovely Christmas time, I thought to myself, yes, why not write about my life.

I began writing in a school exercise book, which I took years to complete. Then I shut it away in my bedroom drawer. In 1975 when Christina was fifteen she asked me if she could read it on the understanding that I should have it back. Eventually she let her teacher read it; she was married to a young historian, John Rudd, who also read it. I was surprised when John rang me to have a talk. He said it should not be put away, that it should be read by people of later generations, so that they could find out what went on in those bad old days and how we had to survive on the *real* poverty line, through hardship and many diseases.

The book, *Her People* was published in 1982. It was all a wonderful experience, and one I shall never forget. I met the Lord Mayor and Lady Mayoress of Birmingham, I signed over 300 books at Lewis's Department store, and in March 1983 I had to go to the Festival Hall in London to receive the J. R. Ackerley Award for Biography. Thanks to everyone. Then, the following year, Central Television did a television version of the book called 'A Baker's Dozen'.

My book has brought me much joy and happiness in my late years. I am now eighty-two. Neighbours and old friends came to congratulate me on my success. I met many people from my childhood, and nieces and nephews and cousins I didn't know I had! I also met many great grandmothers like myself, and many of my school friends, including Mary Steele, who lived in Albion Street; her brother, who is Churchwarden to St Paul's Church where we all played round the tombstones; Lillian Price, from Pope Street; and dozens more. There is one playmate I shall always remember: Matilda Brooks, or Tilly as she was known, who lived at 13 Camden Drive. I hope if she reads my books she'll still remember the stories we used to tell about hop-picking, and how my brother Jack stole the farmer's pig and hid it in the cellar, and the court case that followed, and my Granny in her Salvation Army frock and bonnet, demanding attention, and how my Mum stole a hare, and thought it was a rabbit, and later how she won her black eye.

I must give my many thanks to my wonderful daughters Jean and Kathleen; to Clem and Nora Lewis from the *Birmingham Post* and *Mail*, to my grandchildren and great-grandchildren, to many friends from my bowling club, to many neighbours, to the girls of Virago Press, and to John Rudd and his wife Pat and my granddaughter Christina, without whose help my book would never have come to life.

Where There's Life is my second book, and tells the story of my life from 1914 to 1945. I will be eighty-three next year, and if the Good Lord spares me a few more years, I will try to finish my third book, on my life from 1945 to the present day.

Kathleen Dayus, 1985

1

Granny's Funeral

It was a cold, wet, wintry day in November 1913 when the undertaker brought the coffin with Granny inside it to our house. Before he arrived Mum made us children bustle about making the place 'spic an' span' to create a better impression on the visitors who were expected to drop by to pay their last respects to the memory of a notable local character. I was then aged ten and we lived in a 'yard' of back-to-back cottages in the Jewellery Quarter of Birmingham. My brother Frankie and sister Liza were a little older than I was, so perhaps it was for this reason that I seemed to end up doing most of the chores. I didn't mind; it kept my thoughts off morbid fancies about Granny in her wooden box. The house was buzzing from early in the morning. Mary, my eldest sister, had taken the day off work and had washed the curtains but for lack of time to dry them properly had hung them back up wet. The blinds were drawn to darken our downstairs room where the coffin rested on the table in front of the range. My oldest brothers Jack and Charlie had turned up and were shuffling about, getting in everyone's way, and Dad lit the candles so that the flickering glow shed an eerie light. My attention was attracted by Granny's big black eyes staring down from her photograph on the wall. To my childish imagination it seemed as if she was still alive to what was happening and was show-ing her disapproval. I hadn't noticed this picture much while she was alive, but now she was dead it seemed as if her eyes sparkled with the same vitality that they had appeared to possess when I had seen her lying cold on her straw mattress a few days earlier.

Granny had been living with us for some time. She was a contrary old woman and a match even for our Mum, with whom she was continually arguing. She was Dad's mother and I suppose there was a certain amount of rivalry between them. So it was little surprise to me when one evening after a skirmish Mum had blown up at Dad with more than her normal vehemence.

'I can't stand any mower of 'er. She 'ave ter goo,' she stormed as soon as he got through the door. As usual he tried to smooth things over, but Mum was adamant.

'I mean it this time. I can't stand 'er. If 'er don't goo, I goo!'

Looking back with seventy years' hindsight, Dad might have been wiser to have accepted this offer, but things were different before the First World War and couples might quarrel and argue all their married life as Mum and Dad did but rarely separated and never divorced. As bad luck would have it, just as Mum was shouting, Granny walked in and surprised them.

'What's all the row about? 'Ave yer med up yer minds ter be rid of me?' she demanded. Dad must have recognised the inevitable so he began gently.

'Polly an' me think it's best fer yer ter go ter yer own 'ouse now it's ready,' he told her firmly. Granny had originally come to stay with us while her house was being fumigated but that had been months before and there was no excuse for her to continue living in our overcrowded home. But I could see he looked sad as he added, 'I think it'll be fer the best fer all of us.'

'Oh!' she cried, beginning to gesticulate as she did when excited and then to square up like a boxer. She did calm down shortly, though.

'I know when I ain't wanted. No, I can 'elp meself.'

She turned round and stormed out and I followed her as she marched down the street to Mr Kiniver's 'hire shop' where you could rent a horse and cart for two hours for one shilling. The boy in the stable said that Mr Kiniver was out at a funeral and was not expected back until late.

'Can't wait!' Granny told him. 'I want a loan of one of the 'orses and a cart, now.'

The lad was obviously frightened and backed away from her.

'Giss yer shillin' then,' he managed to mumble. He came forward warily and took the coin she offered and then he went off to one of the stables to fetch the horse and cart. I was glad when we were able to leave that yard. It reeked of wet straw and stale horse manure, and the old nag the lad fetched smelled sweaty. The flat cart was none too clean but Granny didn't seem to mind and was only anxious for the horse to be hitched to it. When this was accomplished she took the reins and walked the old horse down the street. This was by no means an easy feat and she soon attracted an interested audience who speculated loudly about her intentions.

'Where's 'Annah gooin'?' asked one of another.

'I bet yer that Polly's told 'er ter goo,' said another.

'Where's 'er got that old nag from? It oughta be in the knacker's yard,' exclaimed a third.

As they gossiped noisily I followed Granny who was pulling the reluctant animal towards our house. The horse's hooves and the iron cart rims made a terrible clatter on the cobble-stones but at last silence fell as she came to a halt outside our door. The neighbours and their children crowded around to see what was going on and to hear the conversation between Granny and Dad.

'There's no need to get that old nag, mother,' he said. 'I would 'ave helped yer move yer trunk and chair if yer'd waited.' He spoke quietly, but Granny wanted to create a scene.

'Get me things on the cart,' she ordered him loudly.

Dad went indoors and brought out her belongings and placed them as she directed. He looked sad and I knew he didn't want her to leave but I also knew that he hated the constant uproar of quarrelling, so what was he to do? All he wanted was a bit of peace and quiet.

'Well, I'm off now,' she yelled and glared round at the neighbours with her finger on her nose. Then she tried to heave herself up onto the driving seat but couldn't manage without Dad's help. However, when he tried to assist her she pushed him away indignantly.

'I don't need any 'elp from yow. I can get meself up.' And she did, by pulling herself up backwards.

Dad returned to the house but I remained to watch her, seated now erect and looking proud, whip in one hand and reins in the other, for all the world the expert driver as she prepared to move off.

'Gee up now,' she cried, clicking her tongue at the old mare. But she just turned her head and stared at Granny.

'Gee up! Gee up!' she repeated but it was no good, the horse stood still.

Crowds were gathering by now, and many were laughing with amusement. Granny paid them no heed. She reserved her temper for the horse. She yanked the reins and brought the whip down hard upon its bony rump. The toothless old mare only turned her head and gave Granny what seemed like a horsey laugh too.

Granny decided to dismount which she did with some difficulty on account of having to keep her frock pulled down to hide her torn drawers. Once on the ground again she tried pulling the horse, but still it would not budge an inch. At that moment I spotted Jonesy, the son of a neighbour, throw a stone which caught the animal on the rump and caused it to rear up. Jerking the reins out of Granny's hand, it galloped off, leaving Granny standing in the road waving the whip and cursing.

She appealed to the onlookers for help. I would have given anything to have been able to do something, particularly since nobody else seemed interested in assisting, but Granny was a difficult person to help and I was young and afraid of horses. Then Mr Mitchell the muffin man came to the rescue. He jumped off his cart which was nearby and ran after the runaway. He soon had it back with Granny's belongings intact, and I could hardly believe my ears and eyes when I heard her thank him and allow him to lift her back onto the driver's seat, in gratitude for which she kissed him on the cheek. At this Mr Mitchell may have regretted his generosity for he coloured, but nothing could stop Granny when she wanted to create a drama.

'Yer'll be all right now mother, off yer goo.' He gave the horse a gentle slap and the old grey mare, the cart, Granny and her possessions went slowly on their way. However, before she'd gone many yards she recollected herself and turned to the bystanders.

'Yer a lotta nosey parkers. Yow'll never goo ter 'eaven. None on yer!'

I watched her go with sadness in my heart because I felt for some inexplicable reason that I would never see Granny again.

When I returned indoors Dad asked me if Granny had got off all right. I thought he looked upset, so I didn't mention the pantomime I had just witnessed and instead offered to make him a cup of tea. He nodded and returned to his chair while I stoked the fire.

'I want yow and Frankie ter pay yer Granny a visit every Sunday and let me know how she is. Do you understand?' he said, and I replied that I would.

However, each time we called she wouldn't answer the door although we could see the curtain move so we knew she was at home. I told Dad and suggested that if he called she would open up, but he said, 'No. I don't think so. She'll come round if she wants anything.'

So our house got back to normal and our life carried on as before. Then one cold afternoon later that winter when we were all huddled round the fire for warmth from the snow falling outside, Dad sighed, looked at his mother's photo and said, 'I wonder how yer Granny is faring in this cold weather?'

'Perhaps you could take her a lump of coal in yer cart, Katie?' he suggested.

'Goo on then get yer coat on,' Mum told me. Dad said I should wait until it stopped snowing so hard, so I watched from the window, and before very long it did ease and I was sent down the cellar for the fuel. One lump Mum told me to fetch. But I thought to myself, I'll take two when she isn't looking, which I did. Dad saw what I had done but he covered the coal with an old sack, winked and whispered, 'Good girl.'

Mum had a habit, whenever she sent me any distance on an errand, of insisting that I had clean bloomers on, 'in case yer get knocked down by a 'orse', which was why I was scared of them. But for some reason she forgot on this occasion and I did not stop to remind her.

Granny lived about half a mile away, in a narrow street with drab shops dotted between the houses, which were one down and two up, like ours. I was walking down the street, singing happily to myself, when I was startled to hear the sound of hooves on the cobbles. The first thought that came to me was that I hadn't got my clean bloomers on. I looked round to see how far away the horse was and saw there were two galloping towards me. I ran onto the pavement, dragging my cart after me. There was a wet fish shop just there and in my eagerness to escape I darted in. But the floor was wet and I slid along before colliding with a slab of sprats, cod and ice which showered over me. I began to cry. I couldn't pick the fish up because they were slippery and eluded my grasp, and when I tried to stand up I'd slip back again amongst the icy cold debris. I had just succeeded in sitting upright when the fishmonger appeared.

'What yer think yer doing down there?' he asked, looking at me quizzically. I was frightened and began to sob.

'I'm very sorry but I'm afraid of horses and my Mum forgot to change my bloomers,' I blurted out in confusion.

'Well I never!' he exclaimed, laughing. 'I've 'eard some things in my life but that beats 'em all.'

And with that he bent over and lifted me to my feet and told me to be off, which I did not need to be told twice to do.

A few minutes later I arrived at Granny's where I found a crowd of people outside her door. In the middle of them were Mrs Phipps and Mrs Taylor, our neighbours, sitting on the step crying. I couldn't tell what was happening so I asked them to move so I could take the coal into Granny's house.

'Yower Granny won't need that where 'er's gone to,' Mrs Phipps said.

'Where's she gone to then?' I asked, wondering what she meant.

'She's dead. Don't yer Mum know? Everybody else does,' Mrs Taylor replied.

'That's right. She's 'ad 'er chips this time,' Mrs Phipps added.

'I don't believe yer,' I exclaimed.

'Come 'an see fer yerself. I'll tek the coal.' And so saying she helped herself.

I didn't want to go in. I was so shocked I just turned tail and ran home as fast as I could. I stumbled across the threshold but before I could say anything Mum shouted at me, 'Where 'ave yow bin all this time? An' what yer cryin' for now?'

'Granny's eaten some chips and now she's dead,' I stammered, tears dripping off my nose.

'What yer talkin' about? An' where's that lump of coal?' she yelled, shaking me.

'Mrs Phipps took it. She said Granny wouldn't need it where she was going.'

'Oh! She did, did she? Well, we'll see about that.'

She slapped Dad's flat cap on the top of her bun and marched out of the house. She thought more about losing the coal to Mrs Phipps than about Granny, it seemed to me then, but I expect it was the shock that caused her to react in that way. She wanted me to accompany her but I hung back, afraid that she'd find out that I had taken two lumps of coal, and Dad had gone out, so he was not there to protect me.

'Come on. An' don't 'ang back theea. An' bring yer cart along with yer. I might need it fer summat else beside the coal.'

I snatched up my doll, Topsey, and laid her in the cart and ran after Mum who was half way down the street before I caught her up. I was confused and still worried that there might be horses and that I had not changed my bloomers which were wet from where I had fallen in the icy fish. When we arrived at Granny's house Mrs Phipps and Mrs Taylor were still standing outside gossiping with the neighbours. Mum went straight up to Mrs Phipps and demanded to know what she meant by saying Granny had had her chips.

'She's dead Polly. I come in this mornin' to see if she wanted anythink, an' there she was, stiff an' cold.'

This made me shudder but I was brought back to my own worries when I heard Mum demand that she gave the lump of coal back. At that Mrs Phipps began to back away from Mum's fierce stare.

'Oh, I forgot about that. Now she wunt want it will she?'

'No, she wunt, will she,' mimicked Mum. 'Well goo on 'an fetch it.' Mum was insistent.

I watched and held my breath, but to my relief she only brought one lump out of her bag, and that the smallest of the two, which she gave to me and I put it quickly into my cart.

Granny's neighbours were still looking on, watching for further developments, because they all knew Mum's temper. But Mum just gave them one of her black looks and elbowed her way past the two women and went into Granny's house. I followed and peered round. Everything was so still and quiet and there was dust everywhere. I wondered why this should be when Granny was so particular, but I was soon roused from my thoughts by Mum.

'Katie, I want yer ter stay 'ere with yer Gran while I goo out an' get Mrs Taylor. An' don't let anybody in. I don't trust 'em.'

To make doubly sure of this she turned the key in the lock as she went out. At this I was more frightened than ever. Granny was seated in her rocking chair facing the fireplace, but her back was to me and I could only see the paper curlers she had in her hair. There was something strange about these and they seemed to scare me though I could not take my eyes away. I put my hands over my eyes to shut out my fears: I'd never seen a dead person before. But after a bit my curiosity got the better of me and I spread my fingers slowly to peep through. Then I crept forward to look at Granny. I wished I hadn't. I started back petrified. Granny was staring at me with her eyes wide open. I never wanted my Mum so much in my life as I did at that moment. I wanted to run out and scream, but Mum had the key and all I could do was stand stock still, listening to the thumping of my heart. I literally jumped for joy when I heard that key turn in the lock and saw Mum and Mrs Taylor enter with another woman. As they banged the door shut, the vibration set Granny's chair rocking and I put my hands over my eyes. But Mum wouldn't have that.

'Yer don't 'ave ter look if yer don't wanta,' she said sharply, pulling them away.

'We're gooin' ter tek 'er upstairs an' lay 'er out,' she said.

I felt safer now that they'd arrived and I was curious to see what she meant by 'laying out'. So, avoiding Granny's staring eyes, I watched Mum, Mrs Taylor and the big-bosomed woman they called Aggie lift Granny with some effort out of her chair and up the creaky stairs. I stood engrossed by this until I heard the rocking chair creak behind me, and at that I scampered up after them. They stripped off Granny's clothes and then washed her all over. Then Aggie dressed Granny in a brown calico shift which she had brought with her. Then they laid her back on the straw mattress and covered her with a sheet. When this had been done they made to go downstairs again, but I was in front of them going down two at a time. Mum flopped into Granny's chair, heaved a sigh and exclaimed, 'My God, she was 'eavier dead than alive.' And her companions nodded in agreement.

Then Mum thanked them and said she would pay them later for their trouble and invited them to the funeral. Then she showed them to the door. When they had gone I was surprised to see her lock the door again. Then she returned upstairs with me close behind. We entered the room and Mum began to look round, but my eyes were drawn to the bed. I let out a shriek. The sheet had slipped off Granny's face and I was horrified to see that her eyes were still open.

'What's the matter with yer now?' she demanded, shaking me.

'I want to go home.' My voice was trembling now.

'Get outa me way. An' wait,' she muttered irritably, pushing me to one side.

I walked over and looked out of the window into the yard below where several of the neighbours were looking up at me. They must have heard my scream. I couldn't look at them; nor could I look back into the room. I wanted to run away, and if that window had not been so high I believe I would have jumped through it. But I turned round and watched what Mum was doing, avoiding looking at the bed. Then Mum went over and I gazed on as she replaced the sheet and

9

then rolled Granny onto her side and began feeling under the mattress. At last she found what she'd been looking for. It was a small, battered tin money-box. She opened it and took out several half crowns, silver threepenny pieces and some pennies. There were some faded letters but she wasn't interested in those and shoved them back in the tin, unopened. Then, pocketing the money, she placed the box back underneath the straw mattress and rolled Granny onto her back again.

I squatted on the stool at the foot of the bed while Mum searched the drawers, from one of which she pulled a bottle of gin. She consumed the contents quickly before replacing it as she had the box. Amongst the assorted contents of the other drawers she found another small box. Her eyes lit up when she opened it and found it full of farthings. These she slipped in her pocket, then she tidied the stuff away. As she was poking about for more loot I glanced back at Granny and saw that the sheet had moved again.

'Mum, Granny's watching you,' I sobbed.

'Don't be silly. It's only the sheet that's slipped. I'll soon fix that.'

And with that she took two of Granny's pennies from her pocket, put her fingers on Granny's eyes to push her eyelids down and placed a penny over each eye.

'That'll keep 'em shut,' she said with satisfaction and replaced the sheet.

At last she stopped searching and said, 'Come on, there's nothing mower 'ere.' But I was already fleeing downstairs to the door.

When we emerged we found the neighbours still standing around discussing what had happened, but Mum just pushed her way through them without a word. However, we hadn't gone more than a few yards when she stopped and turned around.

'Where's the cart with the coal in? Yer betta goo back an' fetch it. 'Ere's the key,' she said, fumbling in her pocket.

I stood and looked at her, petrified. I could no more return to that house alone than face the devil.

'No! No! No!' I screamed and ran off down the street.

10

I turned to look back once but Mum was nowhere to be seen. When I got in I found the house was empty and the fire nearly out. I felt so miserable. I was cold and wet. I pulled down my damp bloomers and changed them for a warm, dry pair that were hanging on the line over the fire. Then I just sat on the floor and wept for Granny, and for myself.

When I recovered myself and controlled my weeping, my attention was attracted by Granny's photograph hanging over the mantelshelf. She seemed to be glaring down at me with her deep-set, black eyes. I thought about the chips that Mrs Phipps had spoken of and remembered that I had nearly choked on them once. No more chips for me, I vowed. I didn't want to die like Granny had. I was deep in such thoughts when I heard Mum's unmistakable heavy tread coming towards the door. I thought, I'm for it now, but all she said when she'd bustled in and taken the coal from the cart, was, "Ere yar. Tek 'old a this an' mek tha fire up before yer Dad comes in.'

I was only too happy to be busy breaking the coal up with the hammer, pulling out the drawer pan and stoking up the fire with the bellows. Soon Dad returned. I could tell immediately by the look on his face that he knew about Granny, for news travelled fast in our district and nothing was secret for long. I ran over to him.

'Dad!' I cried. 'Granny died from eating chips. Mrs Phipps said so. Shall I die too?'

'No,' he replied. 'It's just a saying.'

'How did she die then?' I asked.

'She was just getting old,' he said sadly.

Now I was talking to Dad I wanted to tell him about how Mum and I had found Granny and what wicked things Mum had done, but I knew Mum's eyes were on me so I thought better of it. Whether she ever told what she'd found I never discovered, but for my own part I only wanted to forget the whole frightening incident. But I never did. That episode has lived with me all my life.

When Dad had eaten his tea I heard him ask Mum if she'd kept the payments up on the insurance policy.

'Course I have,' she told him.

11

I knew this was right because every Saturday I had the job of taking the insurance book and sixpence along the street to the insurance agent's house. Mum didn't believe in paying any premiums for herself, though. 'Why should I waste a penny a week? I shan't be 'ere ter spend it,' she always said.

No matter how Dad tried to explain the principles of insurance to her she didn't want to know. That was how she was. She always looked at every farthing twice before parting with it.

Later, when Frankie and Liza, my brother and sister, came in from playing I told them the sad news, but they didn't seem very upset. This was no surprise: neither of them cared much for Granny.

Mum got me to reach down a tall vase from the mantelshelf. From this she drew the policy and with its lots of pawn tickets. I was given the job of going to fetch the agent, but Dad offered to go and so I went with him. When we got to his house we found he was out so Dad poked a message under his door. Then he told me to go back home and explain to Mum.

'Aren't you coming back with me, Dad?' I asked, surprised that he was leaving me.

'No, I'm going down to the pub,' he answered and he wiped a tear away from his eye.

I felt very sorry for him then. If I'd been older and known the words to comfort him... But I was only a child, so I just stood and watched him out of sight and turned reluctantly to deliver his message.

When I entered our room I found Mum had down two more vases and was sorting out a pile of pawn tickets. Some she discarded and threw into the fire, others she kept.

'I'll be able ter get some of these things out,' she mumbled. 'An' I must set a good table for the funeral.'

Just then there was a knock on the door. Mum lifted the corner of the curtain and peeped out to see who it was. It was Mrs Jonesy, Mrs Phipps and Mrs Taylor.

'An' what der yow three wanta borra?' she inquired sarcastically.

'Can we speak to yer, Polly?' Mrs Phipps asked, ignoring her last question.

Mum opened the door to them. 'Well? Spake up then.'

'We're very sorry about poor 'Annah passin' on, so we thought we 'ad better come to pay our respects.' They stood there with their aprons to their eyes. But Mum knew them for crafty rogues and she hadn't forgotten the coal. She probably knew too that they had been none too fond of Granny when she'd been alive. She made to close the door on them when Mrs Phipps added, 'We're gooin' from dower to dower ter get a collection up for a few flowers. Is that all right with yow, Polly?'

'That's the least yer can do!' Mum replied and stared at them hard and long.

'Well,' Mrs Taylor said. 'We'll do our best, Polly.'

Then off they went but I had noticed that Mrs Taylor was really crying. I liked her. She was always kind to me and she was the only neighbour Mum could really trust.

When Dad returned he didn't speak a word to either of us. He just sat in his chair and gazed up at Granny's picture in its faded gilt frame.

'May God rest your soul, Mother,' I heard him say to himself at last. 'If only I'd 'elped you more you might still be 'ere.' And he put his face in his hands and sobbed. Mum went over and tried to console him but he pushed her gently from him. I suppose his grief was a personal thing which he could not share with anybody.

So that was how we came to be sitting in the darkened room with Granny's coffin on the table, waiting for the neighbours to come and show their last respects. I remember the undertaker asking if anyone wanted to see her before she was screwed down and the people filing past one by one, their heads bowed. Some shed real tears too. Some of them I had never seen before and some were there to satisfy their curiosity. Wreaths and flowers were piled up outside in the yard, waiting to be heaped on the coffin. I remember going upstairs while they were looking at the corpse and writing a note with trembling fingers. It went something like this:

Good bye Granny and God bless you. And please forgive my Mum.
I really did love you and so did my Dad. XXX

13

I rolled this message into a little ball and returned downstairs. Dad was still standing by the coffin and I whispered to him, 'Dad, can I have another look at my Granny?'

He nodded and turned away, and while the others' attention was elsewhere I put my hand down inside the coffin until I felt Granny's cold fingers. My stomach went all queer inside but I managed to push the message between her icy fingers and kiss her forehead before I pulled my hand away.

'Good bye, Granny, I'll try to be a good girl,' I sobbed before I stood back for the undertaker to screw down the lid.

I was pleased he hadn't seen the note or the tears that I left behind on my Granny's face. I wiped my eyes and felt a bit better, knowing that Granny was taking my message with her to heaven. Then I wandered outside to look at the wreaths and the Salvation Army Captain touched me on the shoulder.

'Katie, will you tell your father I'd like to speak to him?' he asked me.

'Yes,' I said. 'Will you come inside?'

I thought I ought to ask him. I could see the neighbours looking curiously at the big box he had with him. I heard him say to Dad how sorry he was about Sister Hannah and how he'd have liked to have seen her before she was screwed down. Then he handed the box over, saying, 'Here's the crocks I promised to lend your wife ... and some extra food. It's not much but it'll help.'

It was amazing how people did rally round at times like this. They didn't bother much at other times unless asked, and then they often had to think twice. But now the Captain was on his knees beside the coffin praying. When he'd finished he stood up and asked Dad the time of the funeral so, he said, he could be there with the other brothers and sisters and the band. Mum kept out of sight until he had left, then down the stairs she came, all dressed up in a long black taffeta dress, which rustled when she moved. She wore new black button-up boots and on her head was perched the largest black hat I had ever seen with a black bird on top.

'Now 'ow do I look, Sam?' she asked as she stood preening herself. Dad didn't take a bit of notice but Mary stared at her.

14

'Anyone would think you was going to a weddin' instead of a funeral,' she let out. 'Disgustin' I call it.'

I looked at Mum and thought if only she was as nice as she looked maybe all our lives would have been better. But I knew this was wishing for the impossible.

Mary was dressed as usual, for she always wore a black tam-o'-shanter and a black coat. Dad, Jack and Charlie just wore a black armband each with their Sunday suits, and I was dressed in a white lace dress with a wide black sash of silk ribbon. I also had real boots for the first time. I remember the argument there had been too between Mary and Mum over keeping her wages back that week.

'What about buying the kids some clothes?' Mary had said. 'Instead of spending all the insurance money on yerself.'

But Mum's reply had been, 'I'll see what I've got left when I've got the grub in.'

'I shouldn't bother yerself if I were you,' had come the reply. 'I'm keeping my wages to buy them some myself.'

So that was how I came to have a new dress and boots and a real ribbon for my hair instead of the usual string. She also bought Frankie new clothes and Liza too, but neither of them was able to attend the funeral: they both had bad colds. Liza had to stay in bed and Frankie was downstairs in front of the fire. Mum said he had to watch the house and the food in case anyone slipped in while we were out and helped themselves.

By this time there was quite a crowd gathered in our little room. There was Mr Phipps, Mr Jones, Mr Smith, the lamplighter and another of Dad's drinking pals, all having a drink and talking quietly. They were to be the pall-bearers. This was all new to me and interesting for that reason. I'd seen plenty of funerals, but this was the first I'd been involved in and I was fascinated by the splendid flowers and the well-groomed horses of the hearse and I forgot, for a moment, my fear. Anyway I had my clean bloomers on.

When we went out the sun had come out and the horses' coats shone like black silk. They were so different from the dustman's horses and those that pulled the water carts. Then the bearers carried the coffin out and the Salvation Army band

15

struck up with 'Nearer My God to Thee' just as we climbed into the carriage.

We passed along slowly so that the cortège could be seen and all could have a last look at the coffin. I looked through the window and there were people lined up on both sides of the street, the women with black aprons and the men with their caps and hats off, bared heads bowed as we passed. Even the dustcart and the draycart pulled over to one side. Shops had their blinds drawn down and the shopkeepers stood in their doorways as a mark of respect. I saw some of my school friends on tiptoe, straining their necks to see.

'Hello Katie,' Annie Buckley called out and waved.

'Hello Annie,' I called back from the half-open window.

At this my sister Mary slapped my face. 'Behave yerself,' she whispered. 'This is a funeral not a wedding.'

But this did not deter Mum who leaned out of the window. 'Some people 'ave got no respect for the dead.' Mary pulled her back from the window and closed it. She was obviously disgusted. 'You're as bad as the rest!' And after that no more was said. Dad sat there quietly throughout.

The church bell was tolling mournfully as the carriage entered the cemetery gate. We stopped outside the church door and the driver handed us down. There seemed to be crowds of people lined up on each side of the door and lots were already seated inside the church waiting for the coffin to enter. Just inside the vestibule there was coconut matting, and seeing this Mum looked about then began to wipe her feet. I thought she was never going to stop until I heard a woman say, 'I see 'er's still showin' off.'

At this Mum turned round and gave her a dirty look before she moved along with Dad, followed by the rest of us. However, it was obvious that she was intent on making a spectacle of herself. She wanted to be noticed in all her finery and as she walked up the aisle she kept stopping to give a little cough on the back of her hand and looking from side to side. Dad simply pushed her forward but I heard him whisper, 'Move along, yer 'olding up the service.' She moved but she still kept glancing about. She would touch her hair then fiddle with her hat and pretend to straighten her dress.

Everybody's eyes were on us, especially on Mum. Then I heard someone say, 'It's disgraceful the way she keeps standin' there preenin' 'erself.' Then another joined in. 'Who does she think she is? The Queen of Sheba?'

All at once people began 'shushing' and those who were not 'shushing' were commenting on Mum's behaviour. Finally Dad pulled her down into her seat. Then everyone fell silent as the preacher entered and the service began. When it was over we filed out to the accompaniment of the organ. It seemed all were anxious to see Granny's coffin lowered into the ground. There were people from everywhere in the district standing around that wet, muddy graveside that day. Some of them wept as the preacher opened up his prayer book and the coffin was gently lowered into the grave. He delivered a sermon during which everyone stood still, until he picked up a handful of earth and spoke in a deep voice: 'Ashes to ashes. Dust to dust.' Before he could continue little Jonesy chipped in: 'An' if God don't 'ave yer, the devil must.' All heads turned as his father gave him such a clip that he landed in the muddy, freshly dug grave behind him. The preacher held his hands together and looking skywards said, 'Forgive them Lord, for they know not what they do.' Then, walking away in disgust, he said, 'I've never come across such a disgraceful congregation in all the years I've given burial services.'

Jonesy was still struggling to get out of the grave, and this he managed only with his father's help, after falling back in once. By now some were laughing openly, but Mrs Jonesy did not think it was funny. She turned round angrily: 'It's no laughin' matter. We might 'ave 'ad another funeral,' she wept.

Then we were walking back towards the carriage, and as we passed I heard Mr Jonesy say to the preacher, 'I'll give 'im the devil when I get 'im 'ome.' But the preacher just walked slowly away, taking no notice of anyone.

When we arrived home Frankie was still sitting by the fire with a coat round his shoulders and Mrs Taylor was there in Mum's starched white apron ready to serve. Mum had given her permission to wear her pinafore. At that time it was a tradition that when someone in a family died there was always a bow of black ribbon draped over the top of their photograph frame. But we had had to make do with black crepe paper, which was the next best thing. It was also said that if the bow should move of its own accord after it had been draped it was a bad omen. While we had been out Mrs Taylor had placed the paper in position.

Then we squeezed round the table – Mum, Dad, the bearers, and several neighbours who had been 'helpful in her hour of need' as they called it. I had never seen such a mouth-watering display of food on our table. There was cheese, pickled onions, corned beef, cottage loaves, pig's pudding and even a gallon jug of ale. However, Mary, Jack and Charlie didn't stop but made the excuse that they had to go back to work. They left, and while the adults were talking and stuffing themselves, I picked up a piece of pig's pudding for Frankie who was still huddled by the fire. I found it was stale so I replaced it and was about to make him a corned beef sandwich when Dad asked, 'Where's Pete?'

'Who's Pete?' the lamplighter asked.

'Our cat. He's usually waiting here for scraps.'

All at once Frankie jumped up, knocking over the stool. 'Oh dear, oh dear!' He sounded worried. 'I forgot 'im, Dad. He went out in the rain and I put 'im in the oven to dry!'

'Yer what?' Dad gasped, dashing to the oven door.

Pete shot out with his hair standing on end like the bristles of a brush. This proved to be only a minor diversion and they quickly settled down to their food and drink again. Frankie did not escape though. Mum went over to him and delivered a hard slap then ordered him off to bed.

After they had consumed all they could the guests began to leave, saying what a good send-off Mum had given Granny. Mr and Mrs Jonesy apologised to Dad for their son's behaviour and promised that he would get 'what's comin' to 'im when we get 'ome'. After they had all left – Dad too – Mum hung Granny's death card beneath her picture then went off to join the others in the local. Now that the house was quiet I filled a plate with some of the leftover food and took it up to Frankie. I found him with Liza sitting on the edge of the bed fully dressed reading a comic.

'Have they all gone?' Liza asked.

'I thought you was ill.' I glared at her. But I suppose she had pretended to be ill because she didn't want to be at the funeral. I turned my attention to Frankie, who still looked pale but who insisted on going downstairs. We sat round the fire with our leftovers and I answered their questions about the day's events. Then I thought of a way to cheer them up.

'Tell yer what. I'll bring in some of the kids who were there and Jonesy can imitate the preacher.' To this they laughingly agreed.

I went into the yard, rounding up those I could find. I knew Mum and Dad would be out until late drowning their sorrows. The pubs didn't shut until eleven o'clock so we would have a good three hours' fun.

I had to go to the next yard to fetch Jonesy. I didn't like him much because he was a terrible liar but it wouldn't have been fun without him. I knocked on his door and when he answered I could tell from his face that he'd been crying. I told him our plan but he was none too eager until I told him we were going to play at funerals and that Frankie wanted him to imitate the preacher; then he came along at once.

When we were all seated in our kitchen Frankie wanted to know who was at the graveyard and what had happened.

'Well I'll tell yer what the bloke said if yer'll all be quiet,' said Jonesy.

With that he pulled Dad's shirt off the line, put it over his head and, pushing his arms through the sleeves, picked up the Bible which was on the sideboard.

'Ashes to ashes, dust to dust,' he intoned, just like the preacher had. We roared with laughter. Then he put his hands together and continued.

'Forgive them Father, for they know not what they do. But my Dad said, "I know what I'm gooin' ter do when I get 'im 'ome."' He changed into an imitation of his Dad. But Florrie Mitchell from the next yard was not convinced.

''E dain't say that did 'e?'

''E did!' he replied angrily. 'An' I've got the marks to prove it.'

With that he replaced the Bible, tore off the shirt and dropped his trousers. We could see the red marks when he bent over but that was not all we saw. We burst out giggling at the sight of his bare bottom and we were still tittering when the door burst open and Mrs Taylor entered. Seeing Jonesy she cried out, 'Pull yer trousers up yer dirty lad.' But he was out the door, tripping over them in his anxiety to avoid another whack.

'What d'yer want?' Liza asked in her surly way.

'Yer Mum asked me to call in and clear away the crocks and tek the chairs outside ready ter goo back ter the mission 'all.' Then she added, 'An' why ain't yer all in bed? Yer'll catch it if yer Mum knows yer've 'ad that Jonesy lad in.'

'I'll 'elp yer ter move the chairs if yer don't tell ower Mum,' pleaded Frankie.

'Very well then,' she conceded. 'But see that yer behave yerselves in future, or I might.'

We were happy helping Mrs Taylor tidy up. I liked her: she was different from the other women. She was always ready to do odd jobs for anyone in need.

She bustled round finishing her jobs and was just about to leave when she noticed that the crepe paper had slipped from Granny's frame. She stood on the stool and reached up to replace it, and when she stood back down again she bent over and whispered to me, 'That's a bad omen, luv. I should get up ter yer bed before there's any more trouble.' I was really scared at this. 'An' remember to be careful what yer say or do, fer yer Granny's eyes will be on yer in the future.' Then she went off.

I tried to remember what my sister Mary had said about ignoring old wives' tales and I tried to put them from my mind, but after that I often caught myself glancing at Granny's picture and it seemed to me that her black eyes came alive and followed me round the room.

2
Mary's Wedding

One day, a few weeks after Granny's funeral, Mary came home earlier than usual from work. I heard her tell Mum the news that she was getting married.

'Why dain't yer tell me before?' Mum said loudly.

'Yer don't 'ave ter shout so loud. I can 'ear yer. You knew I was getting wed. I told Dad weeks ago.'

'Yower like the rest on 'em,' Mum replied irritably. 'Yow tell yer Dad everythink but I'm the last to be told.'

'Oh be quiet and sit down,' Mary yelled back. 'I tell yer lots of things but you never even listen. You always say "shut up" or you've got no time or "tell me later". You aren't interested.'

I could see they were losing their tempers and I wished Dad would come home.

'Don't yer give me any of yer lip!' Mum started going red in the face. 'Yow ain't too old ter 'ave yer face slapped!'

I was afraid, waiting for Mum to raise her hand, but she did not move. Mary was no longer scared of Mum; she stood up to her and matched her temper.

'Strike me if you dare! I don't fear you any more. You can't push and slap me around like you do her,' she said, pointing her finger at me. 'But don't forget, she'll grow up one day too and then yer'll be sorry.'

Mum went quiet for a moment but then she started on Mary again.

'I suppose yower in the family way, is that it?'

'That's 'ow your dirty mind works. Yer'll 'ave ter write the date down and wait an' see won't yer?' Mary must have forgotten that Mum couldn't write.

They were still arguing when Dad came in.

'What's all the shouting about? I could 'ear yer 'alf way

21

down the street.' He loathed the constant uproar of our house and only wanted peace and quiet when he was in the house.

'It's 'er,' Mum told him, pointing at Mary. 'She wants ter get married.'

'Well, what about it?' Dad answered. 'She's old enough to make up 'er own mind.'

'But 'er Gran's only bin dead a few weeks. And I shall miss 'er wages when she goes,' moaned Mum.

'That's all yow ever think of,' Mary retorted. 'Money! Money! Money! Yer'll 'ave ter drink less beer then, won't yer.'

Dad put his hand on Mary's shoulder. 'Now, now Mary. You mustn't talk ter yer Mum like that. Anyway we'll try to manage. I'll put a few more hours in at work.' Mary shook her head, obviously upset, and rushed out into the yard. Dad followed her and I slipped out as well and heard him talking softly to her.

'Don't tek any notice of yer Mum's tantrums, Mary. You know she'll always 'ave the last word, so please come back and tell 'er yer sorry fer yer 'arsh words.'

'No, never,' she told him firmly. But Dad pleaded with her and this had its effect.

'All right,' she sulked. 'But only fer your sake, mind,' she told him.

So we went back in and things were patched up and Mum made a pot of tea and tried to make amends by promising to do her best to make the wedding the best in the district. However, Mary was still upset and sulking and wouldn't have any tea, and with a 'so long' to Dad she walked out, head held high, just like Mum.

I didn't want to stay so I followed her and asked if I could go along with her. After some hesitation she agreed, and taking my hand we went off to her young man's house. Albert his name was, and he greeted her with a kiss when he opened the door to us. He didn't give me so much as a glance. He only had eyes for Mary, especially as she immediately burst into tears.

'Now what's the trouble?' he asked, getting out a white handkerchief. When she'd finished telling him he went wild.

'You're not to go back to that place any more! An' I don't want anything from that house or yer mother,' he told her.

'But I've already bought the new bed, Albert,' she sobbed.

'Never mind about that. You can leave it. We're going to start afresh. My mother will take care of you while I get the house together,' he said, embracing her gently before taking us into the house.

Albert's father was a bookmaker and they were partners in the business. Sometimes Albert's mother helped with the book-keeping in a side room she called 'The Den'. She was a kind woman and whenever I called with a message she would sit me down and fetch me a biscuit or a glass of milk. They were a happy family and very hospitable, but Mary told me I was not to call too often or I would wear out my welcome. So I would walk down Mrs Lewis's street in the hope of bumping into her. Once I met her carrying several parcels and she called to me. I didn't answer at once, pretending to be surprised.

'Oh, hello, Mrs Lewis. Can I carry your parcels?' I asked her.

She smiled at me and gave me two small ones and I followed her to their house. She fumbled in her pocket for the key then let us in the side door. She was a smartly dressed woman, different from the other women in our district, but then she could afford to be because they were very comfortably off. She was generous, though, and helped anyone that was really in need – if she liked them, that is. Our Mum was not one of these and she knew it, but the knowledge didn't bother her; she couldn't care less whether she was liked or not.

I placed the parcels on the table and Mrs Lewis gave me a piece of cake and a penny. I thanked her and left after slipping the coin down my stocking for safe keeping.

When Mary came in from work the day after the row she told Mum that she and Albert had had a talk and that she was going to stay with his parents for a bit while Albert sorted out a house and furniture and the paraphernalia of married life.

'That's nice,' Mum said sarcastically. 'They can afford it with all the money they tek off people, can't they?'

Mary resisted the temptation to answer her back and after a moment's silence Mum continued.

'Yer won't want yer bed then, will yer Mary?' she spoke slyly.

'No, I won't. Albert's told me to leave it.'

This pleased Mum, until I made the mistake of asking Mary if I could sleep in it. Mum scowled at me when Mary said I could have it.

'Huh, we'll see!' Mum shrugged noncommittally.

I vowed to do anything to please Mum so I could have that bed, but I should have known better: it was impossible to please her. I went over to the range to get the kettle and make a pot of tea and listened to their conversation.

'When's the 'appy day then?' Mum asked.

'It'll be soon. I'll let yer know in plenty of time,' Mary answered.

'But yower gooin' ter get wed from 'ere, ain't yer?' Mum asked anxiously.

'Yes. That's the usual thing isn't it?' said Mary, gulping down her tea. I could see she wanted to leave and soon she pushed her chair back from the table and stood up to leave. But Mum put her hand on her arm.

'Will yer 'elp me out? Yer know what I mean. With a little money, so's I can give yer a decent wedding.'

Mary knew what she meant all right. She wanted to show off in front of the neighbours. Mary didn't want the wedding from our house, but she was prepared to concede to get away from Mum as quickly as possible. She even promised she would speak to Albert and see what could be done in the way of money. With that she lifted the latch, but before opening the door she turned to me and asked if I would like to go shopping with her.

'Can I, Mum?' I asked eagerly.

'I s'ppose so, but don't be back late,' she said grudgingly.

I was really glad to be going out with Mary instead of Mum; I don't think Mary had ever asked if she could take me with her before. We boarded a tram which was a treat on its own for me. Finally we got off in a street with enormous

24

shops with beautiful window displays: I could have stood gazing at them for hours, but Mary pulled me away. Liza and I had wanted to go into the big shops in New Street and Corporation Street for ages but we'd never dared to pass the attendant who stood in the doorway ready to shoo small children off. But I wasn't afraid now with my big sister, and while Mary tried on garments I stood gazing in awe at all the sumptuous clothes that hung in the display cases. I would have loved to touch them to see what they felt like but I could see out of the corner of my eye that I was being watched. So I sat down on a chair that stood by the counter and looked around the shop while waiting for Mary to emerge from behind the colourful painted screen where she was trying things on. I was fascinated by the nearly naked figures of ladies in different positions that were painted on it. Some wore only frilly drawers and black camisoles so you could see their bare thighs on which they wore fancy garters and sus-penders. It seemed quite shameless to me then but it would probably seem tame to today's youngsters. I sat there imagin-ing all the pretty clothes I would have when I married a rich husband, but then Mary appeared with the assistant. Mary was carrying a long white veil and dress over her arm. These were wrapped up together with a pair of white satin shoes. Then we left the shop. By now it was getting late and I began to worry. Mary must have noticed my changed mood because she asked why I was so miserable.

'We told Mum we wouldn't be late and it's getting dark,' I mumbled.

'Never mind about Mum. You're with me and you'll go home when I take you.' She was firm. 'Would you like to come with me to Albert's and see his Mum?'

I forgot my fears when she said this and we went off. When we arrived, Mary let herself in the front door and we entered the dining room. My eyes were immediately attracted to the table and my mouth started watering when I saw the home-made cakes and jam tarts laid out on a white lace tablecloth. I was starving; it was hours since either of us had eaten but Mrs Lewis made me wash my hands before sitting at the table.

When I sat down I was handed a plate made of real china which had bread and butter and cakes on it. We only had enamel plates at home and never had food like this. I wished this could go on for ever but I realised that all too soon I would have to return. Just as I was thanking Mrs Lewis and getting ready to leave Albert came into the room.

'Hello littl'un and how are you?' he asked pleasantly.

'Very well, thank you,' I answered shyly as he patted me on the head.

'I think you'd better stay a bit longer and Mary and I will take you home.'

I was only too glad to sit down and wait. Mrs Lewis left the room and Mary and Albert talked.

'Well love,' I heard him say. 'Did you tell your mother?'

'Yes,' said Mary. 'I've explained everything. But you must understand, Albert, I must get married from my home. And we must both help Mum to do the honours. I promised, so if we give my parents some money towards the expenses it will make me very happy.'

'Say no more about it now. We'll both see your Mum and Dad together and make all the arrangements.'

They hugged each other, and then taking me by the hand we went into the street and made our way home. When we arrived they kissed each other good night and Albert kissed me on the cheek before he turned and walked off.

Mum was waiting up for us when we got indoors, but before she could speak Mary began telling her about the agreement she had with Albert to pay for the wedding and this took the wind out of her sails.

'You'll see Albert when he calls tomorrow and he'll give you enough money to get the food and whatever you want to get.' So saying, she turned abruptly to go upstairs. Mum was satisfied with this. She started talking excitedly.

'I'll mek this the best weddin' in the district,' she blustered, but Mary wasn't interested and climbed the stairs without another word.

Next day Mary took Frankie, Liza and me to the shops to buy us some new clothes for the wedding. Liza and I had white satin dresses and shoes with bows on, and Frankie had a suit of small grey and white checked material with a cap to match and a pair of new boots. After the shopping spree Mary took us to a little tea shop for tea and cakes and then we returned happily with our presents.

Mum was pleased as punch when she found that Mary had bought us new clothes, but she was not so pleased when Mary told her she couldn't see them until the day of the wedding and took them straight up and locked them in her trunk. We all knew why: left with Mum they would have been in pawn before we had the chance to wear them.

One afternoon the following week, Mary was coming into the yard having been to hear the banns read for the last time, when she came upon a group of local women standing around gossiping about the wedding. I was sitting on the wall between our yard and the next, so I could hear every word. So could Mary; they hadn't noticed either of us.

'I wunda if 'er is?' asked one.

'An' 'er's gooin' ter get married all in white, orange blossoms an' all,' said another.

'I bet 'er's in the family way. 'Er's deep like 'er mother,' added a third.

I jumped down off the wall and joined my sister who was standing behind them listening. Then she elbowed her way through them with her head high.

'You'll all have to do the same as me and put down the date and see, but if yer want ter know it's the first of May.'

They went quiet at that and moved away. I put my tongue out at them as far as it would go. Mary never liked our neighbours and she seldom even spoke to them, but she knew Mum had invited them all. Even so, she wanted to keep the peace so she said nothing when she got indoors.

I never knew how much Albert and Mary gave Mum and Dad, but they threw money around like water; as Mum had said, she was going to give Mary the best turn-out in the district. She and Mrs Taylor went around the shops ordering what they thought was necessary and Dad and his cronies, Fred the lamplighter and his workmate Willie Turner, went along to The Golden Cup to order the drink. When she returned from the shops, Mum told me to accompany her to the Captain's to ask if we could have the Mission Hall for the wedding. She was disappointed when he told her he was sorry but it was being used for band practice that day. This put Mum in a terrible temper and to make matters worse, when we got home Dad and his friends were there pouring out beer from bottles. I could see at once that they had all had a skinful. This made Mum livid.

'It's all right fer yow. Leavin' me ter do all the dirty work,' she wailed, appearing to burst into tears.

'Now what's wrong with yer? Can't a man 'ave a drink ter celebrate?' Dad asked, continuing to pour the beer. ''Ere, 'ave one an' shut up.' He pushed the mug under her nose.

Mum took the mug from him but she didn't drink it. She slapped it down on the table, spilling some of its contents.

'I wanta know whater we gooin' ter do. The Captain can't let us 'ave the 'all for me daughter's weddin'.' She sagged into her chair and sobbed.

Fred went over to her. 'Can I make a suggestion missus?' he asked.

'Anythink as long as it'll 'elp us out,' she wailed through her apron.

'Why don't yer 'ave yer celebrations in the yard? It's big enough and besides yer'll be near the closets when yer need 'em.' He laughed, as did Willie and Dad, but Mum wiped her eyes and smiled.

'Now why didn't I think of that?'

On reflection, though, she doubted if she'd got enough crocks or cutlery and 'what was they going ter sit on?' After a pause for thought she told Dad that he must go and ask the Captain if he could let them have some cups and saucers and whatever else was available, even if they could not have the hall. Dad was less than enthusiastic about this suggestion.

'No, no, go yerself if yer want 'em. Yer never took the last lot back. 'E 'ad ter come an' fetch 'em.'

'Oh well,' she answered, 'I'll goo meself. Yow carn't do anything in that state any'ow.'

She drank down the remains of the mug of beer and off we went again to see the Captain. Mum pushed the door open wide and marched up the room as if she owned it. I hung back and watched to see what was going to happen. I could see Battling Billy Bumpham, a well-known local 'character', and the Captain seated facing each other at the other end of the room, deep in conversation. At the sound of footsteps the Captain looked around, and frowned when he saw it was Mum bearing down on him.

'What's 'e doin' 'ere?' she demanded, pointing at Billy.

'He's come to sign the pledge and become one of us,' he replied. 'I wish more would do the same.'

Then Mum changed her tone, as she always did when she wanted to wheedle something out of somebody.

'I've come ter ask yer, if we carn't 'ave the 'all, would yer be kind enough ter lend us some crocks an' chairs? Yer see, we're gooin' ter 'ave the party in the yard after the weddin'.'

'I'm very sorry,' he answered sharply. 'I shall be needing them all for the meeting.'

'But what am we gooin' ter do?' she wailed tearfully.

After pausing for a second he must have relented, because he told her that if it was any help she could borrow benches and trestle tables.

'That'll do.' She brightened up visibly. 'I'll send somebody to fetch 'em in the mornin'. Yer see it's tomorra the weddin'. An' yow come yerself if yer like.'

But the Captain didn't reply. He just waved her away and turned his back on us, and while he wasn't looking Mum whispered in Billy's ear: 'Yer wunt ter keep that up fer yer bung!' And with that she dug him in his ribs so hard that he nearly fell off his chair. Then she turned on her heel and we marched back down the hall. When we reached the door Mum called back, 'Good afternoon Captain', as though nothing had happened.

When we got back home Dad's mates had left and he himself was snoring in the chair. Mary was there too. She'd washed her hair and was drying it on the hessian towel. Mum told Mary about the changes in the arrangements but Mary

29

wasn't at all pleased. She threw down the towel and turned on Mum.

'Whatever are yer talking about? I thought everything was arranged for using the Mission Hall?'

Mum tried to calm her but Mary was not impressed by the thought that the money for hiring the hall had been saved. In the middle of the fuss Dad woke up.

'What's all the bloody shouting for now?'

'We carn't 'ave the use of the 'all Dad, and we carn't 'ave the celebrations in the yard neither! Whatever will Albert's people think?' Mary sobbed.

Mum chipped in with, 'They'll 'ave ter think what they like. The stuck-up lot!'

Mary was now in tears. 'I wish I hadn't agreed ter get married from 'ere. In fact I wish I wasn't getting married at all.'

Mum made a half-hearted attempt to calm her daughter down, but Mary shrugged her off and continued sobbing bitterly. Then Dad tried. He told Mary that it would be all right and that anyway it was too late now to do anything else. He put his arm around her shoulder and she wept some more. I could see that it was time for me to make the tea. While I busied myself, I listened to what Dad said to Mary.

'Now Mary,' I heard him say, 'dry yer eyes and listen ter me. It's yer weddin' day termorra and we all want ter see yer 'appy. Yer Mum's done the best she can under the circumstances.'

'But Dad, I feel so ashamed to think that Mr and Mrs Lewis will 'ave ter mix with our kind of neighbours, and you know what Mum's like when she's 'ad a few drinks.' Mary glared at Mum who was pretending not to listen.

'Leave everything to me, Mary. I'll keep yer Mum and everyone else in order.'

But I knew that was easier said than done. It would be as much as Dad could do to keep himself in order after he'd had a drop too much. Dad was a jolly chap sober, or could be, but when he'd had a few he thought himself a bit of a lady-killer. Mum knew this too, which was why she always kept an eye on him when he was the worse for drink.

I handed Mary and Dad their cups of sweet tea and they both smiled. Mum picked up hers as well and we drank in silence. Then when they'd finished Mary and Dad went out together. Mum followed them and I too decided to find Frankie to tell him the news after I had cleared away the crocks. When I got outside I found Mum in the yard, waving her arms about and giving directions to the neighbours whom she was organising for the party.

'I want this 'ere,' she said, pointing. 'An' I want that there,' she said, indicating where the chairs and tables were to go. 'An' bring some crocks, an' knives, an' forks an' anything else we can use.' She was not asking, she was demanding; but they were all used to her ways and were probably scared of upsetting her in case she changed her mind about the invitations.

I slipped away before she spotted me and renewed my search for Frankie, but I could find neither hide nor hair of him, or of Liza either. I finally came to the churchyard, 'Titty-Bottle Park', where there were literally dozens of kids running about the tombstones. Frankie and Liza were there with some of our friends, who gathered round to hear me excitedly telling my tale.

'Better than the Mission Hall,' Frankie said. The others agreed that it would be more fun to eat in the yard.

We wandered back home and when we entered the yard we were called in to go to bed early so we could get up to help in the morning. So it was bright and early when, with a clatter of buckets and bowls, we started to swill down the yard. The lavatories also had a birthday, and Dad left ours unlocked with plenty of fresh newspaper on the nail. The women even cleaned their windows. This was a red-letter day indeed. The clothes lines were taken down and rolled up by the dustbins, together with the props. I couldn't remember such a bustle and hubbub in our yard before. Everyone was singing a different song out of tune and taking no notice where they were throwing the water. Several people ended up with wet feet and all the cats vanished and even the kids who were trying to help got the odd clout for 'gettin' under our feet'. Eventually Frankie and I were called in by Mum and told to get a wash and change as it was nearly time to go. But it was worse in our house than in the yard. We were all at sixes and sevens, getting in one another's way. Mum and Mary kept calling for this, no that, yes that, to be brought upstairs. It was pandemonium. Then to top it all, two of Mary's friends squeezed in with several more parcels. They were what were then called 'buxom young women' and I thought them very pretty. They had come to help Mary dress but there was no room at all when they started busying themselves. Still, they were efficient. They put the parcels on the table and tidied the room while Frankie and I sat on the sofa and watched. Then brother Jack strolled in and he wasted no time in chatting them up. He joked and playacted, then put his arm round one's waist and kissed her on the cheek. This started them both giggling and they fled upstairs in hysterics. But they were no strangers to Jack because he called out 'See yer later Molly' as took his leave.

I was expecting that at any minute Mum would shout down to find out what was going on but she must have been pre-occupied, trying on her new frock. Just then the postman called with more packets and greetings cards, amongst which was also a letter. I recognised the handwriting. It was from Auntie Nellie. Although she was Mum's youngest sister she always addressed her letters to Dad. Mum couldn't read any-way but she always seemed to know when Auntie Nellie wrote and Dad made it my job to hide these letters and give them to him when Mum was out of the way. I never read any of them although it was not for want of trying. But once I'd given them to him I never saw them again so I imagine he must have burnt them.

Auntie Nellie only came to visit on special occasions so I expect Dad must have written to invite her to the wedding. I knew Mum would not have done so because they didn't get on, although I never found out why. Dad had a soft spot for Auntie Nellie and perhaps Mum had something to be jealous about.

I surveyed the scene around me and vowed that when I grew up I would marry a rich man who would carry me away from all this noise and squalor. I little knew then what the future held for me and looking back I can see what a lot I had to learn.

After a while Mary came down with her two friends. Molly removed the rags that Mary had put in my hair and it fell down in ringlets. Then she helped me put on my white satin dress, after which I pulled on my shoes. Frankie dressed himself, and he looked smarter than I had ever seen him in his check suit, waistcoat and matching cap. Liza looked good too. Then Mum came rustling down the stairs in her almost-new taffeta dress with its leg o' mutton sleeves. I could hardly believe my eyes. She looked years younger. Her hair was done on top like a cottage loaf with bits dangling around her ears, in which she had long red glass earrings, and peeping out from under the long russet-coloured dress were her brand new button-up boots. She twirled around the room but Mary wasn't interested and returned upstairs with her friends to complete dressing. Mum kept preening herself in the glass until Frankie could contain himself no longer.

'If yer don't watch out yer'll crack that mirror.'

Mum scowled at him and slapped him hard across the face. However, he wasn't bothered. He'd expected it and just shrugged his shoulders and sat down on the stool. Mum returned to the mirror and replaced strands into the bun which had become dishevelled during the twirling. Then, looking satisfied with herself, she marched out into the yard to see how well her orders had been carried out and, incidentally, to show off her fine clothes. We followed. All eyes turned, filled with admiration and envy. Even Dad looked at us proudly as he paused in his job of putting up the bunting. All our playmates crowded round to marvel at our get-up and touch our finery, but Mum soon put a stop to this and sent us indoors.

'Goo inside, we don't want their dirty maulers on yer clothes.'

We were disappointed but we could still watch through the windows as Mum gave her final instructions to Mrs Taylor and Mrs Buckley. Then we stood down when Mum and Dad came to the house. The young women had come downstairs and Dad, who had already had a skinful, addressed Molly in a jovial manner.

'Why 'ello Molly. I didn't know yow'd bin invited.' Then he pulled her towards him and asked her to give him a kiss, but she pulled away quickly when she saw Mum's scowl.

'No yer don't! I ain't 'avin' none a that in my 'ouse. An' yow,' she turned on Dad, ''ow long 'ave yer known them two?'

Just then Albert put his head round the door and I could see that Dad was relieved that he did not have to go into explanations. Mum turned her wrath on Albert.

'Out! Out! Get out! Don't yer know it's bad luck ter see yer bride before yer married?'

He was probably as glad as Dad to do as he was told and leave and I noticed that Mary's two buxom friends slipped out after them. But Mum's attention was elsewhere. She was upstairs at once to tell Mary what had happened, though I don't suppose Mary paid her much heed. In any case, Mum was soon down again in front of the mirror. She didn't say anything to me and I was too scared to speak in case she started on me, but her mood changed in a flash when Mary came down, and she was all smiles.

'Are yer ready now Mary me luv? We'll be late if we don't 'urry.'

Mary ignored Mum and just smiled at me. I could hardly believe my eyes. She looked a picture, radiant, all in white. Over her orange-blossom headdress she had a long flowing veil which flowed down her back; her dress of white satin rustled and crinkled as she walked. She seemed to glide on her little satin-shod feet. As I watched her I thought Granny would have been proud if she'd been alive to see Mary now. I glanced up at Granny's picture and for once she seemed to be smiling.

Dad came in and I was struck by how handsome he seemed with his moustache freshly waxed and his hair brushed flat and parted in the middle. He wore his best suit which had been redeemed from the pawnbrokers and was freshly cleaned and pressed. He even had on a collar and tie, which I'd never seen before and which he would tug at every now and then as if it were too tight. When he had finished looking in the mirror to put in his buttonhole rose, it was time to go.

Mary picked up her bouquet of white roses from the table and placed her hand through Dad's arm. He looked at her proudly then they turned and we walked out into the crowd. Confetti showered down on us and congratulations were shouted from all directions. Then the people moved aside and we passed through the smiling, cheering crowd, some of whom I noticed had tears in their eyes. I wondered where all that confetti came from; knowing Mum I guessed she must have supplied it, but none of us children were given any. But we'd anticipated this. One night we had sat up late while Mum and Dad were at The Golden Cup and had cut up old Christmas decorations into tiny squares and diamonds and then hidden them in envelopes. Now we hung back and got them out of our pockets and joined in with everyone else. Mary and Dad ducked their heads to avoid the waving arms as they walked along and everyone was smiling, including Mum.

This was not a wedding such as we see today. This was an old-fashioned wedding. There were no wedding cars nor yet carriages. The church was within easy walking distance of our street so everyone went on foot. It was a warm May day and everybody seemed to be out in the street or standing on their steps. There was quite a procession by the time we got to the church, St Paul's, and as we entered the organ played 'Here Comes the Bride'. We walked down the aisle and the church seemed really awesome. I looked from left to right to find somewhere to sit and could see nowhere. Then before I had gone a few yards I felt a tug on my back. It was my friend Nellie who lived in the yard next to ours. She pointed to the pulpit where the parson was beginning the words of the service. Suddenly I was frightened because he had once caught us playing in the churchyard and had shouted at us and chased us out. Nellie and I tiptoed quietly back down the aisle and out of the door. While we waited for the service to finish we amused ourselves rearranging the flowers on the graves. Some had no flowers at all so we shared the flowers out more equally. When we ran out of jam jars we pressed the daffodils and tulips into the earth. I don't suppose that that graveyard ever looked prettier than on our Mary's wedding day.

Then the people came streaming out of the church. We joined the crowd before our handiwork was noticed and watched as Mary and Albert had more confetti thrown over them as they stood on the threshold of the church. Mary was kissed and hugged by her workmates and Albert's back was slapped and his hand shaken by his friends. Mum and Dad and Mr and Mrs Lewis entered into the spirit of the occasion but I thought I could see some sadness in Mrs Lewis's eyes. She didn't smile and this perplexed me because I knew she liked our Mary. But I also knew that she was far from pleased with the arrangements. I heard her say so, though she would not interfere in anything Mum had organised.

When we reached our yard again I could see that Mrs Taylor and her friends had worked hard. The trestles had been put up and were covered with white tablecloths of American oilcloth. They were piled with corned-beef sandwiches, cheeses, sausage rolls, sliced pickled onions, beetroot, all kinds of pickles, watercress, pig's pudding and every mouth-watering delicacy you could think of. And standing in the centre was a two-tiered, iced cake. At one end of the table there were four stone gallon jars of ale, bottles of stout, gin and whisky. There was room on the benches for twenty guests each side, facing each other. We children had a table to one side to ourselves on which were laid out bottles of pop, cakes, buns and bread and jam.

While the adults sat on their forms we sat ourselves down on an assortment of broken chairs borrowed from the neighbours. There was a plate, knife and fork and a paper napkin for everyone. Some, the lucky ones, had a glass for their drink but the rest had to make do with a cup or a mug. After we had settled down, brother Jack stood up and banged the table and called for order for Dad to say grace. Everybody bowed their heads, then as he said 'Amen' they dived into the 'eats'. You would have thought some of them hadn't eaten for days, but then perhaps they hadn't. Many seemed not to know what the knives and forks were for and took the napkins for handkerchiefs.

Mrs Taylor kept an eye on us, ready to rap our knuckles if we got too greedy. As everyone feasted themselves Mum went round with the drink, pouring out gin and whisky or stout as they preferred, making sure to test them all as she did so, while Dad and Fred did the same with the ale. Even the newly converted Battling Billy broke the pledge that day. His wife Maggie kept on eye on him but said it was all right for a special occasion and that he could rejoin the pledge tomorrow. Things were beginning to hum when I noticed Mrs Lewis get up from her seat and go over to Mary. Mum was out of earshot but I could hear. She said, 'Fred and I will have to leave now as we have to catch the early train in the morning, Mary. But we'll see you as soon as we get back from our holidays. In the meantime, I hope you and Albert will be very happy. You have my blessings, my dear.'

'Thank you, mother,' replied Mary with tears in her eyes. 'I didn't want the weddin' this way.'

'I quite understand,' Mrs Lewis assured her. 'But I've never liked your mother and I never shall.' They embraced briefly and I heard her say quietly, 'Remember I shall always love you and if there's anything I can do or that you want, don't be afraid to come to me.' And with that she and her husband left.

Soon after this Mary and Albert got ready to follow his parents and depart. They slipped away unnoticed except by me. I didn't want Mary to go because I thought I wouldn't see her for a long time, and I ran over to her and pleaded. 'Where are you goin'? Ain't you stayin' till the end of the party?'

'No, Katie,' they answered in unison. 'But,' Mary continued, 'you can come and visit us when we've got settled in.'

'But remember,' said Albert, 'only you and Frankie, mind.' And they picked me up in turn and gave me a kiss.

Nobody seemed to miss them, only me. I tried to get Dad to tell me where they'd gone but he was tipsy and only laughed and said they'd gone on their 'funnymoon'. They were all pretty well oiled by then so I went back and sat with the other children. Battling Billy was attempting to sing one of his war songs and Maggie was merry too; if he went too far she would have to help him indoors. Mum was leading the chorus and us kids were singing our own dirty ditties. By now the barrel organ was in action, belting out 'Down at the Old Bull and Bush'; the noise was tremendous. When that number was over people started calling for order so that Mrs Buckley could do one of her songs. Unfortunately Mrs Buckley couldn't sing a note in tune; her throat sounded like it had gravel down it. There was nearly a fight when her husband heard Fred the lamplighter say to Dad that she sounded like 'a constipated canary'. The adults were beginning to get out of hand: some were dancing, having a 'knees up'; others were arguing with the organ grinder about what should be played. Then the men got round to the subject of politics. 'Asquith should be shot,' someone suggested. 'This government's never bin any good,' another agreed. Others sprang to the defence of their rulers and the argument became furious until a heavy fist banged down on the table and bottles and food went flying. This started a real rough and tumble, with people falling or being pushed to the ground amongst the debris.

Us kids were highly amused at all this, but I was distracted from the fun by Frankie who suggested that we gather up the bottles and hide them in the washhouse before they all got broken. We ended up with about a dozen assorted gin, whisky and stout bottles. We hid them in the copper, closed the lid and crept back into the yard, shutting the door carefully behind us. When we emerged the women were still at it. Two were pulling each other's hair and screaming at each other while the men tried to part them. Mum was not taking part. She stood there with hands on her hips, glaring with a face like thunder. However, the disturbance didn't last long because just then there was a cry of 'Hey up! Here's the cops!' They were not joking. It was not only the cops but the Black Maria as well. Dad pushed Mum indoors and Frankie and I followed quickly. Then Dad shot home the bolt, though this didn't stop us opening the window to see the end of the rumpus. We saw Maggie drag Billy from under the table where he was on his knees praying for 'the good Lord to send down lightning and scatter all these wicked people'. The police took one look at him and decided to leave him for later. But while they were hauling various protesting individuals off to the police wagon Maggie got him indoors. Then in a few minutes they were gone and quiet descended on our yard – but not for long.

Just as we'd closed the window and were breathing a sigh of relief there was a loud knock on the door. We looked at each other, scared, thinking it was the police come back for us. Dad whispered to us to keep quiet and not to answer it but then there was an even louder bang and then more knocking. The door rattled and the pictures shook. Granny's crepe paper slipped over one eye and she seemed to be saying 'Serves them right.' Mum whispered, 'That's another bad omen.' Then Dad decided that the banging had gone on long enough.

'I don't think it's the police, Polly. Yer better see who it is.'

Mum was taking no chances. She lifted a corner of the curtain first to make sure it was safe. It turned out to be Mrs Taylor.

'Yer tryin' ter knock our bloody door down?' she shouted. 'What yer want?'

Mrs Taylor stood there sobbing. You could hardly make out what she was saying.

'P-Polly, S-Sam, 'ave yer seen me three young uns? I carn't find 'em. I've looked everywhere. Whatever shall I doo?' she wailed.

'Come on Polly, we better help look for 'em before it gets dark,' Dad suggested.

'Not me,' Mum replied, 'I'll mek yer all a cup of tea when yer get back. They carn't be far.'

Dad and Liza went inquiring door to door while Frankie and I used this opportunity to see if our bottles were safe in the washhouse. They were, and so were Mrs Taylor's twins, Joey and Harry, and little Billy. I tried to lift Joey into my arms but he wriggled onto the slack and ashes on the floor and started giggling. I couldn't understand what was wrong with him until Frankie pulled out the other two from behind the boiler and found them in a similar state.

'They've bin drainin' the dregs outta the bottles. They're drunk!' he cried.

We stood them up. They were filthy with coal dust. We tried to get them to the door but they kept falling about. They looked really comical, and Frankie and I were in fits of laughter trying to help them. Then I spotted Dad down the yard and called out to him. He and Mrs Taylor came tearing down the yard to see what was up.

'Whatever's up with 'em? They're filthy!' he said.

'Yer'll 'ave ter carry 'em, Dad. They're drunk,' Frankie told him.

Then he caught sight of the empties and saw what had happened and began laughing as well. But Mrs Taylor began crying even more, this time with tears of joy and relief that her babies were safe. Dad tucked a twin under each arm and took them home, where we helped to wash and clean them before they went to bed. Mrs Taylor gave Frankie and me a piece of bread pudding each but we didn't like the smell of it so we threw it over the wall on the way back to our house. When we got in there was no tea waiting for us. Mum was asleep in her chair, snoring. Dad motioned us not to disturb her: 'She's 'ad a busy day.' But so had we all. However, we were not hungry for once, so we didn't mind going to bed. Besides, we had plans to make about how to spend the money we'd get for the empties. It was therefore with some disappointment that we faced Dad's inquiries about them next morning.

'How did those bottles come to be in the copper?' he asked. We were afraid to tell Dad the exact truth so we said we'd put them there to prevent them getting broken.

'Good idea,' Dad replied with a twinkle in his eye: he knew why they were there because he went out and fetched them in and later took them back himself. So we ended up with nothing for our trouble.

Thus ended Mary's wedding day. The party did not continue after the police raid. I can't remember who did the clearing up. I suppose the adults must have attended to it. I suppose you could say that the occasion went with a bang.

When Dad went off to the pub with the bottles the following day I followed him. I thought he'd send me home but he didn't.

'Here's a penny,' he said. 'I want you to sit on the step and watch out fer yer Mum and come in and tell me when you see her.'

I sat there a long time, bored, with a cold bottom, and I was about to open the pub door to tell him I was going home when I saw the organ grinder trundling his barrel-organ down the street. He stopped outside the pub and started turning the handle. The music burst forth. I was delighted and decided to stay and watch a while. Then the pub door burst open and two women tumbled out, drinks in their hands, and began dancing and singing. Dad poked his head round the door to see what was going on and to ask if I'd seen Mum. When I told him I hadn't, he disappeared inside again.

After he'd played a couple of tunes, the organ grinder took off his old frayed cap and handed it round the crowd that had gathered. At this the women stopped their knees up and went back in without a look at the man. A few pennies were dropped into it but he didn't look very pleased. I looked at my penny in the palm of my hand. I wondered if he would let me turn the handle if I gave it to him. So timidly I approached him.

'Please, will you let me turn the handle for you?' I asked.

'No!' he snapped. 'Little kids should be seen an' not 'eard.'

How many times had I heard that remark? But I persisted because I loved the sound of the old organ.

'If yer'll just let me play a tune I'll give yer me penny.' He peered down at me and scratched his head as he replaced his cap on his bald head.

'Well littl'un, yer'll 'ave ter stand on yer toes if yer want ter reach the 'andle.' Then he took the proffered penny and went inside the pub, leaving me to get on with it.

He was right, I did have to stand on tiptoe and even then I could hardly reach. I couldn't move the handle and yet it looked so easy when the man did it. I didn't give up; I wanted to get my money's worth. I pushed with both hands but I wasn't strong enough to get a squeak out of it. Then with a renewed effort I managed to get it to moan like a person in pain. I knew that if the handle moved faster it would sound better, so I really exerted every ounce of my miserable muscle power and the handle jerked forward with such force that I was lifted clean off the ground. So with a series of jerky motions I pumped that handle, but all I succeeded in producing was the sound of a set of bagpipes. The noise must have attracted the attention of the people in the pub because the next thing I heard was Dad's voice booming above the bedlam.

'What d'yer think yer tryin' ter do?' he asked. 'I thought someone was bein' murdered.'

Then the organ grinder pulled me away and I began to cry and pull at his coat.

'I want me penny back. It wouldn't play a tune for me.'

At that Dad grabbed the man. 'What's this? Did you tek 'er penny?' he demanded.

The organ grinder, however, did not have time to answer, because the drunken women had pushed his organ which began to roll down the hill. He shook himself free and ran after it.

'Don't yow ever show yer face round 'ere agen,' they shouted after him. Then they drifted back into the pub and left me standing alone. We never did see that organ grinder again and I felt sorry about what had happened. But I really wanted my pennyworth.

3
Our New Neighbour

In the yard next to ours was a tiny cottage squeezed in the corner. It must have been built to fill a space that was left after the five houses had been completed. It had just one room up and one down, big enough only for two people to live in. It was unoccupied, but whether that was because it went unnoticed or because every family was so large it was never taken by anyone, I don't know. So I was surprised when one morning, while filling the kettle at the tap in the yard, I noticed some of our neighbours looking across at this cottage where a painter was taking the 'To Let' sign out of the window.

It was a novelty to see a painter in our district. The landlords didn't bother and people had to look after their houses as best they could. So it was to be expected that this sight should arouse some curiosity, and after putting their heads together the women put down their bowls and kettles and went over to ask the painter who was coming to live there. But he couldn't enlighten them: he only had orders to 'paint the place up a bit'. They wandered back to their chores, clearly dissatisfied with this answer. Here was a new topic for gossip.

I must confess I was as curious as they were so I kept an eye on the cottage to see who came. But it was not until three mornings later that I spotted a horse and cart arrive. I knew then that it must be someone special to have their furniture brought in a van. Everyone in our district used flat hand carts when they moved house – unless they were 'doing a moonlight', when their chattels went on a push cart, pram or whatever else was handy. I dashed back in to make Dad his sandwiches and pour his tea into his billy can. I saw him off to work impatiently, then over the wall I went to see who our new neighbour was.

I watched with growing amazement a succession of beautiful old pieces of furniture go into the cottage. There was a new straw mattress and brass bedsteads on which the morning sun glittered like gold. There were real carpets, not like our old rags. There was a leather armchair and kitchen chairs which matched, and brass firedogs and a fender – in fact things that you never saw under the same roof in our district. However, what caught my eye most was a highly polished harmonium. How I would have liked to play that, I thought, but chance would be a fine thing.

I gazed at this scene thinking that of all of the things I wanted when I was grown up, the one I wanted most was to play a harmonium. Little did I think I would soon be playing, or trying to play, this one. Then the removal men came out of the house for the last time, wiping their brows on their once-white aprons, and then they helped down from the van a little old lady. She was not a lot taller than me. She had wisps of grey hair poking out from under a black lace bonnet and wore a long black lace dress down to her feet. Her face was wrinkled with age but she looked friendly and her voice was pleasant when I heard her talk to the men. She thanked them for their efforts but although they waited for a tip it was not forthcoming, so they went off grumbling. Then she went into the cottage and closed the door and I came out of hiding.

She hadn't noticed me, but she had seen the neighbours hanging out of their windows, spectating. When she'd gone I approached the door timidly. I wanted to ask her if I could run her errands before the other children had a chance. So I plucked up my courage and tapped gently on the door. It opened almost at once and I was confronted by the old lady. I was nervous but she put me at ease immediately.

'Well dear, and what do you want so early in the morning?' she asked, rubbing her hands together.

My voice trembled as I answered. 'I live over there,' I said, pointing to our house on the other side of the low wall. 'I've come to see if yer want any errands fetched.'

She seemed to look straight through me when she continued. 'And what's your name?'

'Kathleen, but everybody calls me Katie,' I told her.

'Well Katie,' she said after a pause. 'If you come back tomorrow I may have an errand for you.'

'But I can help yer now if yer want me to,' I said eagerly. I was anxious to get inside and nose around her furniture.

'No thank you,' she said abruptly. 'My brother will be here later and we shall be busy arranging the furniture. Now run along like a good girl and don't be late tomorrow.'

I walked away disappointed but I was glad I'd found someone new whom I could confide in. I was also excited at the prospect of earning some reward, and I couldn't sleep that night for thinking about visiting her in the morning. But it wasn't till after school the following afternoon that I found time to go. I washed and combed and plaited my hair and rubbed my clogs, then I went round and knocked on the door. I had to stand on tiptoe to reach the brass knocker, which had appeared since the previous day. Then I heard a voice call me to come in so I turned the door knob and entered.

'Come along in Katie and sit yourself by the fire. You must be cold,' she said, but I just stood and warmed my hands: I didn't dare sit down. She picked up a brass poker and stirred up the fire which already burnt brightly in the grate. However, I was too excited to notice the cold or the warmth; I was too excited by the sight of all the beautiful objects that filled the room. There was a copper kettle boiling on one hob and a china teapot on the other and the stove shone clean. Set out on the white lace tablecloth were matching cups and saucers, and a plate with bread and butter and teacakes on it. The old lady made me jump when she told me not to stare but to sit down and not be nervous. I sank into the leather armchair and thought to myself that this couldn't be real; I would wake up soon.

'Now come along, Katie.' Her voice brought me out of my daydream. 'I want you to meet my brother.'

It was only then that I noticed the small man seated in the armchair next to mine. Anyone could tell they were brother and sister they were so much alike, except that he had a little goatee beard on his chin. Like his sister he too was dressed all in black and he had the same habit of rubbing his hands together.

'This is my little friend Katie,' she told him. 'She's going to be my little errand-girl.'

'Good afternoon, Katie.' And he put out his hand, but I quickly wiped mine on my pinafore before I shook hands.

'I like the look of her, Louise,' I heard him whisper to her. 'But the poor little mite looks half-starved.'

She indicated the pretty flower-patterned basin for me to wash my hands in, then I joined them at the table. But I was too excited to eat much. I'd never been surrounded by so many nice things before, not even at the Lewises'. The old lady spoke to me occasionally, but I noticed that she seemed to lapse into quiet moods. This didn't bother me. I just felt this was too good to last and I was right. I had no idea she was using me for a purpose of her own: I was too naive to realise until it dawned on me what it was, a few weeks later.

After tea she wrapped up some fruit cake for me to take back home. With that she saw me off with an invitation to visit her the next day after school but that I was to tell my parents in case they were worried where I was. As if they would be, I thought.

When I got indoors Mum was out but Frankie was sitting in her chair by the fire warming his toes on the fender.

'Where 'ave yow bin?' he inquired moodily. 'I've bin lookin' fer yow everywhere.'

I sat down in Dad's chair and told him all about the old lady and her brother, or at least what I knew, which wasn't much. But before I'd got very far with my story he shrugged his shoulders and said he didn't believe me.

'Any'ow what's 'er name?' he asked suspiciously.

'I don't know, I never asked 'em.'

'Yer tellin' lies,' he said triumphantly.

'I'm not! But I did hear 'er brother call 'er Louise. But if yer don't believe me I'll take yer tomorra to see 'er,' I told him angrily. I felt close to tears to think he doubted my word.

'Is that on then?' he asked, getting excited.

'Yes it is,' I said, although I had no idea what the old woman would say. We shook hands on the promise anyway.

The next afternoon couldn't come quick enough. No one

was at home when we came out of school so we didn't have to explain where we were going. I made sure Frankie washed himself and warned him to behave himself as well.

'I still can't believe you,' he remarked, but he washed anyway and he dried himself on the piece of hessian and then spat on his hands and flattened his hair. I couldn't understand why he did this because his rebellious hair always sprang up like bristles on a brush and never stayed flat like Dad's. I plaited my own hair and then I straightened my ink-stained pinafore and we were ready to go. We had soon reached the old lady's house and rapped on the door.

'That won't be there long,' said Frankie. I gave him a frown and told him to mind his manners because I wasn't sure what the old lady's reaction would be to my brother.

'I don't like you when you're like this,' he said sulking. 'You sound just like our Mum.' But I had no time to reply because just then the door opened and there stood the old lady in her black lace dress.

'Good afternoon, Katie,' she said to me but she frowned at Frankie and said, 'And who is this boy?'

''E's my brother, miss, and 'e's come to pay yer a visit,' I answered nervously.

'You should have asked my permission first before bringing him along. I'm not keen on little boys,' she snapped back.

I could tell she was angry and I was ready to cry, but Frankie pulled me roughly back off the step and we turned to leave. She must have changed her mind because she called us back.

'Well, you may as well come on in now you're here.' And we turned and followed her in. Frankie's eyes nearly popped out of his head when he clapped eyes on the room and its contents, especially what was laid out on the table. It was all neatly laid out as it had been the day before.

The old lady fetched out another plate and cup and saucer, then she checked that our hands were clean and told us to sit down. Frankie, however, flopped into the leather arm-chair, and putting his hands behind his head lay back like a grown-up.

47

'This is the life for me,' he said. I was so embarrassed by his behaviour.

The old lady frowned at him and asked him sharply what his name was and he sat up straight but he answered cheekily.

'My name's Francis William Samuel after me Dad ... but everybody calls me Frankie, except me school mates and they call me ...' But I kicked his shin before he could finish the sentence. To my relief the old lady smiled and said, 'Never mind what they call you, Frankie. But remember not to call here again unless I ask Katie to bring you. Now come along, sit up at the table and have your tea.'

We sat down then and all the time he was eating Frankie couldn't keep his eyes off her or the things that surrounded him. When we'd finished I asked if we could wash up and run the errands but she said she'd already been to the shops with her brother. I was disappointed at this and was afraid she was still vexed at me for bringing Frankie.

'Don't look so sad,' she said softly. 'I shall still want you to come the day after tomorrow.'

'But that'll be Sunday and all the shops'll be closed,' I replied.

'Yes, I know, but if you call early we can have a long talk.' And with that she said 'Good afternoon' and saw us out. As we left I thanked her for the 'nice tea' and off we went.

'I don't like 'er,' were Frankie's first words when we were out of earshot. 'But I loved all that beautiful furniture and the tea she gave us. What about that brown leather armchair? I'll 'ave one o' them when I go to work and don't forget to ask 'er if I can come again. And don't tell Liza!'

'I won't,' I promised and he went off to find his mates while I made my way home to start the chores. For once I was happy doing them because I had the thought of Sunday to cheer me up.

When I returned from Sunday school the following Sunday I wrapped up in my scarf and tammy because it was a chilly day.

'An' where do yer think yer gooin'?' Mum asked when I came downstairs.

'Back ter Sunday school, I've forgotten me test card,' I lied.

'Well, see that yer come straight back. I want ter talk with yer.

This worried me because I could not make out what I had done this time to annoy her. So I decided to return to Sunday school to fetch my card. I ran all the way there and back and handed my test card over.

'Sit in that chair an' listen ter what I've got to say.' She paused for a moment before continuing. 'I 'ear that you've bin runnin' errands an' payin' visits to the new neighbour across at the cottage.'

'Yes Mum,' I answered truthfully. 'I was goin' ter tell yer about that but I thought you wouldn't be interested.'

'I'm only interested in who she is, an' what she does for a livin',' she said sharply.

So I had to explain. I told her the old lady was rich and that she had done the cottage up beautifully. I had found out that her name was Miss Vulcan and I gave her this information as well as telling her that Miss Vulcan had a brother named Freddie who visited her and that he was a little old man who wore a black cap on his head and sported a goatee beard.

'Sounds like they're Jews ter me. I'll 'ave ter pay 'er a visit,' she said more to herself than to me.

'I'm goin' this afternoon, Mum. Shall I tell her you would like to call?' I asked.

'Yes, yer can tell 'er I'll be callin' on 'er tomorra. No, tell 'er I'll come Tuesday, it's washin' day Monday.'

'Yes Mum,' I replied dutifully and left before she changed her mind.

A few minutes later I was standing on Miss Vulcan's door-step. Before I lifted the knocker I gave my clogs an extra rub on my stockinged calf, then I rapped on the door.

'Come along in, Katie,' I heard her voice from inside, so I entered. This time I went straight to the pretty china bowl and washed my hands. As before the table was laid out for tea, but instead of bread and butter there were toasted muffins oozing butter. We seated ourselves and I watched her cut her muffins into quarters. This was a real treat for me. I could hardly remember having muffins before, although I'd seen the muffin man in his white apron, a towel over his arm and a tray of muffins every Sunday afternoon. But we never saw them in our house.

I picked up my knife and attempted to copy the old lady but I soon got into difficulty. The old lady only smiled and leaned over to show me what to do. Thus at my ease, I ate my tea and then I washed up the dirty crocks. After this I was told to sit by the fire beside my benefactor. I sat quietly trying to work out how I was going to give her Mum's message.

'You're very quiet. Is there anything you want to tell me?' she asked me.

'It's me Mum,' I blurted out. 'She's coming ter pay yer a visit and she wants ter know all about you before I can come here again. I don't think you'll like my Mum, Miss Louise, nobody does.'

'Don't worry your little head about me. I'll see your Mum and whatever she wants to know I'll be only too pleased to tell her.' She smiled archly. 'But,' she added, 'would you like me to tell you what I do and how I come to be here?'

'Yes, I would,' I answered, perhaps a little too eagerly.

'First make me another cup of tea and hand me my knitting.'

I did as she asked then settled down again. Then as she knitted she began to relate her life story from when she was a young girl. She went rambling on much as I am doing myself now. She seemed to be talking to herself as she gazed into the fire. I listened, all ears, to hear what she was saying.

'I was only a small child when my parents sent my brother and me to an orphanage. I was twelve and Freddie about fifteen. I was very unhappy after this because I did not want to be apart from my Momma. At first they came to visit us once a month but then the visits became few and far between. I wanted to go home so eventually I ran away. By this time Freddie had already gone home. But I had no idea where I was going. I left early before the nuns were awake but I only got as far as Glasgow before I lost my way.'

I sat stock still, hardly breathing, my chin cradled in my hands. When I looked at her her eyes had tears in them like my own. Her story was like a tale from a book. Then after a pause she started again.

'A young man came along on a bicycle and asked me if he could help but I refused his offer. I didn't like the look of him. Just then two policemen rode past and stopped. They said they were looking for me and I had to go with them back to the convent.' She wiped her eyes with her dainty lace handkerchief and I wiped my own on the back of my hand. She told me how she wrote several letters to her home complaining of the punishment she was given and begging to be taken away but she received no reply until one day her brother paid her a visit and gave her the news that their parents were both dead. After that she went into service and there she stayed until, when she was about twenty-two years of age, her brother came to tell her he was married and to ask her if she would leave her employer and come to look after his wife who was expecting a baby.

I felt very sorry for her by now and for want of knowing how to express my sympathy I offered to make another pot of tea. This broke her train of thought and she brightened up. I made the tea and she drank it, then she continued her story.

'I was surprised to hear that he was married but I wanted a change of surroundings so I packed my few belongings and went with him there and then. He told me he was a money lender in a small way and that he lived in London now. I thought London was a wonderful place but I was disappointed when I saw what a small, tumbledown house my brother and his wife lived in. And to make matters worse I took an instant dislike to the wife. When we were introduced she turned to Freddie and said haughtily. "So this is your sister. Well, she'll have to make herself useful while she's here." Freddie took my few belongings up to the garret where I was to sleep and spend most of my time until the baby was born. I was so unhappy but I had nowhere else to go so I stayed until the baby was born. But it died within two weeks.'

I was fascinated by her story and waited impatiently while she refreshed herself with tea before continuing.

'She blamed Freddie and me for what went wrong but within two weeks she'd died herself; she had never recovered from the birth.' A flicker of a smile passed across her face as she said this. 'Freddie was not sorry and neither was I. I stayed on with him to keep house. I did all the cleaning, cooking and kept his books in order, which was no mean feat because he had a lot of clients call and all the money passed through my hands.'

'Didn't yer want to leave 'im then?' I interrupted.

'No,' she snapped. 'I loved my brother and he needed me, and you must care for people,' she insisted.

'But I do try.' Her words seemed like an accusation. 'But no one seems to be bothered with me. An' when I ask questions no one listens and Mum says I always get under 'er feet,' I added.

'Never mind. I expect she does love you in her own way,' she said gently.

I wanted to hear more of her life so I asked her why she had left London to come to Birmingham.

'My brother's married again now,' she continued, frowning. 'I didn't like his second wife either. She's taken over the household and the book-keeping too. I was treated like a servant so I asked Freddie to find me a place of my own. He wanted me to stay but I'd made up my mind. So when he was in Birmingham he bought me this house, which was going cheap, so that I could start a money-lending business here for him. I have looked after his books for forty years and that's all I know, so he gave me the capital to start and here I am.' She paused. 'You see there's lots of shops and businesses here and we think it's a good place to begin.'

I didn't know what she had planned for me but I understood well enough her meaning.

'But most of the people round 'ere are very poor,' I pointed out. 'They 'ave ter go ter the pawnshop.'

She smiled. 'I can lend them money instead of going to the pawnshop. And that's where you can help,' she said archly.

'But I don't see 'ow I can 'elp,' I mumbled innocently, waiting to hear her reply.

'But you can help me, Katie; I'd like you to spread the word around and tell people what my business is, and that if they need me I'll be able to help and charge only a little interest.'

I didn't understand what 'interest' was but she'd been kind to me and I thought she would be kind to others and help them. She was – but only to suit herself. I learnt this later. At that moment all I wanted to hear was more of her story, but she'd lost interest in that now.

'Off you go now,' she said, 'it's getting dark.'

With that she got up, put her knitting away and said she would go with me as far as our house. She put on a coat, took down her walking cane which hung behind the door and then we left. She held my hand and we walked slowly up the yard. She reminded me what she wanted me to do, then as we neared our house I became frightened that she would fall foul of Mum. So I stopped and turned to her.

'Me Mum won't let yer in,' I blurted out.

'Maybe not, but she will one day,' she said, very sure of herself. Then with a queer, knowing smile on her face she made to go.

'Goodnight, Miss Vulcan,' I said.

'You may call me Miss Louise,' she replied, and with that walked slowly back to her cottage.

It was only after she had gone that I started to ponder why she had confided so much in me. This was most unlike adults of my previous experience. But I dismissed these thoughts from my mind and entered our house. Only Frankie and Liza were in so I decided to tell them both what had happened. I was too excited to bother about my sister's listening, all ears. Anyway, I thought, Liza would do my job for me.

'Where's she going ter get 'er money from?' asked Frankie.

''Er brother,' I replied. 'She says he makes 'er an allowance.'

'That won't last long when the vultures round 'ere get their 'ands on 'er money,' he said. 'Some people are good at borrowing but she'll have to watch them to pay back.'

'Well we'll 'ave to wait an' see. She's kind anyway,' I said.

'I hope our Mum don't start borrowin' off of 'er or she'll never get it back.'

'I don't think Mum will,' I told him. 'I don't know about the rest but anyway I've got to pass the word around.'

'What 'ave you got ter do it for? They'll find out soon enough,' he said.

'I promised,' was my reply.

Next day it was the usual Monday routine: washing,

maiding,* singing and sharing the gossip of the day. The news soon went round the district about why Miss Louise had come live there. Liza took care of that before I had a chance, but I didn't mind this; she was better at it than me. I was fetching a tin bowl of water from the tap in the yard when I heard Mum call out, 'Katie, fetch me a bucket of slack† before yer goo ter school.'

I was scared stiff of going down those cellar steps but Frankie wasn't around to do it so I had to do as I was told. As I was struggling down the yard with the fully laden bucket a few minutes later a neighbour, Mrs Woods, saw me. I tried to walk past her but she caught hold of the bucket.

'We want yow in the wash'ouse,' she insisted. I followed, and on reaching the door I saw Mrs Jonesy, Mrs Phipps, Maggie and Mum, together with two or three more from the other yards, in animated conversation. It was cold and snowy outside so I squeezed in with them. They were chattering like a lot of parrots but I listened to what was said.

'Well fancy that.'

'I carn't believe it.'

'T'ain't true.'

Mum broke in decisively. 'It might be a good idea an' find out,' she said.

'It'd be betta than gooin' ter uncle's,' one said. With this it dawned on me what they were talking about so I became more attentive.

'Well goo on then ask 'er,' said Mrs Woods.

'Well goo on then.' Mum shook me. 'Tell us. Is that the truth? Is she a money lender?'

'Yes Mum,' I told her.

'Right. That's all we want ter know. Yer can get off ter school now before yer late.' She spoke sharply and pushed me outside where it was snowing hard.

---

* Agitating the weekly wash in the household tub, known as a 'maiding' tub.

† Coal dust sold more cheaply than lump coal and was added to the lump coal to make it last longer.

In school the girls kept whispering and turning round to look at me; Liza had told everyone. But it was not until we were in the playground that they could tackle me.

'Make way for Miss Louise,' they choroused, but I was not bothered by their sarcasm: it was the snowballs that some threw that mattered. I was alone; even Liza looked on as the snowballs rained down. I turned to run but slipped over, and that was too much even for my sister who came to my rescue and dared them to throw any more. They did not.

'What's wrong with 'em?' I cried. 'What 'ave I done?'

'I told 'em about you an' the money lender but I didn't know they were gooin' to snowball yer,' she said, pulling me to my feet.

I rather liked the name 'Louise' but not the snowballs, and from that day on until I left school the girls who didn't like me called after me: 'There goes Miss Louise.' It was jealousy, I suppose; the fact that I had spotted a chance they had not, although I couldn't get over the suspicion that their reaction to me had something to do with how Liza had told the story.

When I returned home that afternoon I was surprised to find Dad already sitting in his chair by the fire.

'Aren't you at work, Dad?' I asked him.

'No I ain't,' he answered sharply, which was strange for him. 'An' where's yer Mum?'

She must have been upstairs because almost as if in answer to him we heard her heavy tread on the stairs. I could see the mood Dad was in and all I wanted to do was to make myself scarce before they started to quarrel.

'I don't want any tea Mum,' I called out quickly before she was down the stairs. 'Miss Louise will be waitin' for me.'

'What's all this about?' inquired Dad grumpily. 'What yer mean yer don't want any tea?'

'It's all right Sam, she's fetchin' errands fer the old lady that lives in the cottage.'

Dad stared at her hard before he replied. 'It seems to me that she's always over there.'

'I've told yer Sam,' snapped Mum, 'she's outa mischief, an' besides, it's one less ter feed.'

I didn't realise that Dad was home early that afternoon because he had been put on short time and had had to take a drop in wages in consequence. I was too excited about my new job to stop and think. I made myself scarce as quickly as I could. When I arrived at Miss Louise's door, out of breath from running, I kicked the snow off my clogs and went straight in. The first thing she asked was if I had done what I promised.

'Yes,' I replied. 'Everyone knows.' She seemed pleased with my reply and smiled that crafty smile of hers. Then when we had eaten tea she said she was going to play the harmonium. This pleased me very much because I was longing to hear her play the instrument. Quickly I tidied away and washed the tea things, then she seated herself in front of the harmonium, pulled out the stops and began to play. But after a few notes she stopped and turned round on her stool to face me.

'Would you like to sing for me? I hear you've got a good voice.' I knew there were no flies on her but I wondered how she'd found that out.

'But I only know the songs I sing at school,' I told her warily.

'Well, would you like me to sing for you then?' she asked. I nodded.

She arranged herself in front of the harmonium again and after pulling out more stops began to sing 'On the Banks of Allen Waters'. She played and sang so plaintively that I almost wept, the song was so sad. She taught me the song later, and showed me how to control my voice, open my mouth wide and sing loud or sing softly. I can picture her now sitting at the harmonium in her black lace gown, me standing beside her as we sang together. Another time I was so fascinated by her clicking needles that she offered to teach me to knit as well. That afternoon she took me upstairs to her small bedroom for the first time. I was spellbound by the brass bedstead and all the knick-knacks, but what held my attention most were the knitted bedspreads that were on the bed and draped over the chairs. They were made out of small, knitted squares, all the different colours of the rainbow. What I wouldn't give, I thought, to be able to lie down on that bed, just for a minute. But I was awoken from my daydreaming by her calling me over to the large chest which stood beneath the window. She told me to lift the lid, and there inside were packed hundreds of balls of different coloured wool. She directed me to take as many balls as I could carry and put them downstairs. As I rummaged through the chest, gathering up as much as I could carry without dropping any, I found knitted scarves, blankets, gloves, socks and all sorts of garments of varying sizes. I picked out as many balls as I could manage, then she closed the lid and we returned downstairs.

When we were seated facing each other again she gave me a ball of pink wool and a pair of knitting needles and I had my first lesson in how to knit properly without dropping stitches. As I struggled to follow her directions my natural curiosity overcame me and I asked her how she came to have all that wool and all those knitted garments which were obviously not for her.

'Well,' she said, with a twinkle in her eye, 'if you'll keep a secret, I'll tell you, but first you'll have to promise to keep it a secret.'

'I'll promise,' I said, offering my hand for her to shake, but she only smiled and replied, 'I think I can trust you.' Then she told me about her knitting sideline.

'When I go to my clients to collect I always ask if they have any hand-knitted woollen garments they don't need, and if I'm lucky they give me some. Then I bring them home to wash and I unravel them before they dry. Then I wind them into balls and put them in the oven to dry, and that's how I come to have all those woollen articles to sell.' I thought what a good idea it would be for me to do the same and I kept this in mind.

After a while she examined what I had done. 'You're getting along fine. Keep up the good work.' The more she praised me the quicker the needles clicked. I had soon knitted all sorts of things for her, such as hats, teapot cosies and iron holders. I would have been pleased to own any of these, but after they were finished she told me they were all ordered. All I received for my labour was my tea. I didn't mind this; I was happy just to be there, hoping that one day she would give me some of the pretty wool to make something for myself but she never did. I was afraid to ask in case she said I wasn't to come any more. She was moody at times and easily irritated. Soon she took my visits for granted and I was given the spare key to let myself in the door. I was surprised at this.

'Why do yer want me ter have a key?' I asked her.

'Well, I always take a nap of an afternoon and when you rap the knocker it startles me, which is bad for my nerves.' And she stretched out her hand for me to see it shake.

'I hope you ain't gonna have a fit. I wouldn't know what ter do.' I was frightened.

I don't believe she heard me because she yawned, handed me the key and told me to hang it round my neck so that no one could take it from me. I was very honoured and proud to think she could trust me.

Another afternoon she took me with her to deliver the knitted garments. She said that everything was ordered, and that pleased me because I had to carry it all. We called at several small shops and houses in the better-class district which we called 'the kippers and curtains'. I did not find out how much she sold the garments for because she left me standing outside, but she always looked pleased when she emerged from these visits. When we got back to her cottage she put her hand in her bodice and pulled out a string with her key and a whistle attached to it.

'What's that for?' I asked, pointing at the whistle.

'That's a police whistle in case I'm attacked while I'm collecting the week's takings.'

'But nobody would attack yer round 'ere. At least I don't think so,' I told her, but she just smiled and told me she had no further use for me that day and to call the next day which was to be a school holiday. The following morning I asked Mum if I could spend the day with Miss Louise.

'Yow can, as long as yer do yer usual jobs 'ere first,' she said grudgingly. Although I was helping out Miss Louise I had to get up at six o'clock in the morning to do all the chores before school. I had to fetch the coal up from the cellar, chop the wood, light the fire, make the tea and then take up a mug each for Mum and Dad. Then I went skipping round to the cottage to see Miss Louise before I went to school.

That holiday morning I found Miss Louise waiting for me just inside the door with a pair of old shoes and a pair of slippers in her hands.

'I want you to try these on,' she said, handing them to me. I did as she said but they were two sizes too big for me; they fitted better after she had packed the toes with scraps of wool. She wrapped up the clogs and gave them back to me with the instruction that I was only to wear the shoes when I came to call.

'What about the slippers?' I asked, delighted by these gifts, tatty as they were.

'I'll leave them on the mat inside the door so you can change into them, then your clogs won't wake me up from my nap.'

As I was pulling on the worn satin slippers I thought of the new ones my sister had bought me for her wedding. It was no use thinking about them; they were in the pawnshop with the rest of our wedding clothes. We sat down to knit, but before we had settled there was a loud knock on the door. When I opened it I was surprised to find Mrs Phipps and Mrs Woods.

'Is Mrs Vulcan in?' they chorused, peering past me into the room.

'It's not Mrs Vulcan, it's Miss Vulcan ter you,' I told them haughtily.

'Huh! Puttin' on airs an' graces ain't yer?' Mrs Phipps said sarcastically, looking me up and down. Before I could reply Miss Louise called out, 'Who's that at the door?'

I thought of what my Dad called them and replied over my shoulder, 'It's them two vultures.'

'Now, now,' Miss Louise called back sharply, 'mind your manners and let them in.'

I disliked these two intensely and didn't like being told off for being rude to them, so I told her peevishly that I wasn't staying while they were there and kicked off the slippers, put on my clogs and ran out banging the door behind me. I went home sulking and was still in a mood when Frankie returned.

'What's the long face for? 'Ave yer worn yer welcome out?' he asked none too sympathetically.

'No!' I snapped, with tears welling up in my eyes.

'Why are yer cryin' then?'

I tried to explain that Miss Louise was always short with me when anyone called.

'I s'pose she don't want yer knowin' what's goin' on,' he suggested wisely.

'I know what's goin' on so that's not the reason she sends me away. She said she trusted me but I don't think I like 'er any more,' I said, pursing my lips. 'But I'll miss the teas an' my knittin' lessons so I'll 'ave to go back.'

'Oh you go back if yer want to, but it seems ter me that yow've served yer purpose now an' she don't want yer any more. Does she ever give yer any money for what yer do?' he asked.

'No, she only gives me money ter do the errands an' then I 'ave ter go back twice because I carn't carry them all in one go. She reckons up the change over an' over like she don't trust me,' I admitted reluctantly.

'You know, Katie, she's an old miser and everyone borrows money off her or else they buy the things you knit off her. I even 'eard Mum say the other day she was goin' over there to get a loan. Dad 'eard 'er an' 'e told 'er that while 'e 'ad two 'ands she was not to borrow money off 'er. So I'd stay away from 'er if I was you an' come an' play marbles with me like you used to do.' I knew he was trying to cheer me up but I was determined to go back to my knitting lessons when the vultures had gone.

'Please yerself.' He shrugged his shoulders and went off leaving me to ponder what he had said.

I plonked down on the hard wooden sofa and began musing: was he telling the truth? Would Mum borrow off her? Mum always bragged about never borrowing off anyone but I had noticed that since Dad had been on short time she seemed to have more money than ever to spend and was getting more friendly with the neighbours she could not stand as a rule. Then I remembered an incident not long before. I'd been taking a bucket of slack to the washhouse where all the women were gathered gossiping. They dropped their voices to a whisper when they saw me but I'd seen them taking nips from a bottle of gin. I didn't think too much about this at the time, although I knew they usually only had money for their 'little pleasures' after they'd done the washing and pawned it. Now I understood and I put all the blame on Miss Louise. I determined to discover if Mum was going to Miss Louise like the rest.

I was unsure of my welcome when I visited the cottage the next afternoon. The door was locked but I got out my key and let myself in. She'd placed my slippers in their normal place on the mat so I slipped into them and crept quietly to her chair. She sat very still, her eyes closed, breathing softly and regularly. On her lap lay a large ledger, wide open. I was tempted to look for Mum's name so I checked that she was really asleep, although I didn't care if she woke up or not. Gently I lifted the ledger and placed it, still open, on the table. I looked up again to see that she was still asleep and then I began leafing through the pages, curious to see whose names were entered there. Most of it was double-dutch to me but I could make out the names entered in columns. Some I knew, others I didn't. Beside each entry was the money lent and paid, with the interest and the date. I felt relief when I couldn't find our name, but then I turned a page and there it was, together with those of Mrs Phipps, Mrs Woods, Mrs Buckley and several more of our neighbours. My heart sank. What Frankie had said was true. Mum was as bad as the rest. Sadly I turned back the pages and returned the ledger to Miss Louise's lap. She moved a little but I couldn't have cared less if she awoke. I slipped off the slippers and quietly left the cottage.

As I walked slowly back I kept asking myself what Dad was going to say when he found out. I consoled myself with the thought that he wouldn't find out from me; there was enough trouble at home already. That night as I lay in bed I prayed that it was not our name, only one like ours; I still couldn't believe it. I thought, I'll ask Miss Louise the truth tomorrow, and I drifted off to sleep.

Next afternoon when I let myself in Miss Louise was not asleep; she was seated, upright in her chair, eyes wide open. She looked as if she was waiting for me so before she could say anything I spoke.

'Does my Mum borrow money off you?' I blurted out.

'Yes, you know she does. You saw her name in my ledger yesterday, didn't you?' She snapped angrily and frowned fiercely at me.

I went very hot and felt myself redden. She couldn't have been asleep when I lifted the ledger from her lap and scanned its pages: she must have been watching me all the time. I began to feel ashamed of my nosiness but I hadn't intended to be nosey: I was just curious. I began to dislike her; she looked sly and I felt indignant that she'd spoken to me like that. I replied boldly, 'Yes, I did see our name in that book, along with a lot of others.' Then, placing my hands on my hips like I had seen Mum do many times when in a temper, I looked her straight in the eyes.

'You'll never get paid, yer know, and if my Dad finds out there'll be trouble!' I shouted.

'Well, if yer Mum don't pay yer father'll have to. My brother will see to that.' She answered calmly and shuffled over to the fireplace, but I hadn't had my say yet.

'I don't know 'ow because my Dad's on short time now. My brother Charlie's left 'ome an' sister Mary's married an' Mum 'as to go out cleaning the fish an' chip shop to make ends meet.' I paused to get my breath and this gave her an opening.

'Have you quite finished?' she yelled. 'If so, you may go. I'm very vexed with you!'

'An' I'm vexed with you too!' I retorted and pushed past her to the door. Then, as I turned before leaving, I saw she was grinning at me. I hated her then. I felt that her character had been revealed and, what was more, that she'd been using me.

I went home feeling miserable and ashamed for being such a fool but I didn't have long to indulge my self-pity, for when I entered our house I found my brother Jack and Mum quarrelling loudly. They didn't notice me so I made myself unobtrusive and listened.

'But where're yer gooin'?' Mum wailed, putting on her tearful act and flopping into the chair as if exhausted.

'Not far away. If yer really want ter know I've been courtin' a widow for some time an' we're thinkin' of settlin' down tergether,' he replied.

'Don't goo yet Jack,' pleaded Mum. 'I'm in a lot of trouble with some debts I owe.'

'What debts?' demanded Jack, getting excited again. 'You always said yer never borrowed off anybody.'

'I couldn't 'elp meself,' she confessed tearfully. 'An' I don't know 'ow I'm gooin' ter pay it back if yer leave 'ome now.'

'Pay what back? An' 'ow much? 'Oo d'yer owe this money to, anyway?' Jack was confused but I was not. I knew what Mum was talking about. Then they really went at it, hammer and tongs – so loudly, in fact, that neither of them heard or noticed Dad enter the room. I coughed loudly and scraped my foot on the floor to draw their attention to who was standing quietly listening to them rowing.

'I owe five pounds an' some interest if yer must know,' Mum shouted.

'Oh blimey, whatever'll the ole man say when 'e finds out?' Jack whistled through pursed lips. He always called Dad 'the ole man' when we wasn't about. They finally became aware of Dad and as the penny dropped they both stared at him speechless.

'What's this yer don't want "the ole man" ter know? Something about owin' five pounds, is it?' he inquired quite calmly.

Mum covered her face with her apron and cried noisily, but she got no sympathy from Jack who pushed past Dad and left, leaving her to face the music. Dad slammed the door behind him with an 'An' good riddance!' Then he strode over to Mum and pulled her to her feet, although her face was still buried in the apron and she was wailing louder than ever. He shook her violently by the shoulders and then pushed her roughly back into the chair. 'You can turn yer waterworks off now, Polly. Let's 'ave the truth.'

I was standing mouth wide open afraid of what was going to happen next, but I practically jumped out of my skin when he yelled at me 'to stop gorpin' an' fill the kettle'. I was shaking so much that I had to lift the kettle with two hands when I staggered down the yard. Outside there were several neighbours obviously listening to what was going on in our house, but I just pushed through them. Frankie appeared as I was filling the kettle and offered to do it for me. When we got back to our door Mrs Jonesy and Mrs Phipps were still loitering, all ears, so Frankie deliberately poured some of the icy water on Mrs Jonesy's feet.

'Yow did that on purpose yer cheeky little sod!' she cried out in surprise.

'If yow'd done that ter me I'd ave wrung yer bloody neck,' Mrs Phipps chipped in, but Frankie only grinned and dropped the kettle, contents and all, on her foot. That did the trick! She ran off screaming and hopping down the yard. Frankie picked up the empty kettle and went to refill it but I noticed that none of the onlookers tried to wring his neck while he had the kettle in his hands. He poked his tongue out at them and entered the house in triumph. Indoors Mum was still crying into her apron and Dad was pacing back and forth, fuming.

'I warned yer what would 'appen if yer got into 'er clutches. Yow'll never be able ter get out of 'er debt now,' he stormed.

'But I ain't the only one,' Mum managed to blurt out. 'They all borra off 'er.'

'Never mind the others! It's this family I'm thinking about. Do yer know she can send yer ter prison if yer don't pay? Did yer think about that?' He glared angrily into her face.

'I thought I could pay a bit each week outa yower wages and Jack's, but now 'e's leavin' us,' she wept even louder.

'And a bloody good job!' answered Dad. ''E's gettin' too big fer 'is boots, demandin' this an' that every time 'e enters the 'ouse. I only 'ope 'e finds time ter marry this 'un, whoever she is.'

All the while I stood listening and Frankie sat calmly on the sofa reading his comic as though nothing was happening. During a lull in the shouting I made the tea, and as I was pouring the cups out Mum asked Dad what she should do.

'Goo ter bloody prison with the rest of yer croonies yow've

got yerself mixed up with for all I care,' he bawled in reply, and with that he stormed out slamming the door behind. I looked up at Granny's picture and saw the black crepe paper had slipped again – but then it always did when the door was slammed. Mum jumped up straight away and began rearranging the furniture which had been upset in the commotion. Then she forgot her tears as Jack came back into the room. She pointed at the crepe paper and told Jack it was another bad omen, but he only scoffed at her superstitions and went upstairs to collect his belongings. I poured four more mugs of tea. Mum didn't touch hers and when he came down neither did Jack. He had a parcel under his arm, and much as Mum pleaded with him he wouldn't stay.

'Carn't yer try an' 'elp me out Jack?' she wheedled.

'No! I'm off fer good this time. Yow've drove us all away. Them two will be the next.' He pointed at us kids. Then he paused, put his hand in his pocket and threw four half crowns on the table.

'That's the last yer'll get off me an' don't forget I want my suit from the pawnshop when I come back ter fetch me other things.'

And with that he left, making sure he gave the door a good hard slam as well. The pictures shook and one fell, just missing Frankie's head, but he didn't bat an eyelid and just kept on reading his comic. As I reached for the fallen picture he said to me, 'That door's gooin' ter fall off its 'inges one of these times.'

I looked at him and wished I could be so unconcerned. Frankie always got away with cheeking his elders but I never did. Mum was crying as she picked up the money and slipped it into her purse which she kept down her bosom. I went over to comfort her but she shooed me away. I might as well not have bothered, but then I was too young to know what to do anyway. Tears came to my eyes as I thought that this was my and Miss Louise's fault. If she had not lent Mum the money none of this would have happened. I blamed her and the fact she was a Jew for how she had used us all. Most of the moneylenders and pawnbrokers were Jewish and they had a reputation for meanness. I vowed to have no more to do with her but thought I ought to return her shoes and her key, so I snatched Frankie's comic and tried to persuade him to come with me. At first he refused, then he softened and consented.

'You know I will,' he said and jumped up ready.

We walked together over to the cottage. I had already made up my mind what I was going to say by the time Frankie had rapped on the door. He must have liked the sound it made because he gave it another couple for luck; my courage rising, too, I gave it two more. However, there was no reply, so I opened the door with the key and we entered. I kicked the slippers that were there waiting for me out of the way and then we saw her standing with her back to the fire.

'What's all that noise for?' she asked. 'Why didn't you just use your key, and why have you brought him?' she demanded, pointing her bony finger at Frankie.

''E's my brother an' where I go 'e goes,' I replied defiantly.

Frankie asked why she didn't answer our knock but she ignored this.

'We've come ter bring yer shoes back. We don't want anything more ter do with yow,' I told her.

'Well I never,' she exclaimed, advancing towards us. 'I never heard such cheeky kids in all my life. Get out of here at once.'

'Well, yer 'earin' 'em now!' put in Frankie. 'An' do yer know what ower neighbours an' the kids in the street call yer? An old blood sucker.'

She gave a sly grin at this. 'Oh that's mild. I've been called worse than that round here. Now clear off the pair of yer.'

'Here's yer key.' I flung it on the open ledger on the table. I thought if only I could steal that some time and destroy it, maybe she'd have no proof of what was owed her. But I knew this was a vain hope because the house was always locked securely. I walked over to the door before I spoke to her.

'I'm not coming any more for yer ter use me. It's all your fault. You've upset Mum an' Dad, an' ower Jack's left 'ome. So now I know yer won't be paid, so there!' I put out my tongue and Frankie did likewise, but before we had got out she said, 'You can tell your mother and father that I shall be calling at the usual time on Saturday. And I expect to be paid.'

I'd never seen her look so evil before. This was a side of her nature that she'd kept hidden from me but it made me realise my feelings were justified. I had no regrets as I slammed the door behind me and left the cottage for the last time.

4

Dad's Business Venture

When we got home I was surprised to see Dad sitting in his usual seat because he should have been at work.

'Katie,' he said to me. 'I want you ter take this letter ter your sister Mary. 'Ere's a penny for the tram fare and try to be as quick as you can.'

'Yes Dad,' I answered eagerly. I was glad of a reason to visit Mary in her new home.

I combed my hair, then quickly snatched up Topsey, my rag doll, and took the letter from Dad and went off. The ride on the tram was not far; only a halfpenny each way. When I arrived and rang the bell it was Albert who showed me in. I told him I had a letter from Dad for Mary. But Mary was out so I gave him the letter and began to tell him about the trouble at home.

'I'm not surprised,' he said. 'It's been going on for a long time, but yer Mum's bin very foolish an' so have the rest. Getting into the clutches of a money lender!' As if book-makers were much better, I thought. I gave him a hard look. I could see there'd be little sympathy here.

'I'll give Mary the letter when she comes 'ome. 'Ave you got your fare back?'

I told him I had and left without saying any more. When I returned home I told Dad what had happened and what Albert had said.

'Good girl,' he said. 'Put the kettle on, I expect she'll have a cuppa when she gets 'ere.' But we waited and waited all that afternoon and saw neither hide nor hair of Mary. I could see Dad was worried so after a couple of hours of hanging about I offered to return to Mary's.

'No,' he replied sadly. 'She don't seem to bother about us any more.'

'I can run there and back in no time if you ain't got the money for the tram,' I said eagerly.

'It's not the penny I'm bothered about,' he mumbled almost to himself, gazing into the fire. I wished I could help him then; he looked so down in the mouth hunched up by the stove.

'Can I do anything else for yer Dad?' I asked quietly.

'No, I don't think so. Anyway it's getting late. Yow better get off ter bed before yer Mum comes back.'

I said 'good night' and kissed him on his cheek but he didn't respond. He just sat there, his thoughts miles away. I wept a little as I climbed the creaky stairs, and when I got into the attic I knelt down beside the bed, put my hands together and prayed. I asked Jesus to help us, and to forgive Jack and me and to make Dad happy. I felt exhausted when I climbed into bed and I fell into a deep sleep from which I awoke next morning refreshed and happier. I went down to put the kettle on and while I was doing so in walked Albert.

'Good mornin' Katie,' he greeted me cheerily. 'Is yer Dad in?'

I told him they were in bed and I dashed up the stairs, two at a time, to fetch them. I leant over Mum and whispered to Dad.

'Dad, Albert's 'ere. 'E wants ter see yer.'

I could tell Mum was awake but she didn't offer to move or say anything. She wasn't on speaking terms with Albert.

'Tell 'im I'll be right down. As soon as I've slipped me trousers on.'

When Dad joined us Albert greeted him just as pleasantly as he had me, and I thought at least they're all happy this morning.

'I'm sorry,' Albert began, after clearing his throat. 'Mary couldn't come over last night. She was too upset when she read your letter, Sam. We talked it over and I've decided to let you 'ave five pounds. Yer can pay me back when yer can.' He concluded his speech.

'I don't know 'ow ter thank yer,' Dad said, grasping Albert by the hand. 'I'll see to it that Polly don't get into any debt again, don't you worry.' Albert nodded.

'Remember Sam,' he lowered his voice. 'I'm doin' this for your sake. Not your missus's.' He stroked my head and said as he was about to go, 'Be a good girl Katie, you've got a good Dad under the circumstances.' Dad thanked him again and he left, shutting the door quietly behind him.

I thanked God then for answering my prayer. Dad kissed me on the forehead and asked me to make another pot of tea and he sat down in his chair and smoked a quiet pipe of tobacco looking happier than he had for days. When Mum came down he told her about Albert's offer and she perked up, too. Dad told Mum that Miss Louise would be calling later for her money.

'You'd better be out when she comes,' he told her, but she didn't want telling twice. Soon after breakfast she was off. The rest of us settled down to wait. Dad warned us to be seen and not heard but we didn't need telling either. Frankie read his tattered old comic and I busied myself with the crocks. Just then there was a tap at the door.

'Come in,' Dad called out sharply. The door opened slowly and there stood Miss Louise.

''Ere's yer bloody five pounds,' he said, throwing five gold sovereigns on the table. She stooped and scooped them up. Dad was angry. I suppose he must have resented giving this much money to her; it was a large sum after all.

'Now get out!' he shouted at her. 'I don't want ter see yer round 'ere any more an' I don't want Katie to come near yower place either!'

She just glared back and said acidly, 'What about the interest?'

'Yow can wait fer that. Now get out of my house, you bloody old bugger.'

Frankie peered over the top of his comic, unable to resist the temptation to join in. 'That's tellin' 'er,' he said.

'That's quite enough lip from yow,' Dad snapped at him. 'Get yerself washed an' put that comic on the fire. It's filthy.'

Reluctantly he did as he was told. The comic wanted burning anyway; it was torn and the print was totally obscured by the grimy hands of its previous owners. Miss Louise stood quietly observing this domestic scene, grinning. Dad was furious by now. He made a move towards her and bawled at her to 'get out', which she did but not without slamming the door for all she was worth behind her. Amazingly this must have been the final straw for it, because its top hinge broke and it swivelled on the bottom one, narrowly missing Miss Louise before it crashed to the floor. With that she marched off, and after we'd got our breath, I made the usual cup of tea while Frankie went to fetch nails and hammer from Dad's tool box so he could fix the door before Mum returned and explanations were necessary. In fact the door was mended, and we were drinking our tea when she came in. Dad told her that it was settled but he warned her she must never borrow again. He warned Frankie and me as well. Just then brother Jack came strolling in to collect the rest of his clothes. He went straight up the stairs and a few minutes later came down carrying a parcel of his things. Mum looked pleadingly at him but not a word was said between any of us until he was opening the door to leave and Dad said, 'Bloody good riddance, an' don't bang the door when you go, I've only just mended it.' But he did and once again the pictures on the walls quivered in fear. After that things went more smoothly for a few days, at least until the following Monday.

I got up as usual at seven o'clock to make Dad his cup of tea and his bread and cheese for dinner. We never normally talked in the morning: he got up at the last moment and rushed out without a word. But this morning he spoke to me. He told me to be a good girl for Mum, and that he would give me some money to go to the pictures. I said I would be good and thanked him, and then quite unexpectedly he bent down and kissed my cheek and turned and abruptly left. I loved it when he did that. I couldn't remember the last time he'd shown me so much affection. I pitched into the chores with a light heart, singing to myself as I worked. Then after about an hour I heard the familiar heavy tread of Dad's boots on the cobbles. The door opened and there he was looking pale and worried.

'Did you forget something Dad?' I asked, though I knew he hadn't.

'We've all bin laid off work,' he said simply.

'Oh, dear, whatever will Mum say?' I burst out. Her reactions in situations like this were never predictable.

'Matter a damn what she says,' he muttered almost to himself. 'We'll all 'ave ter go on the parish relief* again.'

Just then Mum, half-dressed, came into the room, but Dad had hardly got a word out before she cut him off.

'I know. I 'eard yer. Whatter we gooin' ter do?' she demanded.

'I'll think of something don't worry, but in the meantime we won't starve. We're all goin' along to see the relief officer,' he soothed her.

'When?'

'Now if yer like,' he said impatiently and went out. I followed him and saw him join some of his mates who were waiting on the corner. Then they all turned and went in a group to the Welfare Offices. This was the same old tumbledown mission hall which the Sally Army used and which all the neighbours used when there was a wedding or some other big function to be held.

I hung back and watched what would happen. The men went in and stated their case to the man in charge, but he merely informed them that they would get nothing immediately and that they were to come back when their money had gone. So there was nothing to be done. The men drifted away and I returned home. By the end of that week things were looking grim around our way. Things were particularly bad for the people who owed Miss Louise because the interest was growing all the time. The women were to be seen hanging around in the yard talking quietly or trying to wash to get a few more rags to the pawnshop. The men idled their time away on street corners or outside the pub, cadging a drink or a smoke. There were more quarrels than usual. We never had much to eat in ordinary times, but we had less now

---

* A weekly dole in the form of clothing and food tokens to be exchanged at local shops. The system was originally set up under the 1834 New Poor Law Act.

and us kids were really glad of the extra slice of bread and jam that we were given for our school breakfast.

The Monday after the men were laid off I came home from school to find crowds of people gathered outside Miss Louise's door chattering excitedly. There was a buzz of expectation about them and quite a few seemed to be smiling and jolly. Mum was amongst the crowd; Frankie and Liza too.

'What's the matter?' I asked Frankie when I had pushed through to him.

'Don't yer know? Miss Louise has died,' he answered.

'That's nothing for them to smile about,' I said, quite shocked at their callousness.

'But they won't 'ave ter pay 'er what they owe 'er now she's dead, will they?'

I had no time to answer; I spotted Dad edging his way through the throng. He must have heard what was being said because he rounded on them.

'Don't yer kid yerselves, yer stupid women. Yow'll still 'ave ter pay. Yow'd better clear off before 'er brother comes.'

At that they began to disperse, chatting and nodding all the time. Mum, Frankie and Liza had been the first to go, before Dad saw them. I was glad he hadn't seen me either as I hurried away in the opposite direction.

This news provided ample scope for gossip in the next few days. Next day Mr Vulcan arrived and the first thing he did was to call on everyone who owed money to his sister. I bumped into him and told him I was sorry to hear about his sister, which I was, despite how she'd treated us. I also hoped she hadn't told him about Frankie's and my rudeness although why I should have been bothered about him I can't think. He smiled, thanked me and patted me on the head before knocking at our door. Dad invited him in and I followed.

'I suppose yow've come for yer interest?' said Dad sharply. 'Well, I ain't got it yet. I'll bring it when I can. No need ter call.'

Dad sat back in his chair, expecting Mr Vulcan to leave, but he paused a moment, looking first at Dad then at me, and I thought, This is it, now what'll he say?

'You have a good girl here,' he began, much to my relief. 'She was good to my sister. I'll forget the interest you owe and cross it off the book as paid.'

'That's very kind of you,' Dad muttered grudgingly, but Mr Vulcan carried on without listening.

'I've locked up the cottage and when I come back in a couple of days I shall sell up my sister's belongings. So if there's anything Katie would like, she can have it.'

'Thank you, Mr Vulcan,' I said as he turned and left. After he'd gone Dad said he would consider what Mr Vulcan had said but I knew already what I wanted and I knew Dad wouldn't object. Those two days couldn't pass quickly enough. Then Mr Vulcan returned from London as he said he would to arrange the funeral.

Everybody in the district came out to watch the coffin being carried away. It was not a grand affair like Granny's. There appeared to be only one wreath. The neighbours didn't have the usual collection for flowers either. Some had tried but the general feeling was that she wasn't one of us. The hearse took her to St Paul's churchyard where the service was to be held. I waited around to watch the burial. I wept when they lowered her coffin into the ground. I'd liked her until the money lending began, and I was sorry for being unkind to her. Then Frankie saw me.

'No use cryin', 'er's dead an' that's that.' And in that breath I thought how like Mum he sounded.

He left me to walk home alone. Later that afternoon I saw a horse-drawn van pull up outside the cottage and soon a burly fellow was fetching furniture out and loading it into the van. I waited for Mr Vulcan to come out with a group of our ever-curious neighbours. At last he emerged and called me in. This caused a murmur of surprise amongst the onlookers. I pushed past them and went in with him.

'I want you to look around, and if there's anything you'd like, don't be afraid to say. I know Louise would like you to have something,' he said quietly.

I hesitated for a while. Then I overcame my shyness and said I would like the coloured wool from the trunk upstairs.

'Very well, go up and help yourself,' he replied. He gave me a pretty cane basket to put it in and I went upstairs, opened the trunk and loaded all the balls I could get into the basket. I looked for the knitted garments that I used to help her with but they must have all been sold. Just then I glanced through the little bedroom window and saw all the women and kids still hanging about outside. Then I closed the lid of the trunk and returned downstairs, tears of happiness in my eyes. As I wiped them on my pinafore Mr Vulcan asked what was wrong with me. I found myself gazing at the harmonium and my memories of the happy times I'd spent listening to Miss Louise play came flooding back and I wept more. Mr Vulcan handed me his black-edged handkerchief.

'I'm happy to have these,' I said truthfully. 'But I was thinking about how we used to sing together.' He looked at me awhile before he said.

'Would you like the harmonium? I have no use for it.' I didn't know what to say: I couldn't believe that I'd heard him correctly. My mouth fell open and I must have stared wide-eyed at him. But I hesitated only a second before I accepted his gift excitedly.

'Run along home then and tell your Dad to come and wheel it away.'

I elbowed my way through the nosey parkers gossiping in the yard and ran home to tell Dad my good news. I fell indoors and crashed into Mum.

'What's the matter with yer? What's in that basket?' she demanded.

'It's a present from Mr Vulcan. Where's Dad?' I blurted out.

''E's down the pub with 'is mates. Why?' She was curious now.

I didn't stay to explain. I dashed out down the street to the pub to get him round to the cottage before Mr Vulcan changed his mind. I'd only gone part of the way when I collided with Dad.

'Well, well, well, an' what 'ave yow bin up to now?' Excitedly I told him what had happened and begged him to let me have the harmonium.

'We'll see,' he answered calmly. 'Don't rush me. If 'e says you're ter have it, it'll still be there.' Then he took my hand and we walked round to the cottage. There the loading was still underway and the women were still hanging about. Dad and I went in and Mr Vulcan explained that he wished to give me the harmonium and that there was a clean bed upstairs if we wanted it. Dad thanked him and said he would return for the bed after he'd wheeled the instrument to our house. Mr Vulcan wouldn't hear of this but offered to send the removal men over with it. I was in tears of joy. I kissed Mr Vulcan: I was overwhelmed. I was the owner of a harmonium as well as the basket and the wool. Then we returned to our house under the gaze of the neighbours.

'I wonder where they got the money to buy them?' I heard Mrs Woods say.

Then Mrs Jonesy replied. 'That Polly's a dark 'orse if yow arsk me.'

Mum was pleased as punch when she saw what we'd got, particularly when the men arrived with the brass bedsteads and a red striped flock mattress. However, she wasn't so pleased with the harmonium.

'We ain't 'avin' that contraption in the 'ouse. We ain't got no room fer it,' she told Dad. Dad scowled at Mum when one of the removal men said to him, 'Yow've got a right one theea mate. I know what I'd do if she was my missus.'

But he ignored the remark and concentrated on bringing the things in. He hauled the harmonium into the room past Mum, pausing only to wink at me. That meant it was mine for keeps. Mum was right though; there was very little room for it and Dad had to move the mangle to fit it in. Mum was furious at this and demanded to know where her mangle was going.

'Inside the pantry,' Dad snapped back. 'An' yow can come an' give me a hand. An' shut that door too before all the neighbours come nosing in.' But Mum didn't lift a finger to help and gave as good as she got.

'Do it yerself. I'm gooin' ter put the kettle on an mek a cuppa tea.' This was a ploy she always resorted to when she wanted to avoid doing something. Dad knew it was no good arguing with her and he carried on with the job.

'That's where the mangle is and that's where it stays,' he told her when he'd done. Mum ignored him. He pushed the harmonium into the place where the mangle had stood, then sat down to sup his mug of tea. He finished before Mum who was still sulking.

'When yow've drunk yer tea, we'll get the mattress and the bedsteads in,' he said impatiently.

'I s'ppose that's for Katie an' all,' she snapped sarcastically.

'No, it's fer Frankie. He's gettin' ter be a big lad an' he's noticing things.'

No more was said except for Mum's moans and groans as she struggled to get the bedding upstairs to the attic. Now there were three single beds in our small room; I had Mary's old one, Liza had the one we all used to sleep in and Frankie had Miss Louise's. I was thrilled with these gifts, especially to have a bed to myself.

When the house was empty I would take the key from round my neck, unlock the harmonium and experiment with pulling out some of the stops. I began trying to play 'God Save the King', but after tapping away for an hour with one finger I hadn't made much progress. Later I improved and graduated to two fingers, and eventually learnt to play the tune using all my fingers. I thought I was ever so clever and I wanted everyone to hear me, so each time I spotted one of the neighbours near our house I would bang out the tune. The noise must have been awful but it was sweet music to my ears.

I was not allowed to play when Mum and Dad were in because they couldn't stand the din, so I had to wait until they were down the pub to enjoy myself. We used to invite in the other children from the yard and I would pretend to be our music teacher and conduct a lesson. One night I dressed up in one of Mum's frocks and Frankie donned Dad's billy-cock hat but in the middle of 'Rock of Ages' Dad returned. The kids scattered quickly and Frankie and I had to explain ourselves; he ignored Liza as usual. We were warned not to dress in our parents' clothes and he threatened Frankie with his belt, but nothing more was said about it.

77

After a few weeks all our money was gone and everything was in pawn so Dad had to go to the relief office. When he returned Mum asked what they had said.

'They're sendin' the visitor termorra to see if we've got anything we can sell. In the meantime they've given me this to go on with,' he answered, throwing our ration card across the table. When Mum had looked at it she cried out.

'We carn't live on that!'

'We'll 'ave ter manage,' Dad replied calmly. 'Other people 'ave to, an' they 'ave more kids than us.'

'That's their bad luck,' screeched Mum. 'I'd 'ave 'ad mower, if yow'd 'ave 'ad yower way.'

Dad was not prepared to stand any more and got out of the chair into which he had just flopped.

'Talk ter yerself, Polly. I'm off out.'

'Where do yer think yer gooin'?' she demanded, but he'd closed the door behind him and left.

The next day the visitor came. He didn't even knock but just walked right in and went through the house looking to see if we had anything of value to part with before we could receive any relief. Dad didn't object to him nosing around but I wondered what Mum would have said if she'd been home; she was out cleaning at the fish shop. Dad looked as if he didn't care what happened any more.

'Is there anything you haven't told me?' the visitor asked Dad, his eyes settling on my harmonium.

'No,' he replied at once, defying him to look under its cover.

'Then what's this?' he said, lifting the cloth.

'That's my Katie's,' Dad told him, snatching the cover off him. 'I ain't partin' with that. It was a gift ter the child.'

'Well,' the man replied. 'I'll have to report it. That's my job and I doubt whether we can grant you anything until it's sold. Good day.'

He went and Dad slammed the door after him. 'Good day and good riddance to you too,' he said angrily.

The next day another visitor called but he said the same as the first. Dad looked sad and worried. I didn't like to see him like this so when the second man had gone I turned to Dad.

'You can sell the harmonium, Dad, if it'll 'elp. I can't play it properly anyway and I know the sound of it gets on Mum's nerves.' He looked at me with a gentle, sad expression on his face.

'Do you really want me to sell it?' he asked.

'No, Dad,' I answered truthfully.

'Then it stays where it is. I'll think of something else ter 'elp us through. Now put the kettle on an' we'll 'ave a pot of tea an' think.'

A cup of tea was our universal cure-all and comforter. We sat and drank our tea in silence then Dad stood up and told me to tell Mum, when she returned, that he'd gone to have one last talk to the relief officer. He'd never told Mum about the words he'd had with the relief officers, which was a blessing really because she would never have shut up about it. I don't know what was said at the relief office but when Dad came back he just threw the ration card on the table in disgust. Mum snatched it up to see what we had got but Dad forestalled the outburst he knew was coming.

'Now don't go off the deep end. I've thought of an idea to bring some extra money in the house.'

'What? Not another one of your bright ideas.' And with that she went off to the shop to collect the miserable amount of provisions that were due.

Dad sat poking the dead ashes in the grate and sucking on his empty clay pipe. The tea caddy was empty too. I had to make do with stewing the old tea leaves. When Mum returned and saw the teapot on the hob she flared up.

'Yow can throw that down the sink! It's bin stewed I don't know 'ow many times. 'Ere's some. An' goo careful with it.' She tossed a two-ounce packet on the table.

This was how we went on then. It was winter and the weather was wet and cold and our life was hard; we survived only on hand-outs from the parish. Soon we were down to our last lumps of coal. Although Mum was working at the fish shop she didn't get much for her labours, sometimes only some fish and chips. Still they helped, especially if we had a loaf of bread to go with them. Dad would go out very early each morning, without even a cup of tea inside him, to tramp round looking for a job – anything to tide us over. Plenty of times I'm sure he stayed out only to avoid Mum's sharp tongue because there was no work to be had for any of the men.

Late one afternoon as I was packing some old boots I had begged with wet slack and tea leaves to use as fuel on the fire the door was flung open and Dad stumbled in. I saw at once he'd been drinking.

'Yer won't 'ave ter do that much more,' he said. 'You'll see. I've got a good idea and this time it'll work.'

I didn't understand what he was mumbling about. He was looking round with a vacant look on his face and I was frightened. Then he suddenly told me to fetch the chopper from the cellar.

'What for?' I managed to ask.

'What for? Never mind what for, just do as yer told at once before I change me mind.'

I fled down the cellar and returned with the chopper. I handed it to him at arm's length, not knowing what he was about to do. He snatched it and I watched, terrified now that something awful was about to happen. He turned and went upstairs muttering to himself. I wished somebody else was at home because I was afraid to be in the house with him in this mood. Loud bangs started upstairs and I imagined all kinds of things were happening. Then I heard him call down from the attic for me to open the stairs door wide. I was too scared to reply but I opened the door anyway and hid behind it. The next moment something heavy came clattering down the stairs. I wedged myself further out of sight. My first thought was that this was Dad lying at the foot of the stairs having killed himself. I clasped my hands tight over my eyes and scarcely breathed. But I knew I had to look, so slowly I peeped round the door. Then I opened my fingers wide and peered down at the floor. With a sigh of relief I dropped my hands, because instead of Dad lying there there was the attic door which had fallen in such a way that it was wedging the door back, trapping me where I was. I called to Dad but he didn't hear me; instead he sent another door crashing down. Then he came down himself, managing with difficulty to negotiate the obstacles on the floor.

'Well I never!' He smiled when he saw where I was. 'I told yer ter open the door wide, not ter get behind it,' he chuckled.

'Katie,' he said when he had released me. 'You know what I'm gooin' ter do? I'm gooin' to sell firewood an' these doors are gooin' ter give me a start.'

'But what's Mum goin' ter say when she sees what you've done?' I began to get worried again.

'Never mind what yer Mum says. Any'ow it'll be all cleared away by the time she gets 'ome.'

He was looking pleased with himself as he dragged the table to the side of the room to make space to work in. He set to with a will and soon the doors were reduced to kindling. After I'd got used to the idea I helped to count the sticks and tie them up in bundles. He tore one of Mum's dusters into strips for this purpose and we busied ourselves counting out sticks and piling up bundles. Then the door opened and Mum walked in. She saw the mess and flew off the handle at once.

'Whatcha dooin'? What's all that wood on me clane flooar? Ain't we got enough broken quarries without yow cracking any mower?' she demanded.

'Sit down and keep calm,' Dad told her. 'Listen ter what I 'ave ter say. I've 'ad this idea for a long time an' if I can get a few customers, we'll be able ter buy some extra food an' we'll be able to rent a better 'ouse, with good strong doors not like these rotten ones.' He waved his hand at the firewood.

'Oh my God!' she shrieked, not waiting for Dad to finish. 'Where's these dooars come from?'

'The attic an' our room. They were hangin' off anyway,' he told her matter-of-factly.

'They wouldn't 'ave bin 'angin' off if yow'd 'ave put a nail in 'em. I don't know what the landlord will say or do when 'e finds out,' she wailed.

''E won't find out if nobody tells 'im and 'e ain't likely ter goo upstairs in any case,' Dad pointed out to her. 'Now put the kettle on Polly an' we'll 'ave a nice cuppa tea then Katie an' me'll get cracking.'

By the time we were drinking it Mum had calmed down considerably. Then she had to go back to the shop to get our fish and chips, so we bundled up the rest of the wood and, as it was dark, ventured out to see if Dad could find some customers for his new business. We couldn't have gone in daylight for fear that Dad would be spotted and reported to the reflief officers; then as now claimants were not allowed to earn money. I pushed the go-cart with the bundles inside covered with a cloth, and Dad strolled behind looking nonchalantly about him. The first shop we stopped at gave Dad an order right away, providing the wood was dry and clean. It couldn't have been anything else but Dad had put out the best wood the first time; some of the rest was rotten.

Dad's business prospered. Frankie helped with the chopping and I went with Dad when he delivered the orders. When the doors were sold Dad went out and bought soap boxes, orange boxes, even smelly fish boxes to use, and Mum was happy with money coming in again. He always said he did best when I was with him.

One day Frankie was chopping a particularly springy orange box when suddenly the head flew off the handle and cracked our only mirror.

'Now look what yer've done!' yelled Mum. 'Another bloody seven years' bad luck!'

'Rubbish!' he snapped back and ran out. He didn't come back for several hours, afraid of Mum's temper but Dad said he would replace the mirror and this seemed to pacify her.

Another day we nearly came unstuck altogether. The previous day the proprietor of a little paraffin shop had asked Dad to deliver the sticks in the afternoon because she was closing early; and to oblige and keep a customer Dad agreed. Off we went the next day and had nearly got to the shop when Dad spotted a relief officer. He pushed me into an entry and we hid there until the man had passed by. Then we hurried to the shop, delivered our wood and hurried back home.

Another day we returned to find an empty space where my

harmonium should have been. I burst into tears because I was sure Mum had pawned it or sold it. Dad moved slowly towards Mum and I could see by the look of him that he was furious.

'Now I warned yow, Polly,' he began. 'Where's it gone?'

She turned round without betraying a sign of understanding what he was on about.

'What're yer talkin' about? Where's what gone?' she asked mildly.

'Yow know very well what I mean!' he shouted. 'Katie's harmonium. If ever yow've parted with that, I warn yer, I'll kill yer!' And I believe he would have too.

'Oh that,' she replied. 'Well we had the visitor call about four o'clock. Frankie warned me he was comin' down the street so we wheeled it into the pantry until he'd gone. But we couldn't get it back agen 'cause one of the wheels 'as come off.'

'Oh, I see,' said Dad, calming down. 'I'll soon fix that.'

Dad fixed it by removing all four wheels and with an effort we dragged it back into position.

'That stays as a permanent fixture from now on,' Dad said. I could have hugged my Mum that day for saving the harmonium but I was afraid if I did she would push me away.

We were all made very wary by this brush with authority and Frankie even refused to go out with Dad that night in case they were spotted by the parish man.

'Yow'll do as yer told!' he was told. 'It's only for another few days then I'll sign off,' Dad promised.

Towards the end of that week the visitor called on us again. We knew he was coming because we could see him calling at our neighbours in the yard first. This gave us enough time to cover the harmonium and clear away any telltale signs of wood.

'Come in,' Dad called out as the knock was heard, but the man was already in the room. Without any preliminaries he began interrogating Dad.

'What's this I hear about you selling firewood?' the man demanded.

'An' who's told you that?' Dad looked the man straight in the eye.

'I cannot divulge any information. You were seen one afternoon this week and I've made inquiries.' His voice tailed off. Dad just turned away and didn't reply. When he could see he would get nothing out of Dad, the visitor continued.

'You know you can go to prison for failure to report a source of income like this?' he said.

Dad turned to the man, head bowed. 'I'm very sorry,' he said humbly. 'I was goin' ter call terday but it's bin snowin'.'

We children were huddled together, scared of what would happen. We knew only too well what could happen to Dad and we were afraid. I began to weep and so did Liza.

'Please don't take our Dad away,' I pleaded with him, and Frankie too chipped in, 'That's quite so sir, he said he was going to sign off.'

We must have looked pathetic because the man paused, looking at us, then he turned to Dad and said if Dad promised to call at the office he wouldn't report the matter.

'I'll come now,' Dad said, obviously relieved. However the offices were closed so he said he would call first thing in the morning. Dad thanked the man several times but he just grunted and left.

'Phew, that was a close shave,' Dad said, flopping into the chair wiping his brow. True to his word Dad signed off the next day and we heard no more about it.

In the weeks that followed he built up a regular round of customers and boasted that it was better than going to work, especially on cold winter mornings. But it was not good enough for Mum. She always had to find fault with everything; she wouldn't have been our Mum else. As the days went by she moaned more and more about the mess the wood caused.

'I ain't 'avin' this mess under me feet every day. Yow'll 'ave ter doo summat about it,' she told him.

It put him off his stroke and the chopper slipped, cutting his finger. Blood spurted and he swore.

'No? But yer 'old out yer bloody 'and when the money comes in, don't yer?'

'Now Mum's goin' ter spoil everything,' I whispered to Frankie.

'No, she ain't!' Dad shouted, having overheard my remark. 'I'm thinkin' of buildin' me a shed where I can work in peace,' he added, sucking his bleeding finger.

'The landlord ain't goona allow it. We owe too much rent,' she replied.

'I'll get round ter that when he calls,' said Dad not to be outdone. Mum didn't bother to reply but went off mumbling to herself, not forgetting to shut the door with a bang after her.

The next day, as it happened, was rent day. No firewood could be chopped up until after the landlord had called so the room was clean and tidy, all except for the odd quarry tile Dad had broken during the wood-chopping. Eventually there was a knock on the door and Dad called out to the landlord, Mr Priest, to enter. Mr Priest looked like an undertaker, dressed in his long black frock coat, top hat, long sideburns and grey whiskers. Dad paid over the four shillings and while he was entering it up in the book said, 'Mr Priest, I was wondering if yer could give me permission to build a small wooden shed facing the house?'

Mr Priest looked up and stared at Dad for a while and Dad stood there waiting for a reply.

'What will you be wanting it for?' he inquired.

'Well, you can see,' Dad replied, waving his arm. 'We have no room for everything an' I thought the place would look brighter if the missus 'ad somewhere to put her buckets an' brooms.' The landlord thought for a bit, stroking his beard, before he gave his decision.

'Now if you'll promise to pay off some of the arrears you can build your shed. But I'll have to raise the rent one and six a week.'

Dad gave his promise and he kept his word. He built his shed which, made as it was of old floorboards from a couple of hovels that had been empty for years, resembled a shack. He was no carpenter but he did his best and he began to sell wood on a larger scale. He supplied shops with the best quality wood which he bought cheap from sawmills; he even sold sawdust to pubs and butchers' shops to sprinkle on their floors. When any of our neighbours wanted firewood theirs was from old fish boxes, but they had it cheap at a penny a bowlful, and 'no tick', 'cash on the nail,' as he said firmly.

Now he was at home more Dad and I became closer. He listened to me more and had time to answer my questions. He still didn't know whose side to take when Mum carried on at us but she never came to the shed while we were chopping wood with him, so we had a retreat. He took us to the pictures sometimes and we shared his intimate refuge from Mum. Each night when we'd finished our various tasks he would look at our hands by the light of a candle and probe with a needle for splinters. We didn't like him doing this for he was rough, but we got used to it and our hands became tough. Kids like us had to be tough in those days.

Liza was like Mum; she never came into the shed to help. She only came to fetch wood for Mum or bring us our cocoa. Dad never bothered about her. He said she was more trouble than she was worth. One night she brought in the usual cocoa and watched while Dad removed a splinter from my palm. Dad looked up and caught her grinning.

'What are yer waitin' for?' he asked her, but she just shrugged her shoulders and held out her hands.

'I ain't got splinters in mine.' She turned to leave, but Dad got off his orange box and grabbed hold of her hands and proceeded to prod her palms with the needle.

'How do yer like that? That's took the smile off yer face,' he told her. 'Now goo an' tell yer Mum that!' She ran off screaming but she never pulled faces at us again if Dad was around.

When we'd finished that night Dad gave us tuppence to go the first half at the Queen's Hall. He told us to hurry back home after the picture had finished because it might get foggy later. He told Frankie to take care of me and so we went off hand in hand. When we got there the chucker-out told us to go in quickly because the film had started. The board over the door proclaimed that it was *The Clutching Hand*. Frankie had seen it before and thought I wouldn't like it and tried to dissuade me from going in. I was determined to see it and I pulled away from him and went up to the box office to pay my penny, hoping he would follow. I started up the cold stone steps to the gallery. It was dark and dismal. There were only two dim lights flickering from two iron brackets high up on the wall. They made weird shadows on the cracked plaster of the walls. I was beginning to get scared even before I'd seen the film. My clogs clattered on the steps and I looked back over my shoulder a couple of times to see if Frankie was following me, but he wasn't. When I eventually reached the gods I hesitated, afraid to push the door open, but after a couple of minutes I became too frightened to stand there in the dark any longer. I pushed the door and went in. I could see that the picture had only just started. Then quietly I walked down the steps and felt for a seat on one of the wooden forms; after being hissed at by several people I found one empty, next to an old woman. She smelt of snuff when she leaned over and said, 'Sit down dearie, yer blockin' me view.' I flopped down in the seat but missed and landed on the floor. This provoked more disapproval.

'Shut yer row down theea,' a voice boomed out from the darkness. This brought the chucker-out to see what the commotion was about, but luckily he couldn't tell what row it had come from because the old woman snatched me up by the hem of my frock and sat me on the seat. Then everything went quiet apart from the piano which was played slower and slower and quieter and quieter as a hand moved across the screen. Then the fingers began to move and the piano got louder and stopped with a final note as the hand fell on to the floor. Everyone was glued to their seats in anticipation of what was to happen next. I was almost too scared to look. I hoped and prayed that the lights would come on so I could fly down those steps. Then the woman took a paper bag out and I thought she had some sweets and might give one to me. But she dipped her thumb and forefinger into the bag and took out a pinch of snuff. She saw me looking at her and thrusting the bag under my nose invited me to take a pinch. I jumped up in fright and in the process knocked the snuff out of her hand. It went all over us. I began sneezing and couldn't stop; nor could several of our neighbours who'd shared in the shower. Someone called out, 'Turn that woman out, an' that brat.' In the confusion that followed the form tipped up propelling us all on to the floor. Then the lights went up and I saw the chucker-out standing over us.

'Who's mekin' all this racket?' he bawled in a thunderous voice.

'Me,' I called out. I would have been only too pleased to be thrown out, and to no one's surprise with a poke and a shove I was. He conducted me back down the cold stone steps by the scruff of my neck and soon I found myself back in the street again.

'Don't let me see yer here agen,' he warned me, but I was off at a run.

Dad had been right; it was foggy and getting thicker so I had to slow down because I couldn't see where I was going. I started to sing to give myself courage and to avoid running into someone. Ghostly shapes loomed out of the fog and then disappeared again. A cat dashed over my feet at one point and I began to think about the disembodied hand in the film. Eventually I reached our yard safely and entered the house breathless. The gas was unlit and the only light was the feeble glow of the coals. Mum and Dad were dozing in their chairs but Dad opened his eyes as I sat down and asked if I'd enjoyed the picture.

'Yes Dad,' I lied. I thought that if I told him what had really happened he might not let me go again and I wanted to see Charlie Chaplin and the Keystone Cops ones that were coming soon.

'Where's Frankie?' Dad continued, scratching his head.

'I don't know, Dad,' I told him. 'He said he'd seen the film once an' didn't want to see it agen.'

'I'll give 'im a feel of my belt when he comes in. I told 'im ter look after yow.' He was annoyed and I had not wanted to get Frankie into trouble. 'Eat yer bread an' drippin' an' drink yer cocoa. Then get up ter bed.'

I was not keen to go yet because I still had a vivid memory of that hand. I offered to do some jobs until the others returned. But Dad told me Liza had already done them, which struck me as a miracle. I asked if I could wait for Frankie but Mum, who I'd thought was asleep, piped up at that.

'No!' she shrieked. 'Tek yer piece of candle an' do as yer told.'

So I took my time over the bread and dripping and I spilt my cocoa on the floor in an effort to play for time.

'That's the last of the cocoa. There's no mower in the jug. An' wipe that mess up,' Mum snapped at me.

In the end I gave in and reluctantly mounted the narrow stairs. The candlelight on the peeling walls made scary shapes that I'd never noticed before. I tried to look straight ahead until I reached the top, then I entered our attic room and stood there as my eyes accustomed themselves to the dim light. My eyes fell on the bed and to my horror something began slowly to stir under the blanket. I let out a terrified scream and scuttled down the stairs. But in my hurry to get away from whatever it was in the bed I missed my footing and fell. As I did so I grabbed the banister to save myself. It broke my fall but the strain of this was too much; it ripped out of the wall and landed on top of me at the foot of the stairs.

'What the devil's the matter?' I heard Dad ask as he jumped up off his seat.

'There's something in my b-b-bed,' I stammered as he bent over me. He sat me down roughly on the sofa and Mum said she was going to find out what I was on about.

'I wonder if it's that Jack the Ripper,' she laughed, and followed Dad out to the shed, leaving me with Liza who had just come in. We clung to each other, the only time I ever remember this happening. Mum came back with the chopper and Dad brandished a heavy lump of wood. They crept up the stairs but can't have got more than half way up when our cat, Pete, came scurrying down followed by the chopper and the lump of wood. Dad stamped back down, leaving Mum to get her second wind.

'No more bloody pictures fer yow me girl,' he said angrily. 'Yow've frightened the life out of yer mother.'

I was so relieved that I began to weep tears of joy but Liza was not similarly affected. She pushed me over and said, 'I knew it wasn't nobody, yow great big baby!' I knew she was just as scared as I was when we heard the cat on the stairs.

Mum flopped down in her chair and didn't say a word but by her look I could see I would suffer for it later. Just then Frankie walked in. He couldn't have returned at a less opportune moment.

'An' where do yer think yow've bin till now?' Dad was in a right lather.

'I got lost in the fog,' Frankie said, looking at his feet.

'An' where's the money I gave yer fer the pictures?' he demanded. 'An' look at me when I talk to yer.'

'Spent it,' Frankie said at once.

'Right! Get up them stairs. There's no supper for yow me lad.' And with that Dad thrust him roughly towards the door. But Frankie didn't care; he always had something hidden away in his tuckbox for occasions like this.

5

Finding Out the Facts of Life

Our next-door neighbours, Mr and Mrs Buckley, had a daughter named Sally who had been staying with an aunt for a year or so. I didn't realise why she'd been away, but when she returned I soon found out. She was three years older than I was. She was mysterious about herself but had plenty to say on the subject of her boyfriends. I was impressed by her self-confidence; I'd never had one boyfriend, let alone as many as she'd had. She used make-up and bleached her hair and was a very attractive girl. The neighbours held their noses in the air when she went out dolled up. Everybody seemed to shun her but I felt sorry for her and we became close friends. However, she didn't suit Mum. The first time she found us chatting in the yard she rushed up and dragged me away.

'Don't yer 'ave nuthin' ter do with that brazen 'uzzy!' she warned me, and when we were indoors she rounded on me. 'Don't yer dare let me catch yer even looking' at 'er agen.'

'Why? What's she done?' I asked angrily.

'Never yow mind what she's done. Yer'll find out when yer older,' she ranted. 'She's the talk of the district. After anythink with trousers on, or off!'

'I don't believe it,' I said, although I knew she had boyfriends.

'Whether yer believe it or not, don't ever let me see or know yer've 'ad anything to do with 'er agen,' she concluded.

Saying this to me was like holding a red rag to a bull: the more anyone told me not to do a thing, the more I tried to do it. So we continued to meet on the sly. I bumped into her one evening when I was out fetching Dad twopenn'orth of twist. We greeted each other and were soon chatting. She asked me if I'd like to meet her current boyfriend and I agreed.

'There's two really,' she said winking. I didn't understand

what she meant by this but she smiled and asked if I would like to go to the 'flicks' the following Saturday. I agreed and we arranged to go to the second house. I would have to wait until Mum and Dad went out to the pub so we couldn't make it to the first. The second house finished at ten so that would give me plenty of time to get home before my parents.

Saturday afternoon arrived and I had the house to myself to get ready. I sorted through my frocks but could find none that fitted me; I'd outgrown them all and was waiting until I'd grown into Liza's castoffs. I tried hers on anyway and after rummaging about for a bit I found one I liked. But it was too big in the bust and too long. I put it back in the trunk, disappointed that there was nothing right for me to wear and wondering what I was going to do, for I wanted to go out with Sally. I decided to go round to her place to see if she had anything I could borrow. Sure enough she offered straight away and gave me some lipstick as well.

'Yow 'ave ter look nice for the boys.' She nudged me, and I, innocent enough to think I could have a boyfriend like her, accepted the dress and the make-up. She was combing out her blonde hair and pouring a colourless liquid from a bottle over her head. She noticed my interest and offered me some.

'It'll make your hair blonde like mine.'

I thought her hair was a lovely colour so I took the remains of the bottle and the other things, thanked her and returned next door. There was still no one home so I was safe to carry on with my experiments in dressing like an adult. The dress was a little too long, but they were worn long at that time so with the help of a pin or two I was able to achieve the desired effect. However, it fitted tight across my bosom. My breasts were developing fast and I was ashamed to see that my nipples showed through the material. I couldn't wear it so I returned to Sally's. When I showed her she lent me a silk shawl to drape round my shoulders and over my breasts. I returned home to admire the effect. I thought I was the cat's whiskers. Then I began combing my hair, wondering if I dared use the peroxide. I'd look better blonde and I assumed that I could wash the colour out before my parents saw: I must have been naive to think that bleach would affect my hair differently from anything else. I was engrossed in these thoughts and just about to drip it on the top of my head as I had seen Sally do when, from nowhere, a hand knocked me to the floor, spilling the contents of the bottle. I was taken completely by surprise to find Dad standing over me. I was petrified; I'd never seen him like this.

'Don't yow ever let me catch yow using that terrible stuff agen!' he bawled.

With that he snatched up the bottle and flung it through the open window into the yard. I was too scared to cry out as he hauled me roughly to my feet and shook me violently. I was in floods of tears. This seemed to calm him down and he spoke more quietly.

'I'll forgive you this time but I'm warnin' yow, my gel, if I catch yow with that stuff agen I'll cut all your hair off an' leave yer bald, and I'll put this strap across yer back!' He pointed to the large brass buckles on his belt.

'I'm off now,' he continued, 'ter meet yer Mum, so when yer've cleared up the table yer can get ter bed.' With that he left, slamming the door behind him. This meant that they wouldn't be back before the pubs closed, but I also knew that if they knew who I was going out with they would have locked me in. I suppose I was kicking over the traces a bit and parental authority seemed as irksome to me then as it does to teenagers today. I fussed about, preparing myself, washing, combing my hair and putting on my borrowed finery. When I'd completed this process I turned to the mirror to look at myself for a last time. Then I received a shock. When Dad had knocked the bottle out of my hand some of the bleach must have spilled down my face because my right eyebrow was blonde. No doubt this would be considered fashionable today but the thought of going out like that mortified me. I'd no idea how I was going to deal with this until my eyes settled on the grate. Then it came to me. I spat on my finger, rubbed it in the soot, then applied it to my eyebrow so that although it was not too convincing at close range, from a distance it looked natural enough. Then, after I'd made sure that I'd left no telltale traces, I was off. There was nobody about to see me knocking on Sally's door. When she came out I stood there waiting to see if she noticed anything but she didn't seem to. Then we took off down the back alleys in case someone saw us and told our parents.

Finally, by the roundabout route, we reached St Paul's churchyard where we were to meet the boys. Sure enough they were there and the smallest was introduced as my date. He was not a bad looker, I thought, and shook hands as he told me his name was Freddy. 'Frederick the Great, that's me,' he said with a chuckle. He placed his arm round my waist, which gave me a pleasurable feeling I'd never experienced, and then we set off to the picture house. He did all the talking. I was very shy but his mischievous grin put me at my ease and we strolled along behind Sally and her beau. We'd hardly gone half way when it began to rain and we had to run the rest of the way to queue under shelter. Just inside the foyer there was a long narrow mirror with an almost naked woman painted on it. How shameful, I thought. I glanced at my reflection to admire the effect and then I got my second shock that evening. The rain had smudged my sooty mascara and it was streaked down my cheek. I looked away quickly. Frederick the Great had been straightening his tie but now he turned round to look at me and after registering a look of surprise he called to Sally and her friend and they all burst into laughter. I was angry and embarrassed in equal measure and hated them. I just turned and ran off. They deserved each other, I thought.

When I got indoors I was still so upset that I tore off the frock, ripping a sleeve in the process, but I didn't care; I was so angry. I rolled it up into a ball and pushed the shawl and lipstick inside the bundle, then I went to put it on Sally's step. As I dodged down the yard I noticed the broken bottle lying in the drain. Picking it up, I rolled that up with the bundle too. I put it on the step, knocked on the door and ran back home. I closed the door behind me then heard the door of the Buckleys' open and close. Nobody saw me, I'd been so quick. With that I washed my face and went to bed.

Finding Out the Facts of Life

I was surprised to find Liza sitting up in bed reading one of her romances. She hid it away quickly as I entered the room.

'What's the matter with yow?' she said when she saw my tears. I had to tell someone so I told her. When I'd finished we began to see the funny side of it and ended up laughing. Liza laughed so much she rolled off the bed onto the chamber pot, spilling its contents on the floor. This caused more hilarity and we ended in hysterical fits.

My first experience with boys was not a great success but it wasn't the last, and later I found myself in worse scrapes than on that first occasion. I had nothing further to do with Sally but she didn't seem to be bothered when I passed her in the street without speaking. In the end I thought it was a good job that I'd cut her dead because I began to pick up the gossip about her and found out that she'd left home when she did because she was pregnant and had had a baby. She was what was known as 'a bad lot' and several times later I saw her standing in alleyways, always with a different man. Mum summed her up when she said, 'Any man can have her, with or without his trousers down.'

This experience renewed my curiosity about the facts of life. All I knew were the half-truths and lies that children were told in those days. I was afraid to ask Mum any details of where babies came from and the word 'sex' was considered a dirty word in our house.

When I saw my first period I was scared to death. I ran all the way home from school thinking I was going to bleed to death. I burst into tears when I saw Mum, and told her what had happened. But all the explanation she gave me was, 'Now yow keep away from the lads an' never let 'em kiss yer or the next thing yer know yer'll be 'avin' a baby. Then God 'elp yer.' I pointed out that I kissed Frankie but she dismissed my puzzlement.

'That's different. 'E's yer brother, ain't 'e. Now be off with yer, I'll see ter yer later. An' don't forget what I've told yer! Keep away from the lads.'

I couldn't make head nor tail of this. Why was Frankie different? I knew he had something more than Liza and me because we'd seen him when he had his bath and when he lay in bed in his short shirt. I was perplexed. If only someone would explain these things to me, but I was too shy and scared to ask. When Mum had left I determined to overcome my embarrassment and go and ask Mrs Taylor. Perhaps she could tell me why I was bleeding. When I told her what was troubling me she just gave me a piece of clean rag and said more or less the same as Mum had.

'Is it true?' I asked her. 'Will I have a baby if a boy kisses me?'

'Well, it's a start,' she answered, smiling, 'but when yer grow older you'll find out.' This was clearly little help either.

I knew when people were married and slept together a baby usually followed, but this didn't enlighten me about the facts of life. In fact, for a while I was almost as afraid of boys as I was of horses and cows. As far as my education on the subject was concerned I was reduced to listening to gossip in the hope of learning more.

I was in the yard one day when all the women were gossiping and Mrs Smith from the next yard happened to pass.

'Hello Nell, I see yer've bin eatin' new bread agen,' Mrs Phipps called to her.

'Yes, an' it's all me own,' she replied, smacking her belly as she walked by.

Then Maggie said, 'Did yer know Mrs Buckley's balloon's up agen?'

'Yes, we 'eard,' replied Mrs Jonesy.

Mrs Phipps gave Maggie a cold look and said, 'Why is it yer've never 'ad your balloon up, Maggie?'

'That's my affair,' Maggie replied. 'Any'ow my Billy ain't got much, an' what 'e 'as got 'e's keepin' it fer 'imself.' And they all burst out laughing.

I didn't make much of this but Mrs Smith's daughter was a friend of mine. Her name was Nellie and she was in the same class as me at school and her family had not long moved into the neighbourhood. Nellie was not a bit shy or timid like I was, and I was attracted by her outspoken ways. Sometimes after school we would visit their house and she would show me all her nice clothes. Nellie promised me one of her old dresses when she had a new one. Then one afternoon Mrs Smith came in and found us and asked who I was.

'It's Katie, my school friend,' Nellie replied.

'Well, sit yerself down Katie. Don't be shy, I'm not going ter eat yer,' she said, busying herself untying the parcels she had with her.

She was a pretty woman and would have had a good figure had she not been pregnant. She had a pleasant dispositon and always had a twinkle in her eyes. She had a soft voice and always put me at my ease. We watched her untie the parcels which turned out to contain pretty blue woollen baby clothes. When Nellie saw them she asked, 'Why 'ave yer bought blue?'

'Because I know it's goin' to be a son ... Anyway,' she said, 'I'm 'opin' it is.'

The next parcel contained a new dress for Nellie. It was bright pillar-box red with a white lace collar and cuffs. When her Mum undressed her to try it on I couldn't take my eyes off the lovely white underclothes she wore. I turned my head away then, because Mum always said it wasn't decent to watch people undress. Evidently Mrs Smith thought differently.

'Don't be shy, Katie,' she said. 'Yer can turn round now.'

Nellie looked sweet in her new frock. Then she asked her Mum to find something for me. She was the same size as me so I knew that her clothes would fit me. Mrs Smith went to the wardrobe and brought out a yellow dress with pretty flowers and leaves all over it.

'Take your dress off and try this on. It should fit.'

I must have looked embarrassed when she handed it over because they both turned their backs while I slipped my old dress off and slipped the new one on. After fastening all the buttons up the front I said meekly, 'You can turn round now.' I felt great when Mrs Smith said I looked pretty and that I could keep the dress. I was so overwhelmed that I started to cry.

'What's all this for?' she asked kindly.

'Mum will never let me keep it. I've only got old ones an' this one will go to the pawnshop.' I wiped the tears with the back of my hand.

'Never mind that. Wipe yer eyes and then we'll go upstairs and see what else we can find,' Mrs Smith soothed me.

Nellie had a pleasant bedroom all to herself. If I had a room of my own, I thought, I would knit and knit to make it as pretty as this or as Miss Louise's had been. We girls sat on the bed while Mrs Smith sorted out some underclothes for me.

'Now, don't be shy. Yer can undress in front of Nellie and me,' she said. 'But if yer like we'll go downstairs.'

'I'd like Nellie to stay,' I whispered. I was shy of undressing in front of adults. So Mrs Smith left us alone and I stripped off in front of my friend although I made her turn away when I came to my combs.* Then I dressed in the vest, bloomers, camisole with pink ribbon threaded through the top and bottom, a pretty lace underskirt and finally the yellow dress. I felt like a princess.

'You look lovely, Katie,' Nellie said. 'Let's go an' show Mum.'

They both enthused over my new look and I became weepy and wailed that I couldn't keep them.

'But they're yours to keep, like I told you,' Mrs Smith said gently.

'No, they'll end up in the pawnshop,' I sobbed.

'Oh, no they won't. Nellie, you go upstairs and bring down Katie's clothes,' she said.

What was she up to, I thought. She wrapped them up in a parcel and took them out to the dustbin. She was about to pop them in when we heard the strains of the rag and boneman's cry. Round the corner he came, pushing his handcart with balloons flying high. She gave him the bundle and he opened it to examine the contents.

'What yer want fer these, Mrs?' he inquired.

'Oh, just give the kids a balloon each,' she told him.

'They're only worth one,' he grumbled.

'Right! I'll put them in the bin then,' she replied, but before she could get them off the cart he handed us the balloons.

We went in and I stayed a bit longer; then, with many

*Combinations.

thanks to Mrs Smith, I left for home, anxious to tell Mum about my good fortune. When I entered our kitchen Mum stared at me, dumfounded, until she recovered and found her voice.

'Who's got yow all dressed up?' she demanded, shaking me.

'Mrs Smith gave them to me,' I told her.

'An' where's yer own?' she snapped.

I was too scared to admit to her what had happened to them, so I said Mrs Smith would tell her. Now our houses backed on to each other, with only the party wall between, so she just picked up the poker from the fender and started banging on the wall so that the plaster showered a cloud of dust in the room.

'Are yow theea, Mrs Smith, cos if yow are I want some words with yow!' she bellowed.

Mrs Smith came immediately, with Nellie behind her. Neighbours who had heard the noise were gathering round the door and chattering noisily. However, Mum had found her mistress in Mrs Smith. She drew herself up to her full height, hands on hips; quite a figure.

'An' what's the matter with you?' she asked sarcastically. 'Yer trying' ter knock the 'ouse down?'

'Where's me daughter's clothes yer've took off 'er? I want 'em back.'

Mrs Smith was unimpressed by Mum's overbearing manner but simply grinned and replied calmly, 'Sorry my dear, you'll have to ask the rag an' boneman for them.'

'WHAT!' yelled Mum.

'Yes,' Mrs Smith nodded.

Mum knew then she had met her match and tried to retreat indoors, but Mrs Smith left her foot in the door so that she had to listen.

'They weren't worth keeping so I swapped them for a couple of balloons.' Mum's face reddened visibly.

'Oh, I could tell all yow a thing ter shock yer,' she said wagging her forefinger. She continued to splutter and threaten. 'An' don't let me catch yer layin' another finger on 'er,' she said, pointing at me. 'I'll 'ave the law on yer.'

'Let me tell yow if you ever lay a finger on her yerself, I'll 'ave the authorities on yer,' Mrs Smith was not to be bested. 'And don't yow take them clothes away from her either,' she concluded, just as Mum saw her chance and slammed the door shut, leaving me standing there with Mrs Smith, Nellie and the neighbours.

'Come on you two,' she said to us. 'I never 'ave anything to do with trash if I can 'elp it.'

I went round to their place again and we had toast and tea with real cow's milk, not the Handy Brand condensed milk we always had at home. After tea we went out to play. I was afraid to go back home for fear of the trouble I'd be in from Mum. When I left Nellie I hung about waiting for Dad's protection but he didn't appear. I went to several pubs looking for him but nobody had seen him, so, as it was getting late, I turned to go home to face the music. As I dragged reluctantly along past Mrs Smith's house who should come out, deep in conversation with Mrs Smith, but my Dad. They were smiling and when Mrs Smith saw me she called out cheerily. 'It's all right Katie, I've explained to your Dad.'

I ran up to him and took his hand in mine. He said 'goodbye' to our neighbour and thanked her for 'everything', and he squeezed her hand. 'That's all right Sam, any time you're passing,' she told him. I was puzzled about what had been going on but was pleased that Dad, at any rate, was in a good mood.

'Come on Katie,' he said. 'Let's face the music.'

Before we'd set foot over the doorstep Mum had started. 'What yer think about 'er round the back? Tellin' me what ter do with me own kids. She wants ter look after 'er own.' She stopped to draw breath which gave Dad his opportunity.

'Now yow be quiet, Polly. Yow don't want all the neighbourhood round yer door do yer?'

'Oh, she's told yow the tale 'as she?' Mum didn't miss much.

'Only the truth, and I admire her for it. She's one person yow can't push around like the rest of yer cronies.'

Mum could see she was getting nowhere so she tried

shedding a tear or two. This was an old ploy when she couldn't get her own way. Dad was having none of this.

'Yow can turn yer tap off, I'm going up to bed and you, Katie, better get off too,' he said, handing me a saucer with a stub of candle on it. I didn't wait to be told twice and I made myself scarce.

After that Nellie and I became close friends and so did her Mum and my Dad. Mum never said a word when I invited Nellie into our house but I could tell she didn't like her. We played the harmonium and sang together and Dad sometimes gave us money to go to see a picture at the Queen's Hall. When Nellie's Mum was very large and the baby was due she wouldn't let Nellie go far in case she needed to fetch the midwife. All this time I still wondered about the origin of babies, and one night I raised the subject with Nellie. I began by asking her if she like boys. She said she did 'a bit' but she was also afraid of them 'a bit' as well. I asked why and she gave me a reply I hadn't expected.

'Well, my Mum told me not to let boys fondle me or kiss me now I've started me periods, otherwise, if I did, I'd soon be having a baby.'

I told her that I was surprised at that because my Mum had said the same and I hadn't believed her. Was that how Nellie's Mum came to be having a baby, I wondered?

'But I like it when boys whistle at me,' she continued.

'Me too,' I agreed, 'but my Mum says she don't want me growing up like Sally Buckley.'

'Do you know 'er?' she asked in apparent surprise.

'Everybody knows 'er,' I said.

Then I offered to tell her my secret if she didn't tell anyone else. I told her about the date at the pictures with the two boys and about the disaster with the bleach.

'How lucky you were,' Nellie laughed. 'Yer never know what would 'ave 'appened if it 'adn't rained.'

'Nellie,' I said, 'd'yer know where babies come from?'

'Course I do, silly. Don't you?'

'No.' I shook my head, a bit shyly.

'Well you know when mothers get fat and their stomach

sticks out like a balloon? Well, they carry that for nine months, don't they? Then when the time comes their belly goes pop with a bang and the baby pops out.' That seemed to make sense to me.

'I wondered what the belly button was for,' I said. Nellie was always right about things.

'Tell yer what,' she offered. 'When my Mum's about to have her pains I'll call for yer and we'll sit on the stairs and listen.'

Although I was anxious to be there I didn't get the chance because Mrs Smith gave birth to a baby girl in the early hours of the morning later that week. We were both disappointed but Nellie said we could wait until the next time.

I also wondered about why we never saw Nellie's Dad and eventually I asked her about him. Nellie rounded on me angrily and asked me why I wanted to know. Then I told about the tales the neighbours were telling about her Mum and her men friends. She replied that she knew where he was but she didn't want to discuss it. 'What my Mum does is her affair.' She was adamant. She must have know what her Mum was up to but I didn't question her any more on the subject.

We were still at school when, later that year, the First World War broke out. We were in standard seven, the highest class, which meant we could leave school early, when we were thirteen, which would be another eighteen months at least for me. We were both monitors and I helped the teacher with the younger children, teaching them how to knit socks and balaclavas for the soldiers at the Front. We put little messages wishing the Tommies 'good luck' in them to cheer them up. I loved knitting and do to this day. I won first prizes for the best garment and for the most knitted in my class. The only thing I didn't like was the monotonous khaki wool. One day I asked the teacher if it wouldn't be more patriotic to knit some items in red, white and blue. She smiled at this and said if I wanted a change I could knit up navy blue wool for the Royal Navy, which I did. I won another prize for this as well, and I was presented with a beautiful work basket lined with red satin by the headmistress, Miss Ford. I had to stand in front of the whole school which gave me ample opportunity to observe the envy on some girls' faces because knitting for the troops was a popular pastime then. In fact, everybody seemed to be busy finding some job to help with the war effort, except Mum who continued to clean at the Gingold's chip shop.

My two eldest brothers, Charlie and Jack, volunteered for Kitchener's army as most boys of their generation did. Even Dad tried to enlist. He told the recruiting officer that he'd been a sergeant in the Boer War and boasted that he knew more about the Army than all these whipper-snappers who were waiting to join with him. He was told to strip for a medical examination but he wasn't up to scratch and failed, and so never got his chance. Nevertheless he was determined to do his bit, so he gave up the firewood business and went back to the casting shop to make shell cases. This was more patriotic than wise because he had to work long hours and came home coughing; you could smell the sulphur on his clothes. But he said he didn't mind as long as he was helping the war effort, and anyway it would all be over in six months and he could go back to selling firewood. Little did we imagine then that the war would last until November 1918.

Frankie left school and Dad found him a job with him, fetching and carrying sand for the men. He was a strong, healthy lad and as pleased as punch to be working with Dad. He began to put on airs and think he was a grown-up who could boss us around until Dad checked him for it. Liza left as well and got a job on the munitions with Sally Buckley, which boded no good. There were rows at night over her staying out late with Sally. Mum always stood up for Liza, her longtime favourite, telling Dad she had enough sense to know what was right and wrong, but I doubted she did. Dad wasn't convinced either.

I wanted to help too but I was still too young to leave school. There was work for everyone. People were doing all kinds of jobs to earn money; even the married women who could get nothing before were able to take in washing for the posh folk whose maids were earning more in a week in the munitions factories than they could in a month skivvying.

Mum would have none of this: she was not going to do other people's dirty washing and she stayed at the fish shop all the war years.

It was ironic that now everybody in our district had plenty of money for food they couldn't obtain it because everything was rationed. Still, this left all the more to spend on drink. The pubs were doing a roaring trade, what with this new-found prosperity and the constant flow of soldiers on leave with money to spend and precious little time to get rid of it. There was plenty of scandal about the Australian and Canadian troops being out with other men's wives or, worse, being seen in doorways or entries with them while the black-out was on. Women whose men were away at the war were still having babies. Several times I was given money to go to the chemist's for bitter aloes or penny royal or a bottle of gin from the outdoor. Miscarriages procured in this way often led to death or malformed births.

Brother Jack wrote each week while he was in training on Salisbury Plain with the Royal Field Artillery. Mum always opened the letters but I had to read them for her. He would write that he was 'doing fine' and that the war would be over soon. He also asked her to keep an eye on his widow because he had heard about the carrying-on with the women-folk. 'And', he underlined the 'and', 'keep an eye on our Liza.' I always wrote the replies and told him the news and reassured him that Mum was watching his widow, which it gave her great pleasure to do. I knitted him socks as well and slipped packets of Woodbines in with them. It was through the need to obtain money for this that I took the part-time job with Mrs Morton and her husband, Weary Willy. They were the school caretakers but my job helping them didn't last long.

Another incident which sticks in my memory from those final years at school concerned a friend of mine, Nelly Mitchell. I'd discussed the mystery of child birth with her as well and she'd offered, like Nellie Smith, to call me when her mother, who was pregnant, was about to give birth. I was playing jackstones in the street when Nelly Mitchell ran up with the news that she was going for the midwife. We ran and knocked on the midwife's door and Mrs Bullivant seemed to know who it was without looking, for she called out for Nelly to run and get newspapers and hot water ready.

When we got to Nelly's the fire was low, but while she was collecting newspapers I filled the kettle and using the old leather bellows stoked up the heat. Mrs Mitchell called out for Mrs Bullivant from upstairs and at that moment in she came. She was the only midwife in our district and if the women couldn't afford her the neighbours helped, a practice which often ended in tragedy. As Mrs Bullivant, carrying her bag of instruments, mounted the stairs, Nelly's Mum began to cry out in agony. We looked at each other, scared stiff, but we followed Mrs Bullivant upstairs. She was a small, round woman with eyes that seemed too small for her face which was flushed red; it was as much she could do to struggle up, rolling from side to side and, I noticed, smelling of drink. When we followed her into the bedroom she ordered us out, saying it was no place for kids. We went outside but could still see because the door didn't quite close. As soon as she thought we were out of sight she reached under her apron and produced a small bottle from which, tipping back her head, she took a swig. Then she replaced it and went over to see to Mrs Mitchell who lay on the top of the bed dressed only in a calico nightgown groaning as she writhed about. Then the midwife lifted up the gown and rolled her roughly on to her side. I almost screamed out but Nelly's hand stifled any sound. I saw the largest bare belly I'd ever seen in life. The belly button was protruding and it looked ready to burst. I'd seen enough. I didn't want to wait for the baby to appear through the navel. I tried to back down the stairs but Nelly kept hold of my frock and prevented me. Just then the midwife told Mrs Mitchell to get up and pace the room and simultaneously we crashed against the door and ended in a heap on the floor. I expected a slap but Mrs Bullivant just stepped over us saying she'd be back later, after she'd attended Mrs Groves who was having her first. Then she was gone.

Nelly begged me not to leave her, and plucking up courage I stayed. Nelly held her Mum's hand while I dipped a sponge into the cold water jug and mopped her brow which was sweaty from the pain she was in. I became frightened; I thought she was going to die and I felt sick. It was the first time I'd seen anyone in labour and I made a silent vow that when I was married I wasn't going to have any babies if this was how you had to suffer. A few minutes later, when Nelly was preoccupied, I'm sorry to say my cowardice got the better of me and I crept out of the room, down the stairs and ran off home.

For hours I couldn't put those dreadful cried out of my mind and I imagined that with every breath my own stomach was swelling and about to burst. I had a nightmare that night which ended with me rolling out of bed and landing on the floor where I was sick. Next morning I cleaned up the vomit and got myself ready for school but I still had a nasty taste in my mouth and I was hot and achey. When I peered at myself in the mirror I screamed. My eyes were puffed up and my face was covered with red spots. My scream brought Mum up to see what was wrong and when she saw my face she ordered me back into bed. I had measles and had to stay isolated in the darkened room for two weeks.

I was dosed with saffron tea which tasted foul and I couldn't see anybody. By the time I'd recovered I was skinnier than ever, having been rationed to an orange a day. After a few days I was allowed downstairs and began to eat proper meals again, and two weeks later I started back at school.

On my way there the first morning I noticed that Nelly's house had a 'To Let' sign in the window. I ran to catch Liza up and when I asked her where they were she hesitated before replying.

'She's dead,' she said. I was dumbstruck.

'Who? Nelly?' I stammered. Then Liza told me that Mrs Mitchell had died in childbirth and that Nelly herself had been taken to Wolverhampton to live with an aunt and uncle. I felt miserable and blamed myself even more for not staying that night or fetching a doctor, but I didn't realise and I was so scared. I was too upset to go to school. I went and sat in the churchyard and wept for Mrs Mitchell and Nelly and prayed for myself to be forgiven and for them to be looked after. I was not missed that day either at school or at home. I didn't forget Nelly who had been a good little friend to me, and eventually we did meet up again, several years later.

6

The World of Work, 1917

At Christmas 1916 when I was nearly fourteen I was preparing to leave school. The Great War was still going and there was still plenty of work for young people in our district. I got an inkling of what was in the wind when I came home early from the Band of Hope* and overheard a conversation between Mum and Dad.

'She don't look strong enough ter work on a press,' said Dad.

'But that's where the big wages are, on munitions,' Mum told him. 'Anyway,' she continued, 'we'll soon fatten 'er up if we give 'er plenty ter eat.'

'All right,' Dad said, 'I s'ppose yer know what's best for 'er.'

'She's gotta earn 'er keep like the rest of 'em,' Mum concluded.

I was amused when I was given two thick slices of bread and half a cow heel before I went to bed but I didn't take long to devour it. This was a treat and no mistake and I sucked all the bones clean I was that hungry. I was even offered more, and I could see the writing was on the wall. Every mealtime for the next few weeks it was as if I was being fattened up for the slaughter. I had as much as and more than I could eat for a change. And I was putting on weight so fast that my clothes wouldn't fit. I was also getter taller. Mum said she couldn't afford to buy me a new frock and that I would have to have one of Mary's old ones cut down. She cobbled it together which black thread so I felt a proper charlie, but she said it would have to do until I earned my first week's wages.

---

* The Band of Hope was a youth temperance organisation run by the Salvation Army. Entry was dependent upon signing the pledge not to drink alcohol.

I wasn't going to wait until then. I'd been saving pennies and halfpennies up for ages for this moment. Next day when the house was empty I bolted the door and ran upstairs to the attic. Pushing the iron bedstead across the room I got on my knees and with a knife prized up the floorboard and pulled out a mice-nibbled newspaper package. I emptied its contents on to the bed and counted out three shillings and ninepence-halfpennny, all earned running errands. I put it in my rag purse, replaced everything, unbolted the door and went off down the street to an old woman who sold second-hand clothes from her front room.

When I got there I looked through the window and there as luck would have it was the prettiest pink crepe-de-chine blouse I had ever seen. It had lace trimmings on the cuffs and round the high collar, and down the front it was fastened with six round pearl buttons. I had to have it. I pushed open the door and went in, a rusty bell clanging a warning to the owner. At first I couldn't see her and assumed she was in the back but then I saw her sitting on a stool sewing, amidst heaps of old clothes. Suddenly she looked up, glared at me and shouted, 'What der yer want, comin' in 'ere like that?'

'H-how much is that blouse in the window?' I managed to stammer.

'Who wants ter know?' came the reply.

'Me,' I said. 'I want ter buy it.'

She stared at me in disbelief until I shook my bag and she heard the chink of coins. That livened her up and she grinned a gummy smile and said, 'Ter yo' it's 'alf a crown.' She then proceeded to extol the garment's virtues and the 'fine lady' who originally owned it. However, I had to explain that although I liked it I couldn't afford that much because I wanted to buy a pair of boots as well and all I had to spend was three shillings and nine-pence-halfpenny. I explained that I wanted it for an interview for a job because I was leaving school and she began to soften.

'All right,' she grinned, 'yer can 'ave a pair of second 'and button-up boots an' the blouse for three an' ninepence an' I'll throw in a camisole. Now come on through the back so's yer can try 'em on.'

I held on to my money though until I'd satisfied myself the clothes were worth what she wanted for them. She handed me the camisole which was frayed and yellow with age but which looked clean, then she shuffled through to the window to fetch the blouse. I was pleased when she handed it to me to see how nice it was, and when I tried it on it looked better on me than it did in the window. So she wrapped them both up in some newspaper. I next tried on several pairs of boots until eventually I found a pair that fitted. They were a bit down at heel but with blacking I could see they would look better than the ones I was wearing.

'Yer got a bargain,' the old crone cried, counting the pennies. 'Now be off with yer before I change me mind!'

All I had left was a halfpenny, but I was pleased with my purchases which I hid under the straw mattress until I needed them. The following Friday I shook hands with my teacher for the last time, listened to her lecture on 'my new life', was handed a book for good attendance and walked home feeling grown up, at the tender age of fourteen.

When I got in I showed Mum my book and told her what the teacher had said but she didn't seem interested. All she said was that my sister was coming to tea and she wanted me to fetch some errands.

'I want yer ter go ter Jefferson's an' fetch two ounces of tea, two pounds of sugar an' a tinna condensed milk. Oh, an' 'alf a loaf, an' see it's new. An' don't forget me change.'

I remember Mr Jefferson vividly. He was a short, fat man with a red face and a bald head. He reminded me of Humpty Dumpty. He kept a well-stocked, tidy shop where you could buy almost anything. I ran all the way to the shop and rushed in, pushing open the frosted-glass door and making the bell clank noisily. I went straight up to the counter. I climbed on the hot-water pipe that ran along the floor and peered over the top where I could see Mr Jefferson's bald head. I blurted out my order without drawing breath and jumped down to the floor.

He glared at me over the counter and said, 'Be quiet, an' wait yer turn.' Then for the first time I noticed three well-dressed women looking daggers at me. Then they began whispering and looking down their noses at me.

'Serve her, we can wait,' one said.

While he was fetching Mum's order I had time to observe the women as they dithered over the glass cases of biscuits, trying to make up their minds which to have. Then I remembered the blacking I needed for my boots and I picked some up. That I paid for with my halfpenny. When I got back Mum was in a lather again. 'About time,' she said and snatched the bag off me and started checking it was all as she had asked for, even squeezing the bread to check it was fresh. Just then Mrs Taylor tumbled into the room and Mum looked up with a glare on her face.

'Yower Mary ain't comin' terday, she told me ter tell yer 'er mutha-in-law's took bad.' She collapsed breathlessly into a chair.

''Er thinks mower of 'er than she does of me,' Mum fumed, sitting down in the other chair. I could see signs that they were going to be some time nattering so I crept up to the attic and rummaged through Liza's trunk. I found an old, long black hobble skirt which I knew she didn't want because she'd grown out of it.

With the hem turned up and some elastic in the waist I thought it would be just the thing to go with my blouse. When I heard the two women leave a little later, I went down and set to with a needle and thread. I took some elastic from a pair of bloomers and pretty soon had a serviceable skirt to go with the other things.

On the following Monday morning Mum gave me two-pence for a bath at the public ones in Northwood Street where I went now that I was 'a big girl', and sixpence for my medical which I had to have before I could work in a factory. I bundled up my new clothes and set off. It was heavenly to stretch out in such a big bath and soak in gallons of hot soapy water; I could have stayed there all day, but I knew I had to go out and look for a job before long. I stepped out of the bath and dried myself and admired myself in the mirror; I'd certainly filled out. I felt so clean and fresh. I put on my stockings, clean bloomers, my camisole and skirt then my blouse. It felt a bit tight when I fastened all the buttons up but I thought, I won't burst open if I don't breathe too deeply or thrust my chest out. Then I buttoned up my boots which were now polished and I felt ready to face the adult world. I folded the old clothes into a bundle and standing on the lavatory seat I pushed them behind the iron cistern. Then I walked out into the street. Imagine my surprise when the first person I bumped into practically on the steps of the bath, was my old friend Nelly Mitchell.

We threw our arms round each other and exchanged greetings. She told me she was in lodgings round the corner. I asked her why she hadn't been to see me before but she said she'd only been there a few days and had only just moved from her aunt's in Wolverhampton. Her aunt had died and now she was with a friend and looking for work like I was. We walked along arm in arm exchanging news, oblivious of anything else. Then I noticed how well dressed she was and she told me about the good times she had with boys. It seemed so exciting, but my first thought was to find a job and I began to miss what she was saying. Then as luck would have it we turned a corner and saw a notice on a factory gate which read: 'WOMEN AND GIRLS WANTED TO LEARN PRESSWORK'. I knew it was heavy, manual work, swinging the handles of the heavy mechanical presses which were used to stamp out metal components, but many young girls like us were doing this sort of work because so many men were away at the Front.

'You go in and ask first, Katie, while I wait here. Then you can let me know how you got on and I'll go in after.'

I agreed as long as she waited for me, because I didn't want to lose contact with her again. Up the narrow stairs I went, trying to avoid slipping on the grease which covered them. I reached the top and pushed open the door and found myself inside a small cubicle just big enough to hold two people. I tapped the wooden panel and suddenly a small trapdoor shot up and I jumped with fright as a woman's face and shoulders appeared in the gap.

'What yer come for? The job is it?' She had to shout to make herself heard above the noise of the presses in the room behind her.

I was suddenly nervous. Why, I wondered, didn't Mum come with me for the interview like other mothers did? Now I was fourteen I had to stand on my own two feet, she'd said. I stared at the woman's stern face until I found the courage to speak.

'Yes, ma'am,' was all I could manage. She eyed me up and down and asked me my age.

'Fourteen. I left school last week,' I told her.

'An' yer sure yer want ter work on a press?' she asked.

'Yes, we do,' I answered without thinking.

'We, who's we?' she snapped gruffly.

'My friend Nelly. She's downstairs.'

'Well, send 'er up. Let's take a look at 'er.' Then the trapdoor slammed shut.

I ran and fetched Nelly and we both returned to the cubicle. Up shot the door again.

'So you're Nelly?' she snapped. 'Well, yow'll do.' She had to bellow.

She gave us a note pad to write down our names and addresses and when we handed it to her she told us to return at eight the following morning with our birth certificates and medical certificates. 'An' I mean eight, not five past!' she shouted.

'Yes ma'am,' I replied while Nelly tried to peer over her shoulder into the workshop beyond.

'Yower ter call me Madam. I'm the forewoman,' she snapped.

'Yes Madam,' I replied timidly. With that the trapdoor shut again and we were alone in the cubicle.

'I don't like 'er, she's an old battleaxe,' said Nelly as we made our way down the iron stairs and back into the street. Then Nelly asked about the pay.

'Didn't she tell you 'ow much the wages are?' she asked and I had to admit that I'd forgotten to ask.

'Well, you'll 'ave ter go back and ask 'er then, won't you,' she snapped.

'You go!' I retorted.

'Anyway I didn't ask for the job an' if you don't want ter go I'll look round for something else that pays better. She don't look like she pays much,' she pouted.

'Oh, all right.' I sulked my way back up the stairs again. I noticed it was always me who had to do things.

When I entered the cubicle the trap sprang and Madam appeared wanting to know what I wanted.

'Please Madam,' I asked,' 'ow much will the wages be?'

'Twelve an' six a week, eight o'clock till six and one o'clock on Saturdays. Yow get fifteen minutes for lunch and one till two dinnertime and yow'll clock in and out. I'll put yow right, an' if yer be'ave yerself an' work 'ard you get a rise to thirteen shillings at the end of the month.' And with that the trap closed again and her hard face was gone.

I thought on twelve and six I would be rich in no time. Mum could have ten shillings and I could have the half crown for myself. I could do a lot with that much. But when I told her Nelly didn't seem very pleased and suggested that it was not wise to take the first job that offered itself but to look around for something better.

'But Nelly,' I told her. 'She's got my address an' if my Mum finds out I'll be in trouble.'

'Yer Mum won't find out an' anyway she won't mind more money.' With this I had to agree.

We went off down the street in high spirits, looking in all the shop windows, planning what we would spend our money on. Then we thought we'd better look for an alternative job. By now it was one o'clock and the boys were coming out of the factories. They began to whistle at us and although I didn't want anything to do with them, Nelly stopped to talk to them. I was so scared I ran round the corner and hid. Eventually when Nelly appeared she said she'd made a date with one of them. I was shocked at her brazenness. How could she? I thought. She was only the same age as me but a lot more forward.

We stopped at several other workshops that were advertising for women and girls, at each of which I had to make inquiries. Nelly was not so forward at this, it seemed. None of them wanted to pay more than ten or eleven shillings and one small place only seven and three pence with overtime. So we decided to take the first job at the factory in Vittoria Street.

Then we thought about going for our medical. We walked along the street, arm in arm, as the trams clanged past, their bells ringing. Posters were pasted up everywhere there was room. Life-size posters of Kitchener looked down on us proclaiming 'Your Country Needs You'. There was the odd Union Jack, and hand-painted slogans saying, 'Down with the Hun', and 'Votes for Women', and rude ones like, 'Fuck the Kaiser'. I was shocked when I saw this. Bad language was frowned on even in poor households and you didn't see the graffiti you do today. Finally we arrived at the clinic. There were several women waiting with their children. Nelly and I sat down on the bench beside them to wait our turn. The women and girls stared at us; we were the only ones without our mothers. We watched the steady stream go in and come out until it was our turn, when Nelly pushed me in front as the voice called loudly, 'Next!'

I steadied myself and entered; I was very nervous. The doctor was sitting at his writing table. Without looking up he said, 'Sit down!' I sat down on the chair and took the opportunity to have a good look at him. He was a thick-set man, very dark-skinned with wavy black hair. I couldn't make up my mind what nationality he was but he wasn't English. When he'd finished writing he suddenly swivelled round in his chair and stared at me, and his black eyes seemed to look through me. He stood up and bent over me and with his pen he lifted up my plaits.

'I ain't got ticks in my hair, doctor,' I told him, but he didn't answer but instead shone a little light in my ears. 'Hm, hm,' he repeated. 'Hm, open your mouth and put out your tongue.' I did as I was told. When he was satisfied with that he took his stethoscope and put it to his ears. Nobody had told me there'd be all this rigmarole. I thought he just asked you questions and you paid the sixpence for your medical certificate; I had already put it on the table. I was beginning to wonder what he was going to do next when he snapped at me:

'Open your blouse!'

I was rooted to the spot with fright; I wanted my Mum or Nelly to walk in to come to my aid.

'Come along, open your blouse. I can't stand here all day,' he said becoming impatient.

Slowly I fumbled with the first button, then the second, but for the life of me I was not going to open my blouse any further than that. I felt unclean as he looked at me and the next thing I knew he had pulled my blouse open wide and the lovely pearl buttons had gone pop, pop, pop and were rolling about the floor. I was unable to move, terrified of what was to come next. Then he put his cold hands down inside my camisole and lifted out my bare breasts. He felt them for some time, then with another 'hm' slowly returned them – but not before he'd smiled and squeezed them. I slapped his hands as hard as I could, and clutching my blouse fled out of the room with 'Next!' echoing in my ears. I had no time to tell Nelly who was through the door in a flash and I collapsed on the bench in tears over my beautiful pearl buttons. In no time at all Nelly emerged, all smiles.

'He's nice ain't 'e?' she said.

'No! 'E's not an' I don't ever want ter go through that again,' I replied still sobbing.

'Yer too modest,' she laughed. 'Anyway, 'ere's yer buttons an' yer medical certificate 'e gave me ter give yer.'

Birmingham's Jewellery Quarter near where we lived was an area of old Georgian and early Victorian houses that had once been fashionable but were now run down. As the tenants left the landlords would rent off the rooms singly to craftsmen in the many trades of the area. Workshops were built at the back of these houses and the whole area was a warren representing many of the city's 'thousand trades'. Some people in the district I knew let off their front room, undertaking outwork for the jeweller who moved in. All kinds of gold and silver objects were made there: diamond rings, tableware, anything you could think of in that line; it still is to this day.

When I was a bit older I would go on a Friday night to a

pub called The Jeweller's Arms with some of the girls I worked with. Many's the time I have watched the gaffers of these thriving little businesses exchanging hundreds of pounds or packets of diamonds in corners of this and other pubs in the area. The factory where Nelly and I started work was not far from this pub. It was called The Birmingham Brass Works. The front door led to a small office and the workshop was down the entry.

At five minutes to eight the next day we were standing outside the gate with several roughly dressed women. They pushed Nelly and me to one side when the gate opened, clocked in and went off up the yard, disappearing up the steps without exchanging a word. We were standing there, hesitant, when a voice boomed out 'Follow me'. It was Madam, the forewoman, dressed in a khaki overall. She was elderly, tall and straight and very serious: I never remember her smiling. She showed us how to clock in with our timecard and then we followed her along the cobbled yard and up the greasy steps into the workshop.

The women who we'd seen previously were already busy operating the presses. At the end of the shop were smaller machines driven by an electric motor on the wall which worked the leather pulleys that ran along the ceiling. The workshop was dirty and reeked of oil. In the centre of the room was a large, battered pipe stove filled with glowing coke, the smoke from which went up the pipe and out through a hole in the roof. Every now and then smoke billowed into the room and when it did Nelly and I began to cough, but no one else seemed to be affected. They just sat there busily swinging the handles of the presses.

We were each handed khaki overalls like the rest had on; mine came almost to the floor and my cap, when I tried it on, kept slipping over my eyes. The forewoman told me it was the smallest they had. Nelly was taller than me and had more hair to fill her cap with.

'Come along you two,' she snapped at us. 'You can work the guillotine,' she said to Nelly.

As soon as she had Nelly settled in she came back to me and

117

showed me how to use the press to cut brass blanks from strips of scrap metal. I soon picked the job up but she came several times that morning to see how I was getting along.

'We don't want any scrap left,' was all she said. She examined the blanks that I had made and seemed satisfied, and that made me work harder. Then I noticed the other women along the bench were giving me black looks but I had no idea why.

At break time when I was standing eating my corned beef sandwich, one of the women shouted over to me.

'Yow've got my job, an' it's the best in the shop!'

They were all about to join in when Madam appeared and warned them if there was any more trouble they would be reported to the gaffer. They went on eating in silence. One of the women came over and offered me her place by the fire but I was too scared to move and anyway it was too late because just then the bell rang for us to start work again. I hadn't finished my sandwich so I wrapped it up and put it in my overall pocket. I was surprised I hadn't seen Nelly but I found out later that she'd walked out because she didn't like the place or the work. But I did. It was satisfying work cutting out the shilling-sized blanks and stacking them in three dozens. Afterwards I took them to the drilling machine where Minnie, the woman who had offered me her place, showed me how to drill four holes in them. I was proud to be doing my bit for King and country when I was told they were brass trouser buttons for the Army.

When one o'clock came and I was clocking out, Minnie came up to me and spoke. She was a small, thin woman, very pale, and came, she told me, from the Black Country. I asked why she couldn't get a job nearer home but she said she had seven children and a husband to keep and this was the best-paid job she could find. We became very friendly. She looked as old as my Mum with her lined face but she told me she was not yet thirty. She explained why the other women were nasty to me. Apparently they were on piecework, although I hadn't realised this, and I had one of the best jobs. That made me work harder. But when I got my first week's wages I received a shock. Instead of the twelve and six I expected there was only ten shillings and ninepence. I was too embarrassed to ask the other workers why so I plucked up courage and tapped on the office door.

'Come in!' came the voice of the Battleaxe from within.

I edged in timidly and asked if there had been a mistake in my wages.

'No!' came the reply. 'If you read the notice, you'll find it's correct.'

'What notice?' I asked; this was the first time I had heard about a notice.

'The girls will show you, now be off. Can't you see I'm busy?'

I went over to Minnie and asked her and she pointed to a notice on the wall at the end of the machine shop. It was small and splashed with oil and almost illegible but I could make this out:

STOPPAGES EACH WEEK
TO BE COLLECTED FROM WAGES

6d.   FOR XMAS FUND
3d.   FOR THE SWEEPER
3d.   FOR THE LAVATORY CLEANER
6d.   FOR THE TEA LADY
3d.   FOR THE LOAN OF OVERALLS AND CAP

I thought about it and reasoned that since we all had to take our turn sweeping and cleaning the lav then next time it was my turn I would receive my fair share. When my turn did come I found that they were dirty, smelly jobs but I did them anyway thinking of my reward at the end of the week. But when the wages arrived I found the same amount as usual. I demanded an explanation from the other women but they just laughed.

'Silly girl. All the money's pooled together for our outing and Christmas party.' Unfortunately for me I went on neither.

119

When I returned home with that first week's wages I was afraid to tell my Mum because I knew there would be hell to pay. She would have turned workshop and the forewoman inside out, so I gave her the ten shillings that she expected and made do with the ninepence: not much for a hard week's work.

I went back on the Monday after I'd discovered my error over the deductions but I was determined to find myself another job. However, during the morning the forewoman came over to where I was pressing the brass buttons and offered to put me on piecework like the others, although I hadn't been there as long as you normally had to have been for this to happen. She told me I could earn more money and I deserved it because I was a good little worker. When she'd gone the other women sent Minnie over to find out what she'd wanted and when Minnie told them they started to laugh and titter. I ignored them and set to as hard as I could; so hard that by the end of the week my fingers were bleeding from many cuts I had from the sharp brass discs. The others tried to compete, I suppose because they still resented me, but I worked even harder. I even slipped back in, unknown to them all including the forewoman, and worked through my dinner hour; at the end of that week I'd earned fifteen shillings and fourpence clear. I didn't tell the others but the following Monday the forewoman told me how pleased she was with my 'output'. I didn't tell Mum either; she still had her ten shillings and the rest I hid under the floorboards.

The following week the pace began to tell and I had to slow down because I was tired and lifeless. All I wanted when I finished work at six o'clock was my bed. I was in more trouble at work as well. The women crowded round me, jostling me and shouting, making all kinds of threats. I had no idea why until Minnie told me that the piece rates were being cut and it was my fault. And sure enough at the end of the week all I had earned was seven shillings and threepence. It was not even the day rate. That was it! I decided there and then to leave, and I did. I was only glad I had enough to make up Mum's ten shillings.

I didn't move far because my next job was at a firm only a
few doors away where they were advertising for a young girl
to learn case-making. I went along the next Monday and rang
the bell of the workshop which had been someone's front
room. It was opened by an elderly man, small with a grey,
pointed beard. On his head was a black velvet cap and round
his waist a long, well-worn leather apron. He smelled horribly
of glue, as did his little workshop. I told him why I'd called
and after looking me up and down while he fingered his beard
he took me inside where there was a long bench from one end
of the room to the other on which were laid sheets of red and
blue covered cardboard and plywood. Sitting at the bench
with their backs to me were two women and a young man
busily making boxes out of the cardboard. These, he told me,
were jewel cases. I didn't get much chance to see what was
going on here because he led me into a smaller room at the
back which I could see had been somebody's kitchen. There
was a gas stove with two pots of molten glue on it, and on the
other side of the room was a bench with scissors, a tape
measure and a small roll of velvet.

He told me I was to work here and that my job was to cut
out the pieces of velvet and pass them through to where the
women sat glueing. I enjoyed this job because although it was
smelly it was clean and wasn't hard work. He said my wages
would be fifteen shillings a week if I could be trusted and I did
what I was told. I spent a happy month there until an incident
happened that scared me off.

It happened one Friday night. The boss asked me if he
could trust me to take a packet to a woman who would be
waiting outside The Rose Villa, a nearby public house, which
stands on the corner of Vyse Street. With that he brought a
Bible out of his desk and asked me to swear on it that I would
not tell anyone what I was carrying or where I was going. I
agreed and after I'd kissed the Bible he handed me a small
leather 'dolly bag' which he said I was to give to a tall woman,
dressed in a fur coat, who would approach me and say, 'I'm
Di.' In return she would give me a packet which I had to bring
straight back. I must, he emphasised, be very careful that

nobody saw me hand the bag over. My immediate reaction was to be thrilled to be trusted with this important errand and when I said I would hide the leather purse round my waist under my apron he just smiled and told me to be off. Before I had even reached the pub the woman approached me and said the password. Then taking me by the hand she led me up an entry. I retrieved the purse from underneath my frock and in return for this she handed me a large flat envelope which I could feel contained banknotes. Then she was off, without saying another word. I retraced my steps as quickly as I could and found my boss waiting for me outside the workshop door.

'Good girl,' he smiled and whispered, taking the packet. 'Now come in an' warm yer 'ands while I make up the wages.' As soon as he'd disappeared upstairs one of the other women came over to where I was warming myself by the stove.

'I want ter warn yer,' she whispered, glancing towards the stairs. 'Yer don't want ter goo on them sorta errands.'

'Why?' I whispered too although I had no idea why.

'Yer know what yer was' carryin?' I shook my head. 'A bag o' diamonds. He's too scared ter tek 'em 'imself in case 'e gets caught or somebody knocks 'im down. Tek my advice, yow leave before it's too late or yow'll get caught or worse!' she hissed.

I was terrified. I didn't want to go prison or get killed, and as soon as he gave me my wage packet I was off, never to return there again. When I'd calmed down enough to open my wage packet there was the fifteen shillings I had been expecting and in addition a ten-shilling note and a message which read, 'Thank you, this is for you.' I wasn't sorry to be clear of whatever racket it was that they were up to, but the ten shillings helped me over the time until I found another job. I couldn't be out of work and I couldn't tell anyone why I'd left my last job.

I went to several factories asking for work; I'd decided I would be safer working with lots of people. I had a couple of jobs at factories in Frederic Street and Vyse Street, still in the Jewellery Quarter, but I spoilt the work, not being very experienced, and was given the sack. Eventually I settled for a job learning to enamel brooches and badges and motor plates at Fray's in Tenby Street North. It was an interesting job although all I was doing was learning how to 'lay on'; that is, apply the powdered glass on the metal prior to firing in the kiln. I wanted to learn all the other aspects of the process from grinding the enamel to firing, filing and polishing. I suppose I was impatient and there was a kind of informal apprenticeship system in operation in the trade to prevent somebody like me learning enough to set up in competition with the existing gaffers. I found out that I would have to spend three years laying on before I was likely to move on to anything else, and at that rate I would be middle aged before I was expert in all the processes of enamelling. However, I was not to be deterred so easily and I decided that if I couldn't learn everything at one firm then I would move on and learn more somewhere else. That, in fact, is what I did. I changed jobs, making sure that when I moved I was taken on to be trained in a process that was unfamiliar to me, and in that way I picked up the entire trade bit by bit. In no time at all I knew it inside out, but I'd learned enough to make sure that it was never me who was responsible for getting the piece rates reduced again.

7

Love and Marriage

I had steady work in the enamelling trade until 1920. By then the War to End all Wars was over, but so too was the boom in the metal trades of Birmingham. It was no longer easy to flit from job to job until you settled for something you fancied. Plenty of people were laid off and many girls, particularly married women who had found no difficulty getting jobs in munitions and such like a year before, were now reduced to whatever odd jobs they could find. In short this was the beginning of the Depression which, unlike what many people think, began then and went right through until the Second World War brought another period of full employment to Birmingham. That time too it brought destruction of life and property in the Blitz. It was during those two decades of grinding poverty between the wars that I grew to womanhood, experienced love and marriage and children and had it all taken away, all my hopes dashed. I was brought to the very edge of complete and utter despair before I was able to drag myself back from the abyss of sorrow and re-establish myself and my family. But this is jumping the gun, and a lot happened to me and to Birmingham before that came about.

Mum was not so strict with me now I was contributing to the household. I placed my wages beneath the faded, bobbled mantel fringe every Friday night and I was free to go out to the pictures with the girls I worked with.

'Keep away from the boys,' she would warn me, wagging a finger at me as I was leaving. 'An' don't forget if yer bring any trouble 'ome 'ere I'll 'ave ter put yer in the workhouse.' She still enjoyed ranting, but I would shrug my shoulders now: it was an old record I had heard throughout my childhood. I needed maternal love and affection and I needed to understand what really happened between men and women, and what it was I was to avoid, but I didn't learn any of these things from Mum.

I worked with a lot of pleasant girls mostly my own age and I suppose you would say I was enjoying life. I was young, had money in my purse if I needed it and a sort of independence. I remember Christmas Eve 1919; Florrie, a girl I worked with, had invited me to a party at her mother's house. I agreed and when I told Mum she said it was all right, although not without the usual cryptic warnings. I'd saved a few pounds over the years since I'd left school and this particular Christmas I decided to celebrate be ceasing to be a regular customer of second-hand shops and splash out on some brand new clothes. As Christmas Eve approached I began to look around the shops for something suitable for the party, but then as now with my grand-daughters, the clothes I wanted were too expensive. So this particular evening, since I could find nothing in the shops in town and it was near to closing time, I decided to go to the Bull Ring markets where the shops kept later hours to try my luck. I caught a tram into the city centre and alighting from it bought a twopenny bag of roast potatoes to eat as I went along. The streets were crowded with late-night shoppers, young couples and the inevitable drunks weaving along the pavement. Eventually I arrived at the Bull Ring where the barrow boys lined the pavements, naphtha flares casting an unnaturally bright light on their wares. There were crowds of people pushing and shoving, trying to get a bargain, and the noise was like a fairground on a Saturday night. The barrow boys shouted to outdo each other and the Salvation Army band was there too, competing for the attention of the people.

One of the barrow boys shouted at me, 'Come on duckie, fower a penny oranges, all sound', but I moved quickly on, clutching my purse tightly. When I reached the open-air fish market I saw two down and outs, disabled soldiers still in their khaki overcoats. One, a man with only one arm, had a card round his neck saying that he had a wife and six children to support. The other was trying to play his concertina above the hubbub. These men were not unusual then. There were several disabled soldiers in our district alone who were reduced to busking for a crust. When these two saw me stop and stare, the one pushed his cap towards my crying pitifully, 'Please 'elp an old soldier, missy.' I dropped a coin into the cap, wishing it could have been more, and then I went on my way to the little clothes shop I was heading for.

It was in Moat Row, near the Rag Market, and when I arrived I found the woman closing up. I pleaded with her to serve me, telling her what I wanted, but she said she was sorry but her 'ol' man' had taken all the best stuff home. However, when she saw my tears she relented.

'Oh all right, wait 'ere while I get me basket carriage an' lock up, an' then yer can come 'ome with me an' try a few things on.'

I knew she only lived round the corner because Mum had taken me there one Sunday morning. The proprietress was a small woman, not much bigger than me. She had untidy hair and a dress that dragged on the floor, and around her shoulders she swung a black knitted shawl while on her head she slapped a flat black straw hat. Then she set off wheeling the basket carriage full of clothing in front of her. I offered to help but she said she could manage. We were soon at her house and she kicked open the door and pushed the carriage inside. I followed her into the room which was piled so full of clothing old and new that you could hardly move.

'Come on in the back,' she said as she made her way through a pile of coats strung across the room. We entered the back which was only slightly less crowded, and there she introduced me to her husband who I could see was in a drunken sleep in a chair. I was glad she didn't wake him because I knew I would be there ages talking about my Dad and Mum who they'd known years ago when they lived in Deritend near the Bull Ring. She asked me what I wanted and how much I had to spend. I had three pounds fifteen shillings and sixpence and I wanted a skirt, blouse, stockings and a coat.

'Can't let yer 'ave all them for three poun's fifteen,' she said.

'Well, that's all I've got. I haven't bin able ter save more,' I told her.

'Oh well, let's see what we've got,' she said, rummaging through things.

So instead of new I had to be content with nearly new, which is little different from second hand but sounds better. I tried on several pairs of shoes until eventually she let me have a new pair of black patent leather which were the only ones that fitted. I'd always wanted a pair of these since I'd seen a woman wearing some in Jefferson's years before. I also chose two pairs of lisle stockings, a black hobble skirt, a white satin blouse with a frill down the centre and a brown velvet cape. She threw in a dress that was frayed along the edge saying that if it was cut and hemmed I'd be able to wear it for work. I was very pleased with my purchases, which she folded up for me and put in my string bag.

While she was doing that I opened my purse to pay her but when I did I couldn't believe my eyes. Inside there were only three pounds, two half crowns and a sixpence. Where was the half sovereign? She saw me fumbling and stopped what she was doing.

'What, yer mean yer ain't got the money?' she demanded.

Then I remembered. 'I must have given the half sovereign to those two soldiers,' I said, getting very upset.

'What soldiers?' I could see that she didn't believe me. I tried to explain between sobs that I must have dropped that coin into the man's cap instead of the sixpence I'd intended.

'Yer wunt see that or them again. They're more likely ter be in the pub now suppin' ter their good fortune. Anyway dry yer eyes an' give me the three pounds. Yer can pay the other after Christmas.'

I gave her the money, and the two half crowns I slipped back in my purse. Then after thanking her I made my way back through the heaps of clothes towards the door. She warned me not to stop or talk to anybody on my way home.

'Pretty little thing like yow shouldn't be down a rough quarter like this at night. I'd send the ole man along with yer but yer can see 'e's in a drunken stupor.'

I was glad. I thought I'd be safer without him. Her last words to me were, 'Now off yer goo, an' mind what I said, an' a merry Christmas.' I returned the compliment and hurried off with my bag on my arm. I returned the way I'd come. The barrow boys were thinning out by now, sweeping their speckled oranges and apples into the gutter along with the other rubbish. I thought of when I was little when I would have been glad of these, and indeed there were some small children scavenging. But now I could afford to turn up my nose at this scene. I half hoped that I would see the two soldiers still begging when I reached the fish market but they were nowhere to be seen. I guessed they were in the nearby pub and I was debating whether I dared go in to look for them when I was startled by a gruff voice behind me.

'Want ter buy a coupla puppies missy?' it said.

I turned round and saw a man I took to be one of the barrow boys holding a straw basket with two black and white puppies in it.

'It's me last sale, three bob the two,' he told me, lifting them out of the straw. I was fascinated by them. They licked my fingers and looked like they were saying 'please take me'. But even if he'd given them to me I knew that I couldn't take them home because Mum would have turned them out into the street. While I was thus occupied he thrust them into my arms and said, ''Ere tek 'em. Yer can 'ave 'em fer 'alf a crown.'

I've always been soft-hearted and I could not resist them, so I gave him the money, hugged them to me and walked off thinking I could find someone to give them a home. A few yards down the street I saw two lads sitting on the edge of the pavement sorting through the rotten vegetables that the stallholders had left there. These are two likely lads I could give them to, I thought.

'Here, would you like these?' I asked them, holding out the puppies.

''Ow much?' the taller of them asked.

'You can have them for nothin',' I replied.

'Goo-on, we don't believe yer, do we Jimmy?'

'No we don't,' Jimmy replied and continued sorting the rubbish.

I bent down and handed them over. ''Ere,' I said, 'if you'll promise to give 'em a good home and be kind to 'em you can 'ave 'em for nothin'.'

'Really missus? Yo' ain't kiddin' us are yer missus?'

With that they tucked them under their ragged waistcoats and darted off down the street with a 'thank yer an' a merry Christmas'.

I had some misgivings about letting them have them but it was no good my keeping them. By this time I'd missed the tram so I set off to walk home and by the time I got there it was past eleven o'clock. The house was deserted and the fire only embers. It seemed damp and cold and I set to to put some life into the fire with some wood and coal from the cellar. I found a penny and put that in the meter and got the kettle going and then went up and put my purchases in my trunk. I had very little money left but I reflected I'd bought all my Christmas presents so there was nothing else I needed. I had got Dad a new clay pipe and an ounce of twist, a black apron for Mum, two packets of Woodbines for Frankie and a box of chocolates for Liza. For Mary I had a box of white handkerchiefs. Just as I was about to sit down Mum and Dad appeared, both well oiled. They pulled their chairs up to the fire and began singing 'Only a Rose'. I'd heard enough drunken singing on my way home so I went to go to bed. But before I'd got to the door Mum called me back and told me to hang up some holly she had bought and some 'mottoes'. As I was sticking the oval mottoes up I thought what it was to put up the message 'GOD BLESS THIS HAPPY HOME' in our house. There were not many happy homes in our area now that the war was over and there were so many unemployed. When I'd done this I grabbed some bread and pickled beef from the table and tiptoed up to the attic where I sat on my bed eating my meagre supper, listening to Mum and Dad's feeble attempts at harmony before getting undressed and popping into bed.

I was too old to hang up my stockings now I knew who Father Christmas was, but even though he was out of a job Dad gave me a shilling and kiss. 'Thank yer me wench, just what I could do with,' he said next morning when he saw his present. Mum gave me a pair of fawn-coloured lisle stockings and a Christmas card with lace edging. Frankie had a tin of toffees for Liza and me. We thanked each other with kisses that were only exchanged in our house at the festive season. After breakfast Dad went out to find his mates and us three helped Mum clean the house and prepare for dinner. We had a stuffed goose and sausages and roast potatoes with Christmas pudding to follow. Mum couldn't afford to put silver three-penny bits in that year but I'd made the pudding and had slipped in four anyway. This meal was what passed for a real 'blow out' in 1919, but it wouldn't rate much for Christmas today.

After we'd washed up the dirty crocks Dad produced half a bottle of rum from the cupboard. He said he'd won it at a fair but I could see Mum didn't believe him. That didn't stop her from helping him empty the bottle though. Then they went upstairs to have a 'nap' as they termed it. As soon as they'd gone Frankie and Liza went out, leaving me alone, but I didn't mind; I went up to get out my clothes in readiness for Florrie's party that evening.

I bolted the door then stripped and began putting them on. First I put on the camisole, then clean bloomers, stockings and so on, until I was competely ready. Then I combed my hair, parted it in the middle and tied it up in a bun on top. I was ready to face the world. I looked in the mirror and thought I looked just 'swell'. My cheeks did look a little pale and since Liza always hid her carmine away I spat on my finger and rubbed some red off the wallpaper and rubbed it gently into my cheeks and lips. At last I had it right, I thought.

It was a cold frosty night that Christmas but I hadn't far to go. I was hurrying along past The George and Dragon when I heard the strains of 'The First Noel', and looking towards the pub doorway I saw six small, ragged children, four boys and two girls, trying to reach the top notes. I stood at a little distance – they hadn't seen me – and listened. It brought tears to my eyes, recalling as it did the night when Frankie, Liza and I, equally ragged and runny nosed, had sung carols on those very steps. Like us they were not having a lot of luck. So I opened my purse and gave them all I had with me, sixpence; a penny each I thought, not much. But I was late so holding my hobble skirt above my knees I hurried on. Lights were on in many houses and the sounds of jollity drifted on the night air; somewhere a gramophone crackled out a popular tune.

I could hear that Florrie's party was going with a swing before I reached her house. I knocked on the door but no one heard over the noise so I walked in boldly. As soon as I entered a churus of voices sang out, 'A merry Christmas, Katie.' I knew most of the boys and girls from the works and I felt relaxed and at home in no time. Florrie introduced me to her Mum, who was sitting at the piano about to play.

'Hello,' she said cheerfully. 'Go an' 'elp yerself to the eats and have a glass of port.'

Mrs Chatwin, Florrie's Mum, was a youngish woman with fair hair done in a bun on top. She had a pleasant smile and made me feel welcome. As the notes of 'Hearts and Flowers' sounded from the piano I helped myself to sandwiches and a glass of port as she'd directed. I stood by the piano listening to the tune and reflecting that Florrie was lucky to have such a nice Mum and homely home. I thought, I can never ask her to my home, I'd be too embarrassed. I moved across to stand by the log fire which was blazing in the grate. After a minute or two Florrie's young man came up and invited me to have another glass of port, but before he could take my empty one, Florrie had whisked him away.

'Come on, we haven't finished our dance,' she pouted. I saw at once she was jealous but he ignored her for the moment and fetched me my drink. Then I was left to drink alone. Everyone was paired up and I began to feel left out. They were all dancing and nobody had asked me but I couldn't dance anyway, so I made the best of it and enjoyed the scene. I couldn't dance because I'd never been taught and was definitely not allowed to go to dancehalls. The second glass of port I could feel warming me, and I had another for 'Dutch courage'; then I had a fourth because by now I was beginning to feel merry. After that I became bright and gay and finally tipsy.

'I'll show 'em,' I thought, 'they'll regret ignoring me.' I walked boldly, not a bit unsteadily, over to the piano and requested Mrs Chatwin play 'Annie Laurie' and I would sing. I had a good voice and as she called for quiet and the first notes sounded I let rip. When I had finished there were calls of 'encore', and as they pressed round me I felt dizzy and faint. One of the girls took me outside for a breath of fresh air and a glass of cold water. I couldn't go home looking and feeling like I did, so I was taken back in and made to sit on the plush green sofa.

My first party was not turning out to be a success and I determined to leave as soon as I felt well enough. I was making my way over to the door when a young man in soldier's uniform came in.

'Don't go yet, Katie,' Florrie urged me as she dashed over to greet the newcomer. 'I want you to meet Harry's friend, Charlie.'

I looked up into his face and I knew in that instant that I didn't want to leave. As soon as he'd entered he removed his cap, showing his dark auburn hair. He had light blue eyes and a fresh, ruddy complexion and a few freckles. I thought him most handsome. I must have stood there staring, too shy to speak, but he soon put me at my ease.

'So, your name's Katie? I've seen you lots of times coming home from work but I didn't like ter speak to yer when you was with the other girls.' I felt myself go hot all over and blush at this.

'Don't be shy,' he said gently.

'She's just leavin', Charlie,' Florrie called out, but I didn't want to leave now. I wanted to stay.

'Would you like me to see you home then?' he offered.

'I only live two streets away but if you don't mind you can see me part of the way.' I didn't want him to see the yard where we lived; I would have been too ashamed.

I said my good nights to everyone and as I did so noticed that Florrie seemed to be fuming, but I couldn't have cared less about her. When we got into the street we found it freezing hard and icy. Neither of us spoke as we walked along the pavement. I was too shy and perhaps he had nothing to say but every now and then when I slipped on the ice his arm went round my waist to steady me. To tell the truth I slipped purposely a couple of times so that I could feel the slight pressure as he gripped me. If it had been anybody else's arm I should have knocked it away, but each time he tightened his hold I experienced a certain thrill that I'd never known before. All too soon we reached the corner at the top of the hill which led down to Camden Drive where our yard was. He was as keen as any young man ought to be to see the girl he is escorting right to the door. However, I dissuaded him by telling him that I was not quite eighteen and that my parents would object if I was brought home by a boy.

'Can I see you tomorra night then?' he asked me and without hesitating I replied, 'Where?' We were looking straight into each other's eyes, the way only people falling in love do, as he replied, 'Outside the Mount Zion, seven o'clock.'

I knew the chapel in Graham Street he meant; I'd gone to Sunday school there as a child.

'Now, you're sure you'll be all right?' he asked, bending to kiss my cheek.

I felt a little disappointed he'd not taken me in his arms and kissed me properly but as I walked down the hill I heard his footsteps behind me, and as I turned he took me in his arms and squeezed me so hard I thought he would squeeze me to death. I was thrilled; I wanted to stay like that for ever. At last he released his grip and whispered, 'Good night, and don't forget your promise or I'll come knocking on your door.' With that he hugged me again and kissed me full on the lips, then turned to walk away. As I walked down the hill towards the Drive I felt I was walking on air; I was in love for the first time in my life. I had had a few boyfriends but nothing that felt like this.

The next night, Boxing Night, Charlie looked so handsome in his navy blue civilian suit, white shirt and dark tie, and as he doffed his cap to greet me I noticed his auburn hair highlighted under the street lamp. He kissed me on the cheek and took my hand. We walked and talked as young people have done since Adam and Eve. He told me he was twenty-two and lived with his sisters nearby in Nelson Street and that we were going there to meet them. I was too shy to meet any of his relatives and so he agreed I should meet them after Christmas. In any case he knew of a party in Nelson Street so we decided to go there.

He introduced me all round but he could see I looked uncomfortable so we didn't stay long and, having one port (I had learnt my lesson of the previous evening), we left. We strolled along the Sandpits and went into a pub called The Stores. He knew some of the customers there who asked me to have a drink, which I did though I stuck to lemonade. Everyone was singing and making merry and we joined in. Then all too soon it was eleven o'clock and 'Time gentlemen, please!'

We stopped on the way home to kiss and cuddle and parted with a promise to meet again outside the Queen's Hall, off the Parade. Before meeting Charlie the next night I took special pains with my dress and my hair, parting it down the middle and pinning it back into a tight bun. I kept looking in the mirror and back at the clock whose hands seemed to be standing still. At last it was time to leave. We met as planned and it was then, sitting in the dark, that he told me he loved me.

In the next few weeks we went for walks or to the pictures and each night before we parted we stopped to kiss and cuddle in an entry. In fact we stopped in one regularly near Stern and Bell's in Arthur Place, which was lined either side with larger, bay-windowed houses. It was an alley between two of these houses and at its end was Moseley's toffee factory. There was nowhere else to go and it was at least warm and out of the wind. One night we were seen together by my sister Mary who questioned me later. She wanted to know if I was going with Charlie steady. So I told her. I wasn't like Liza; I love him, I said, and when I was older I would marry him. She tried to warn me, tell me the facts of life, but I was too much in love with love to listen or care.

We were invited to a New Year's party where we both drank

too much but we were so happy and so terribly in love nothing seemed to matter. Going home he stopped me and, putting his hands on my shoulders, sang, 'I'll take you home again, Kathleen'. He had a good voice and I shall remember his singing that song to my dying day. We sang together and laughed and giggled all the way to our courting place. That evening I forgot my sister's warning and we made love for the first time. We stayed there for a long time after, our arms around each other, huddled together until the thin light of dawn began to streak the night sky. Eventually we did part and I floated home without a care whether my parents were waiting up for me or not. When I got home and tried the door I found it bolted on the inside. They must have assumed I was already in bed so I was left with only one alternative; I had to lift the cellar grating and get in that way. I slid down the heap of slack on my bottom and landed amid the cobwebs on the floor. I pulled myself to my feet, felt for the stairs, climbed up and entered the living room. I dusted the cobwebs from my hair, took off my shoes and crept up the bare wooden staircase, hoping it wouldn't creak too loudly and wake them. I could hear Mum and Dad 'sending the pigs home to market', as they used to say, and reaching the landing I felt safe. I quickly undressed and jumped into bed and had hardly hit the pillow than I was waking up the next morning.

As I awoke what had happened the previous evening came flooding back to me. Now I finally knew the facts of life: there was no doubt in my mind at all where babies came from now, and I felt ashamed and worried in about equal measure. What if I have a baby and he won't marry me, I thought. There were girls in our neighbourhood who had babies and were not married. Would Mum turn me out into the workhouse as she'd always threatened she would? All that day I was worried sick and when I met Charlie that evening I was that upset I broke down and cried. I hung my head, I was too ashamed to face him. But Charlie lifted my face to his and kissed my wet cheeks and smiled.

'Don't get upset Katie. I really do love you an' as soon as we can save enough money, we'll put up the banns and in the meantime we'll save 'ard an' look for a 'ouse.'

Of course, then as now, this was easier said than done. We met only at weekends, when Charlie took me to lodgings where he was staying since he had left his sisters'. That was only temporary while he sorted himself out after his discharge from the Army. I cleaned and cooked for him and was happy that we had things worked out between us. I managed to save a pound a week and Charlie likewise. I put it away safely and our savings began to grow. The first of February was my birthday: I was eighteen. I told Charlie I was going to tell my parents that I was courting but he dissuaded me, saying he would tell them himself in a while. I was reassured by this and each time his landlady was away at the weekend we made love. Towards the end of March I felt out of sorts, and one morning couldn't face my breakfast. I felt nauseous and frightened. I pushed my food away untouched and Mum noticed I'd turned pale.

'Wot's the matta with yow? Ain't it good enough for yer or summat?' she said.

'Yes, but I feel sick.'

'Sick or not yer betta 'urry yerself fer work or yow'll be late agen,' she yelled.

I knew that I was pregnant. I'd missed my period and now I was feeling sick in the morning. I wanted to confide in Mum but I was too scared: I knew she wouldn't understand. I should have brought Charlie home before so she could have got used to the idea of my getting married.

When I returned from work that evening Mary was waiting for me. Straight away she said. 'Mum says yer've been outta sorts the last few mornin's. What's the matter with yer?'

I just broke down and cried. 'I think I'm going to have a baby, Mary,' I wailed.

'Oh, my God! Are you sure?' she gasped.

'I hope not, but I think I am,' I sobbed.

'You'd better come upstairs an' let me see,' she told me. She made me strip, and when she felt my breasts and belly, sure enough, the evidence was there.

'Is it the young chap I've seen you with?' she asked, and I nodded my tearful reply.

'Then he better marry yer before Mum finds out. Or anyone else round 'ere for that matter, yer know how the tongues wag,' she added.

I got dressed, feeling miserable, and followed her downstairs. She made tea and we drank it.

'Now we'll talk,' she said sharply. 'An' stop yer snivelling.'

I told her all that had happened and when I'd finished I could see she was not impressed.

'You should both be ashamed! If it had been Liza I could understand but not you!' she said harshly. 'I warned yer, didn't I.' At that I flared up.

'Yes, you warned me, but too late!' I snapped back. 'I was always asking you an' Mum to explain things to me years ago, but no, you never did!' "Yer'll 'ave ter wait until yer older", that's all I ever heard from Yow. 'Ow old 'ave I got ter be, tell me that?'

'Well, why didn't you bring 'im home?' she asked.

'What! Bring 'im ter this hovel!' I shouted at her.

'Oh, well, I'll see what I can do to 'elp,' she said, getting up to leave.

Next night I came home from work to find Charlie, Dad and Mary already there, discussing me. I looked from one to the other, shaking in my shoes, wondering what was going to happen. But Charlie came over and put his arm round me.

'It's all right, don't worry Katie. Your Dad's given 'is consent, so we can get married in a few weeks' time.'

Hearing that I threw my arms round my Dad and hugged him. There was no one like my Dad.

'Be good to 'er lad,' he told Charlie. 'She's a good girl. But I don't know 'ow her mother is goin' ter tek this,' he added.

'You leave 'er ter me,' Mary said firmly. She was quite strait-laced was Mary. She was married for the second time now and also a bit of a snob.

'Come along, lad. Let's go out an' 'ave a drink an' leave these two to sort things out,' said Dad.

As soon as they had left I asked Mary how Charlie came to be here.

'I thought it was about time he found out what his

responsibilities were and had a talk with Dad, so I made it my
business to find out where he was lodging.'

'But Mary, I can't face Mum. What am I goin' ter say?'

'You should 'ave thought of that before getting into this
trouble! Any'ow you better slip upstairs and wait there while
I try to explain.'

I rushed out of the room and hid. I was so confused and
upset I just lay down and wept. I would sooner have faced the
devil than face our Mum. It wasn't long before I heard her
voice below.

'Oh my God! Oh my God!' she shrieked. 'Whatever will
the neighbours think?'

Then I heard Mary's voice very angrily. 'Never mind the
neighbours as you call 'em. It's your daughter upstairs you've
got to think about now, and stop crying. That won't mend
matters.'

'I warned 'er, I warned 'er wot would 'appen if she brought
disgrace on us,' she wailed.

'Don't be stupid, mother. And wipe your eyes. We're to
blame really for not explaining the facts of life to her years ago
when she asked us. Anyway it's too late now; she's getting
married in three weeks' time.'

'Who ses so?'

'Dad and the young man she's been going with. He seems a
nice fella, Mum, and I know you'll like 'im too.'

'We'll see,' I heard her say more quietly before adding, 'yer
betta call 'er down while I mek a cuppa tea.'

When I heard Mary's voice from the foot of the stairs I felt
too ashamed to come down to face them. But I knew I would
have to sooner or later; better face Mum now while Mary was
present, I thought, than wait till we were alone. Slowly I crept
down the stairs and finally stood facing Mum. It was then that
I got the biggest shock of my life. She threw her arms around
me, drew me to her bosom and wept.

'Why did yer do it? Why?' she sobbed. I was in tears now
as well, thinking I'd been forgiven. I should have known
better: Mum was never one to forgive or forget. She was like
the weather and whenever we were alone together she kept

harping on about the disgrace I'd brought to the family, and each night I cried myself to sleep. I felt I could never be happy there any more and on the following Friday, after placing my wages as usual under the mantel fringe, I put some of my belongings in my string bag and prepared to leave the house. There was only one place where I'd be welcome now, I felt. Then, just as I was opening the door, in walked Mum.

'An' where do yer think yer gooin'?' she demanded.

'Charlie's. He's made arrangements for me with his land-lady,' I replied at once.

'All right!' she snapped as she pushed past me. 'Yer can please yerself but wotever yer do from now on I wipe me 'an's on yer.'

I walked down the hill in tears. If only she'd offered to forgive me, taken me in her arms and meant it. That was the impossible, and it was not until later when I was raising my own family that we came to understand each other better and became closer as mother and daughter.

8

Married Life

Charlie and I were married on 25 April 1921, by which time I was three months' pregnant. I would have loved to have been married in white with a flowing veil like Mary, but she had said that it would be a 'sin' and 'a mockery' and no matter how tightly I laced my whalebone stays, she said, the neighbours would know the truth when they recollected the date of the wedding. So I was wed in a pale blue frock and coat, both much out of date, with a blue straw picture hat and white shoes and stockings. I had begged Mary to lend me some money which I'd promised to pay back from my wages each week so that I could put on a better show on my wedding day. However, she refused, saying she'd enough money owing to her already. It was then she told me she was going to America to make a fresh start, and this was another reason, I suppose, why she wouldn't lend me anything. Perhaps she thought I should be punished as well. In any case we quarrelled and were never truly close after that.

They did do us the courtesy of coming to the church though: Dad, Mum, my brothers and sisters, as well as a few of the neighbours and some of my friends from work. After the ceremony we received the usual congratulations and Mum was the last to kiss me. I noticed a real tear in her eye, but I was past caring then; I was what is known as 'a happily married woman'.

Charlie and I returned to our lodgings to pack our weekend case ready to catch the early train to Blackpool next morning. I'd saved the money to do this in a 'diddleum' club,* run by a

---

* A diddleum club was a savings club organised by the workers with the aim of going on an outing such as the one described. It was so called because it was often said that you were diddled out of some of your money.

Mrs Chapman with whom I worked. I'd never seen Blackpool so we thought this would be a good idea for a honeymoon: we couldn't afford anything better.

The following morning, Saturday, found us waiting on the platform for our train when several women from my works, together with their men friends or husbands, appeared. They were already the worse for drink, rolling around and looking bedraggled, as if they'd not been to bed. Had the train not drawn up when it did we would have foregone the diddleum money and returned home.

'Good 'ealth, me wench,' one of the women cried out to us as she tipped back the contents of a bottle.

'Mind wot yer doin' ternight,' another shouted, amid howls of raucous laughter. The only two who were sober, I noticed, were two spinster sisters who lived in Sloane Street.

When the train stopped we jumped on and found an empty compartment. We pulled the blinds down, then we were alone and happy. We could still hear the off-key singing from along the corridor, but we weren't disturbed.

When we arrived at the boarding house we had to be shuffled about because there were too many guests and some had to go next door, but our landlady had the pick of the bunch before sending the others off. In our group there were the two maiden sisters, prim and proper, two women friends, Mr and Mrs Chapman and Charlie and I. The landlady was a small, plump, middle-aged woman; a typical seaside landlady. She motioned us upstairs and off we trooped. Our rooms were on the first floor; small bedrooms made from partitioning one large room into four with plywood walls. Although our room was virtually empty apart from the bed it was clean. The bed was only three-quarter size and stood in the middle of the room. There was a washstand by the window with a crock bowl and water jug on it and there was also a small piece of Sunlight soap and a threadbare towel. There were only nails on which to hang our clothes and no carpet or lino, just bare floorboards. Yes, and beneath the bed there was the regulation china chamber pot. Pinned to the door were the house rules regarding lights out and breakfast time which was 'nine o'clock sharp'. Over the bed was another handwritten message: 'Please Be Quiet As Other People Want To Sleep'.

Before she left us she said, 'I'll send Fred up with your bag,' and as she opened the door she paused and said, 'You're the newlyweds?' We nodded and she left, smiling.

There was a strong smell of disinfectant about the room which seemed to emanate from beneath the bed. I turned down the bedclothes and the mattress to check for flea or bug powder but everything, though threadbare, was clean. Charlie and I sat down on the edge of the bed and giggled. We'd expected something better than this but would make the best of it.

'When am I going ter see the sea?' I asked him.

'As soom as we're ready ter go downstairs,' he replied.

'No, it's too dark now. Anyway, the landlady says its about fifteen minutes' walk unless we go by tram. We'll wait till morning and we'll go an' explore before the others are awake,' I told him.

So we settled down to wait for the supper bell, and while we sat there we became aware that every movement and word that went on in the rooms adjacent to ours was distinctly audible. Then the bell sounded and we went downstairs to see what was in store for us. We entered a large kitchen where the landlady was standing beside the large, black range ladling out soup.

'Sit yerselves down.' She motioned with the ladle when she saw us standing, politely waiting.

We all found seats at a large table covered with American oilcloth and waited while Fred served us plates of thin, watery soup and chunks of dry bread. The two old maids sitting across from us whispered, 'Is this all we're gooin' ter get?' This produced a black look from Fred but we did get a good meal of roast mutton, carrots, cabbage, peas and roast potatoes. Fred and his wife sat down and had their meal with us and we had a pleasant conversation. When we'd finished the other guests asked us if we'd like to join them for a drink in a nearby pub but we couldn't afford to go drinking. Fortunately, before we could refuse Fred came to the rescue.

'You young 'uns don't want to start drinkin' your time o' life. Anyway if yer like ter stay in an' keep me an' the missus company we've got a drop in,' he offered.

Charlie and I were happy to accept this offer because apart from anything else it was now raining heavily. Fred and his wife turned out to be a jolly couple and they made us feel very welcome, and as we sat round the range supping stout and ale we became very talkative. Fred regaled Charlie with his exploits in the Navy and Charlie in turn talked about his time in the Army while 'the missus' and I talked of our families and what I was going to do when I got a home of my own. We seemed to chat like this for hours until, when it was time to go to bed, I felt quite dizzy, not being used to drinking much. Charlie too, I could see, had had enough but we thanked them without difficulty and said 'good night'. However, when it came to the stairs I needed some gentle pushing from Charlie to get up. As soon as we had entered our room and lit the gas jet I flopped down on the bed. The others were already in their rooms, as the laughing and giggling we could hear testified, and when Charlie had removed his boots and trousers and was standing beside the bed in his shirt I was infected with the giggling too: I could see all he'd got.

'What's there ter giggle about?' he asked huffily. 'Get me the pot, I want ter mek water.' But before I could reach it he bent down and we both somehow managed to topple over. We lay there giggling hysterically as the floor began to resound with thumping on the ceiling of the room underneath ours.

'What's goin' on up there?' we heard Fred shout.

'Sorry ol' man,' Charlie replied, 'I 'appened ter fall over.'

'All right, but think of us what wants ter sleep,' came the annoyed response and we could hear our neighbours laughing at this exchange.

'I wonder just what they think we're up to,' Charlie said close to the partition.

We sorted ourselves out and I held the pot for Charlie to stop his making too loud a noise. I was embarrassed. I closed my eyes and turned my head and giggled and while he made water I must have raised the pot higher. I'd forgotten there was disinfectant in it and I suppose his penis must have dangled in, because the next thing I knew the pot and its contents went flying across the room.

'Oh my God! Oh my God!' he kept screaming as he shook it and chased me round the bed. 'I'll kill yer,' he shouted, 'I'll kill yer!' By the look on his face I could believe him.

Before I could reach the door it was flung open and there were Mr and Mrs Chapman and the two old maids, their eyes almost popping out as Charlie showed them what I'd done. I fled down the stairs and fell into the landlady's arms. She had to sit me down and administer whisky before I could explain coherently what had happened. Then she and Fred began to laugh but I'm afraid I couldn't see the funny side of the situation so she sent Fred up to see what could be done. He took a bowl of cold water and a sponge. When he returned, still smiling, he said there was no real damage done, only that the pot was broken and Charlie was a bit sore but that it was safe for me to go back upstairs. I was scared, though, and the landlady had to go with me to see that all was all right. She pushed me through the door and I sat on the edge of the bed while she cleaned up the floor and removed the broken pot. Charlie all the while lay in bed, staring up at the ceiling. Not a word was spoken for a long time until he began to cough. I threw my arms round him and whimpered.

'I'm sorry Charlie, I forgot there was disinfectant in the pot.'

'No good bein' sorry now. It could 'ave bin worse. Now get undressed an' get inter bed before yer catch cold, an' stop yer snivelling.' He sounded far from pleased.

I undressed slowly and lay nervously beside him. Then he took me in his arms and kissed my wet cheeks and I knew I was forgiven. That's how we lay, in each other's arms, until we fell asleep.

The next morning the landlady knocked on our door and brought our breakfast in on a tray.

'I thought you'd like ter say in bed late. 'Ow is it this morning?' she asked Charlie, who replied sheepishly. 'Not so sore this mornin', thanks.'

'Well, you can stay in bed an' I'll call yer later, 'ows that?' she told us.

We thanked her as she left the tray on the foot of the bed. We sat up and I poured the tea as well as I could without spilling it, but before we'd begun to drink it Fred arrived with a wooden stool and another chamber pot.

'Yer won't be able ter break this un, it's enamel,' he informed us jovially before leaving us to our eggs, toast and marmalade.

After putting the dirty crocks and tray on the stool Charlie decided to slip his trousers on and go downstairs to the outside toilet, and when he returned I asked him if he was still sore.

'No, it's wearin' off a bit now, but we won't be able ter mek love until I've seen the doctor,' he said.

'But I wasn't thinkin' about that,' I replied angrily.

'Now, now don't lose yer temper. Let me get back inter bed, it's freezin' out 'ere.'

And there we lay just huddled together to keep each other warm until the dinner bell rang. Then we hurriedly washed and dressed and went down to the dining room, not the kitchen as before, where we found that the others had already started theirs. I could see by their exchanged glances that they knew what had happened the previous night. So we finished the meal in silence and then it was time to get our things together to catch the train back to Birmingham. We'd not seen a great deal of Blackpool on our honeymoon except what we'd glimpsed after our arrival the previous afternoon.

We were lucky enough to have a compartment to ourselves again for the return journey and as the train puffed slowly out of Blackpool station I observed to Charlie, 'We never did see the sea, did we?'

'Never mind,' he answered, putting his arm round me. 'We'll come next year an' stay a whole week. I promise yer we'll 'ave a real good 'oliday.' But I was to be thirty years of age before I ever saw the sea: the only water I saw till then was the canal. However, we both looked forward to a happy future that spring day and perhaps it was just as well that we didn't know what fate had in store for us because neither of us would have had the strength to face it.

When we arrived home late that Sunday night our landlady greeted us with bad news.

'Yer'll 'ave ter find yerselves new accommodation,' she said. 'I'm sorry but I let the 'ouse ter me brother an' 'is family an' they want ter move in next week.'

Charlie called her a liar. 'Yer want ter get rid of us because my wife's 'avin' a baby,' he told her and she didn't deny it.

'Well, yer've got till next week anyway,' she conceded. All that week we searched desperately but we had no furniture to put in a house even if we could afford one which we couldn't. Furnished rooms were difficult to come by as well, particularly when the landlady found out I was pregnant. By the end of that week we were at our wits' end and there was only one thing to do as a last resort. We went to see Mum and Dad together and explained that in a few days we'd be out on the street. Mum said she knew a Mrs Larkins who lived on the corner of Arthur Place next to The Leopard public house who had a furnished room to let. Mum thought that Mrs Larkins would give her first chance of the room because she'd often cleaned for her.

We were able to take the room, which was very scantily furnished, for eight shillings and sixpence a week, but while we were there we saved enough to buy some second-hand furniture including a couple of chairs and a large oak wardrobe. There was a bed and a table and odd crocks that belonged to Mrs Larkins and we had to manage without other things until such time as we could afford them.

Mrs Larkins was soon to go to Australia to visit her son and it was arranged that I should pay the rent to Mr Dykes at The Leopard Inn. In the basement of the house there lived Mr and Mrs Penny. She was a small woman and although she had very little herself she was always kind to me and gave me what she had. She often came up for a chat, a cup of tea and sometimes some cake if she'd been cooking. Soon, however, they had to leave because they couldn't pay the rent and the room was taken by a couple I hardly ever saw.

Now that I was living just a stone's throw from Mum and Dad they came to visit us often. Dad would call in at The Leopard for a pint and a game of dominoes while Mum dropped in to chat and tell me what to get for my confinement. We were closer now than we'd ever been and I was glad, because now I was going to have a baby I needed her more than ever. She told me she'd booked a midwife, who turned out to the same Mrs Bullivant who'd attended Nelly's mother. When I told Mum she'd died Mum sprang to Mrs Bullivant's defence.

'Yer carn't blame the midwife fer that. Any'ow yow ain't gooin' ter die, yer too young an' 'ealthy, an' another thing, she's brought 'undreds o' babbies inter the world. It ain't 'er fault if any died,' she concluded.

She convinced me and I ceased worrying and set to to knit the little garments the baby would need. With Mum's help I washed and ironed the nappies, nightgowns and 'belly binders'* that would be needed.

When my labour pains started Mum came at once while Charlie ran for the midwife. Mum was right. I had a trouble-free confinement and on 7 October 1921 my first child, a boy, was born. He was a fine, healthy baby weighing in at 6 lbs 12 oz. It was the custom then to bind babies and after he'd been washed Mum fastened his belly binder round him before she put on his nappy and wrapped him in his nightgown. Then she held him close.

'My little gran'son,' she whispered, and as she put him on my breast there was a tear in her eye. She bent over and kissed me too. At that moment I felt the happiest woman in the world; I had my son, my husband, my Dad and finally my Mum.

Charlie and I had our son christened Charles Samuel, after his father and grandfather, at St Paul's Church when he was a month old. By then I was back at work, doing press-work, with Mum looking after little Charles, but I had to pay her

---

* A bandage which was put around the baby's waist and left there for several months to prevent the belly button protruding.

five shillings a week for his milk and rusks. My husband was now on short time and we were very hard up. Between us we were earning two pounds ten shillings a week which had to cover rent, food, coal, lighting and the boy's food, as well as 'club money' for sheets and blankets which I was buying on hire purchase, the 'never-never'. I'd scarcely stopped breast-feeding my first and my milk had only just dried up when I found I was pregnant again. Mrs Larkins, who had returned from Australia, found out from the neighbours' gossip and she told us we would have to look for other rooms.

Mum had angry words with her but Mrs Larkins was adamant. So Mum said I'd better get my few 'traps', as she called our belongings, and move in with her and Dad until Charlie found a better job. Dad agreed with this but it was the last place I wanted to live. Liza was the only one still living at home and Mum said she could sleep in their room and we could have the attic. When Charlie returned footsore from looking for a place we discussed Mum's offer and reluctantly decided to accept the room, at least for the time being. When he heard, Dad said that we should have all our belongings in our room to avoid any arguments with Mum. I was happier living up there, out of Mum's way, but first I had to scrub and disinfect the room which was filthy. I paid Mum eight and sixpence a week for that small room, plus the coal which she rationed out and the washing.

I worked until a week before the baby was due and my second son was born eleven months to the day after my first, on 7 September 1922. He was christened John Ernest after my eldest brother and my husband's brother. Charlie was out of work altogether by now and we were in terrible straits with two small babies to look after. With no money coming in I had to go back to work a few weeks after my baby was born and leave my two sons with Mum. How hard I persevered to get us away from that hovel no one knows; I even went office cleaning after I'd finished my press-work at the factory and had fed and put the boys to bed. I literally worked all hours God made to earn a little extra to take care of their needs, but as hard as I worked we seemed to be no better off; it was like treading water to stay afloat, we were always short of money. We tried to find our own place but that was just as hopeless; nobody wanted two small children.

Charlie tramped the streets day after day looking for a job but to no avail. Finally in desperation he decided to go to the timber mills and buy bags of sawdust to sell to pubs and butchers' shops. This he did, but it was an ill-fated venture because he made very little profit from it, only managing to give me two shillings or half a crown a day. And, more important in the long run, he started drinking heavily. I suppose visiting all those public houses to sell sawdust presented too much temptation and he would have a drink in each; by the time he rolled home he was very much the worse for drink. This went on for two years, during which time things went from bad to worse. It was more than anybody could stand; our situation never seemed to improve, and we seemed destined to a life of grinding poverty – what would be called 'deprivation' today. For me and those who lived through similar experiences it was just plain misery.

Dad was out of work as well. He was ill and at home with asthma, the legacy of his years in the casting shop, and Mum was at her wits' end. In the end there was no alternative: she went on the parish again and when the visitor came to inspect the house we had to hide because Mum had told them that she and Dad were living alone. She got away with this subterfuge and no one in the yard split; how could they when they were in the same boat themselves? As the reader can imagine I was utterly exhausted each night after leaving my second job and I would crawl into bed with the babies and pray to the Lord to get us away from all that poverty. I cried all the time. I suppose in retrospect that I was emotionally as well as physically drained.

Dad was not one to give up, though. He bought himself a last and mended the boots of everyone who could afford to pay, even some of the firemen at the Albion Street Fire Station. This helped us for a while, but soon Dad became too ill even to do this. Then to cap it all I became pregnant again and had to give up my job and fall on the parish. Needless to say when they found out that Charlie was selling sawdust I was refused help. This time I had a daughter, christened Kathleen like me, born on 13 March 1925.

It was during this period that I had two lady visitors from the welfare call with clothes for the children and blankets and sheets for the bed. Later we became entitled to Salvation Army soup and bread, sometimes a meat dinner, but you had to be in the queue early or the food would be cold. To me at that time all this seemed like history repeating itself, and I could see no way that I could do what I wanted most which was to ensure a better future for my children. Charlie had lost his spirit and seemed content making the sawdust rounds for a few coppers a day, most of which went to finance his heavier and heavier drinking. It was enough to break your heart. We quarrelled often but the rows did no good and only increased the bad feeling. I threatened to leave him but then what would become of my babies? Charlie himself stayed out more and more and we seldom saw him, and then rarely sober. There was only one alternative for me. I would have to go back to work and hope that the children would be all right without me.

One day not long after Kathleen was born I was taking the children for a walk when I happened to spot what I'd been hoping for: a notice in a window that read, 'EXPERIENCED ENAMELLER WANTED, YOUNG AND MUST BE USED TO BADGES AND MOTOR-PLATES'. I could hardly believe it: it was just up my street. I left the two boys sucking a toffee apple on the step and, carrying the baby in my arms, I went in. The boss, a Mr Butler, looked me up and down and asked me how old I was. I told him twenty-three, though I was a year younger than that. He asked what experience I'd had and I told him that I'd worked at B.H. Collins, Frederic Street, and Joseph Fray's, Tenby Street North, but I didn't tell him about all the other jobs I'd had. He seemed satisfied with this and fetched out a motor-plate and asked me how I would enamel it. I showed him, and with that he said I could start the following Monday morning at thirty shillings per week. I couldn't get home quick enough to tell Mum the good news, and later that week I pawned my wedding ring and with the money I bought coal and extra food. Mum too was glad of the money I gave her for looking after the children while I was working, and Mr Butler was pleased with my workmanship and I received two increases in wages in consequence. I was able to save, after all was paid for, about five shillings a week, but I should have known that this was too good to last.

When I found out I was pregnant with Jeanette I was afraid to tell Charlie and I certainly didn't want any more babies. I couldn't adequately feed and clothe the children we had already, and in the absence of child benefit and family income supplement and the other support that the Welfare State provides, another child was simply another mouth to feed, reducing a family's ability to care for the children it had already. I was so desperate that many times I made up my mind to ask one of the neighbours to abort me, but fear rather than conscience prevented me – fear of what would become of little Charles, John and Kathleen if I should die. I knew of many young women who had died through trusting the ignorant old women of the neighbourhood to terminate their pregnancies. Abortion was also a crime, and prosecution would surely follow if you were found out.

The reader is probably asking at this point why Charlie and I hadn't taken precautions to prevent another pregnancy, and the answer is simple: I had no idea that contraception existed, nor did I until after my fifth child was born. It is not appreciated today when the pill is so universally available to young women such as I was then that the subject of sex was completely surrounded by ignorance, myth and misunderstanding throughout the working-class community. I cannot speak for those who were better off and better educated, but in our neighbourhood these things were never spoken of.

Despite the poverty-stricken circumstances of my early married life there were some happier moments. I remember Dad and Charlie spending many happy hours with the children when I was at work and Mum was too lazy to see to them. They organised games for the kids in our yard like 'kick

the can' and 'tip cat' and if the weather was fine and windy
Dad would make a kite from newspapers and take them all to
the recreation ground in Goodman Street where they would
take turns in flying it. I also remember young Charlie worrying us because he'd not got a ball to play with like the other
boys at his school; he must have been five then, and he
couldn't understand that we couldn't afford to buy him one.
So one day his Dad brought him home a golf ball he'd found
or been given. My son treasured that little white ball, even
putting it under his pillow at night. Then one day the
inevitable happened and it was kicked through the window of
a nearby shop and we had to pay the proprietor half a crown
we could ill afford. A crying match followed and eventually
Charlie promised to get him a ball that would do no damage.
How he managed this shows the lengths parents had to go to
then to provide even the simplest toys for their children. One
of Charlie's customers on his sawdust round was Knight's,
the pork butcher, on the corner of Great Hampton Row and
Tower Street, Hockley, and he asked the butcher there for a
pig's bladder. What fun we had trying to inflate it! In the end
we succeeded and Dad, Charlie and my two sons had many
happy hours playing football with it in the yard.

Those were the good times, when I or one of the neighbours was able to play with Kathleen and the other little girls
in the yard. We would hold the skipping rope for them or
they would play at marbles or with their spinning-tops or else
draw a grid with chalk on the bricks and play hopscotch,
games that children of this present generation seem to have
forgotten. The pig's bladder football was not to Mum's liking
though. When she first saw young Charlie bring it indoors she
exclaimed, 'I ain't 'avin' that stinkin', greasy thing in my 'ouse
an' if I see it about it'll goo on the fire.' So to avoid his
grandmother's wrath Charlie dropped it down the cellar
grating at night before coming in to bed and then retrieved it
to play with the next day. Until one afteroon when he
returned from school and went down the cellar to fetch it and
found it had gone: the rats had eaten it. There was another
tearful scene before his Dad brought home another one. To

avoid a similar fate Charlie hung this one high up on a nail outside the attic window where it was safe from the rats' gnawing teeth.

My fourth child, Jeanette Elizabeth, was born on 3 Septembe 1927 after I'd been rushed by ambulance to Dudley Road Hospital. There I experienced a proper childbirth with real medical attention and I was well looked after, even being given a bottle of stout every evening. This would give me strength while I was breastfeeding I was told. While I was there I was very concerned about my other children and received a reprimand from the matron for worrying. 'You'll lose your milk,' she warned me. She was right because when I returned home I found that the neighbours had each taken it in turns to look after them. We were all in the same boat and there was always help at hand if needed.

I was shocked to discover that Dad had been taken into the poorhouse on Western Road while I'd been away. As soon as I could I went there to see him. The workhouse was a forbidding-looking building and I shuddered as I walked through the heavy wrought-iron gates and across the cobbled yard. I was standing not knowing where to go when an old man in grey corduroy trousers and heavy boots approached me and asked who I was looking for. When I told him he led me into the building and up several flights of steep stone steps to the second floor. When I entered the ward and looked around I saw that it was filled with men of all ages lying on their beds in an eerie silence. They stared at me and looked so dispirited that I felt like bursting into tears. I searched down the ward for my Dad but couldn't see him. Then a male nurse came up and showed which bed he was in. When I reached his bedside I couldn't believe my eyes; he'd changed so much in the ten days since I had seen him last. He looked old and drawn and had a faraway look in his eyes, as if he was looking at something a long way away. I just broke down and wept; I was so shocked to see him like this. I took his hand which seemed pitifully thin and wasted in my own and kissed him.

'Dad,' I managed to say, 'it's me, Katie, I brought you some oranges and some twist.' But he didn't answer or move at all but continued to stare into space as if I wasn't there. The male nurse, seeing my distress, told me that he'd had a stroke, and as he led me away, still crying, I wondered if Dad knew what a terrible place he had come to.

I couldn't believe that my father would end his days in the poorhouse when he'd been good, honest and kind and had always worked hard when there were jobs to be had. I visited him several times but his condition didn't change. I have often wondered since if he was conscious of what was happening but had simply suffered a temporary paralysis. Either way, his suffering, if suffering it was, didn't last long and a few days later a policeman called at my mother's house with the news that Dad was dead. My mother began to wail and cry when she heard this, and soon a crowd of our neighbours had gathered round to offer their sympathies, but to me these were only crocodile tears and I couldn't believe she would mourn his loss long. Dad had always been my favourite. I loved him and came to rely on his kindness and sound advice and I never forgave my Mum all the pain and suffering she'd caused him over the years. After Dad's death she took to drinking more heavily, which she was able to do because she was receiving ten shillings a week widow's pension. As we laid Dad to rest I reflected on my own life: twenty-four years old, I'd seen nothing of life, only poverty and hardship, and it seemed to me then that I'd been born simply to breed. Yet I couldn't afford the luxury of self-pity for long; life had to continue and my four little ones had to be cared for.

By now both Charles and John were at school. I'd refused to send them to St Paul's School in Camden Drive, the school I'd gone to myself, but had insisted instead that they go to Nelson Street, off the Sandpits, where the school had a better reputation and I hoped they might get a better start in life than I had had. While I was at work and the boys at school, Mrs Taylor, my long-time friend, looked after the girls and we were able to cope sufficiently for me to cast aside the *Daily Mail* boots that were always blistering the children's feet and buy them ones that fitted properly. Again things were looking up for us – if only I didn't become pregnant again.

Each Saturday evening Mrs Taylor would look in – Mum was hardly ever at home any more – and when I'd put the children to bed she would keep an eye on them so that Charlie and I could go out together.

'If yer want me ter mind 'em, it's no trouble, as long as yer bring me back twopenn'orth o' snuff,' she would say.

I always cherished these Saturday nights when Charlie would embrace me and say, 'Get yer togs on, I'll tek yer out.' I knew well enough where we would be going. We would take a penny ride on the tram to the terminus at the top of Snow Hill, outside the railway station, now sadly demolished. Our first stop would be to buy a tuppenny bag of baked potatoes or roast chestnuts, then off we'd stroll, arm in arm, to the Bull Ring markets where we would haggle with the barrow boys for our fruit and vegetables or whatever we needed. Then when we had made our purchases we'd call in The Nelson where Charlie would have a pint of bitter and I would have a stout, sometimes two if we had the money to spare.

We had the house to ourselves more now as well, including the room downstairs. Mum was often away. She took trips to Gloucester, she said to visit relatives, but I knew of no relations there. However, I did not ask questions, being only too glad she was out of our way. I'd lost whatever interest I had had in her, and despised her for the drunkard she was turning into. When she'd collected her pension and our rent money she would disappear for days at a time. Things went more smoothly then. I even managed to save a few pounds without Charlie knowing. This was for a 'rainy day' or, perhaps, my dream – to get away from this bug-infested hovel I'd lived in all my life. I imagined being able to bring my children up properly, without their arses hanging out of their trousers and in a clean, tidy house in a pleasant district. But this was just not to be.

The next blow came just as things were beginning to look up for us. One Monday afternoon there was a knock at the door and there stood a policeman. He had come to break the news of my son Charles's death. Even now, nearly sixty years later, I cannot describe how I felt and feel about the loss of my eldest child. He'd been knocked down by a butcher's delivery van on his way home from school at lunchtime, and I never forgave myself for the foolishness of insisting on his going to that school in the Sandpits rather the close, safe school at the top of the Drive.

I was out of my mind with grief and guilt and although people were kind in their sympathy, nothing seemed to help. I kept breaking down and crying, and I suppose I had what today would be classed as a nervous breakdown but then was not understood as other than a mother's natural grief. People came from all over the district to his funeral but this simply made me worse. I couldn't face them without breaking down and I isolated myself from contact with people. I experienced frightening nightmares and refused to allow my children out of my sight lest something should happen to one of them too. I suppose I was trying to give them the protection that I felt in my misguided way I hadn't been able to give Charles. Looked at rationally I had nothing to reproach myself for, but logic is not what guides one's actions or thoughts in the state of shock following bereavement. Eventually, I had to send John back to school because the man from the school board threatened us with a summons if I didn't. Still I hid indoors with the girls, more mad than sane. Each time I looked out of the attic window and saw the old pig's bladder hanging there it started me off. Then one day it was no longer there. I asked Charlie what he'd done with it and he said he'd buried it next to our son's grave in Warstone Lane cemetery. Strangely enough, that act was like laying a ghost, because although I still grieved after that I began to pull myself together. I realised that I was making Charlie suffer, and the children whom I was neglecting, to indulge my own feelings. I still had a heavy heart but I determined to get on with life which did, after all, have to go on. I went back to work and resumed my role as the main support for my family.

Charlie was still out of work. He did have a few odd jobs but nothing permanent, and he continued with his sawdust round. In truth his health was not good. The doctor had warned him, but every penny he could lay his hands on he drank. He had spells when he drank less but often he came home raving and would fall asleep at the foot of the bed. I think he was probably just as upset about little Charlie as I was and his drinking was a form of escape for him.

This was how the first few years of married life went for me, hardly fulfilling the childish fantasies of a bright prosperous future that I'd cherished when Charlie and I had met that Christmas only a few short years before. Since then it had been a seemingly inevitable cycle of pregnancy, hard work, poverty and grief, but although, by today's standards, life for me was rough, it was no rougher than it was for thousands of other people like us in Birmingham in the 1920s.

9

The World Collapses Around Me

After my son's death I returned to work. I couldn't return to Butler's because my timekeeping was not up to standard, so I applied for a part-time job with a Mr Brain in Tenby Street North. He took me on at once and I joined his workforce, which consisted of his two elderly daughters. His workshop was an old converted redbrick house, and his business was enamelling the round, metal Union Jack badges for Standard cars.

After working there about a week I confided in one of the sisters that the job was getting me down because I had to rush home to breastfeed baby Jean. She must have mentioned it to her father because Mr Brain told me that if I still wanted the job I could bring the baby along and feed her during my working hours. Creches are by no means a normal facility today and then they were unheard of, but this arrangement suited me perfectly; John was at school, so Mum had only Katie to take care of.

I borrowed a pram from a neighbour and was then able to push Jean to work and leave her in the pram in the entry beside the workshop. I could work and listen for Jean's cries to tell me she was ready for her feed. The sisters were kindness itself to me. Each day they would bring a little something in the grocery line for me to take home for the other children. Often they would change Jean for me if she was wet. And thus by such little kindnesses they made working life bearable and at the same time I was able to provide food and clothing for my family. I was even able to supplement my earnings by making toffee apples and selling them to the children as they came out of school. I sold them two a penny and every penny I earned I had to spend. It was useless trying to save anything now Charlie was drinking more heavily and contributing next to nothing to the family income. Mum was boozing more too and causing more quarrels as a result. I survived by closing my eyes and ears to what was happening and concentrating all my attention on the children and their needs.

It was too good to last, I knew, and sure enough one morning I arrived at work to find Mr Brain alone, packing his tools into a tea chest. I was too horrified to speak when in response to my shocked enquiry as to what he was doing he told me was being forced to close because of lack of orders. I stayed to help him pack his things away. Then he handed me my insurance card and three days' pay that was owing. He did say that if he should start up in business again I would be the first to know, but this was scant consolation to me now that I was out of a job again and penury was staring us in the face. There was no alternative: I would have to apply for relief again. Mum suggested we take in washing and ironing and I agreed since there was no other way of earning money. This arrangement was doomed, of course. After two weeks she demanded a larger share of what little we were able to earn and we quarrelled.

'Well, they're my tubs an' mangle, an' coal, yower usin',' she insisted.

After that the situation quickly deteriorated. Her constant nagging got on my nerves and the strain began to tell. One night it finally became too much for me to cope with any longer and I almost did a terrible thing.

I washed the children as usual and put them to bed. Katie and Johnny slept between Charlie and me. I could not bear him near when he was drunk, which he was every night now, and we had not made love for nearly a year. Jean's bed was a makeshift one in the wardrobe drawer. This particular night she wouldn't stop crying for me to feed her, but my milk was drying up and she got little satisfaction from my breast. Then as I was putting her back in her drawer cot, Mum began banging on the ceiling with a broom.

'Stop that babby cryin'. I want ter get some sleep!' she bawled.

'I'm doin' me best,' I shouted back from the top of the stairs.

'About time yow got 'er a dummy,' came the reply.

I'd never used a dummy because I'd seen too many little children drop them in the filth and then pick them up and put them back into their mouths. It was no wonder to me that so many children died of gastric diseases, diphtheria and the like. I returned to try to comfort Jeannie without resorting to a dummy but then the broom banged again. At that moment something snapped inside me. I flung my baby into the drawer and kicked it shut before collapsing on the bed exhausted. It must have been several minutes before I'd calmed down sufficiently to realise what I'd done. I jumped up and pulled the drawer out. It was just in time; another few minutes and she would have suffocated. I took her in my arms and wept. I could have fallen asleep and let her die. I might have been hung for murder, I thought, and thanked the Lord that I'd come to my senses.

I tried one more trick to quieten my wailing baby. I smeared condensed milk thickly over my nipple and gave her that, and for a wonder it worked. She lay contentedly sucking the empty breast and I thought with great relief that Mum could bang the ceiling as much as she liked; Jeannie was safe and if she cried we would both have to put up with it.

The next morning I went to see the doctor, Doctor Mackenzie, who had a front-room surgery in Arthur Place. His manner was abrupt but he could be kind and he listened sympathetically while I told him what had happened.

'How old are you?' he asked when I had finished.

'Twenty-four,' I told him.

'And how many children have you got?' he asked.

'Three now, doctor,'

'Any miscarriages?'

'Two.' Both had been brought on by doing heavy press-work.

After asking several more questions he gave me a bottle of 'Parish's Food' and told me to take two teaspoonsful at night and to return to see him in a week's time. I found that his prescription seemed to do me good and that I experienced a good night's sleep for a change. I must confess that I also put a teaspoonful in Jeannie's milk bottle and she seemed to thrive on it; so did Katie and Johnny. But instead of the medicine lasting a week it was gone in two days. It was like a drug: I wanted more. So I went back to the doctor and lied.

'You again,' he snapped when I entered the surgery. 'I said a week's time.'

'I'm sorry doctor. I had an accident and the bottle broke.'

'Very well, try not to break this one.' He handed me another bottle.

I went easier with that bottle and when I visited him again he gave me a panel note. This meant that I could draw sick pay, which wasn't much but enabled us to manage better with the little my husband was bringing in. It might be enough to tide me over until I was strong enough to work again. The rules about entitlement to sick pay were strict. You had to be indoors when the visitor called, otherwise your benefit would be stopped. You could only draw sick pay for six week; after that you had to submit to a means test and see the doctor again. When he re-examined me the doctor wrote out a letter.

'I want you to take this letter to 161 Corporation Street and have your chest X-rayed,' he told me as he wrote. This alarmed me.

'What's the matter with me chest?' I asked tentatively. 'Have I got consumption?'

'Nothing to be scared about. This is only routine and in the meantime I want you to take this medicine.'

I was hoping for some more Parish's Food but no such luck. I took the other stuff as directed, but two days later I developed a cough so decided to do as I had been instructed and go to be X-rayed. It was a bitterly cold morning as I readied myself to make the journey into the city centre. Mum and Charlie were out and I was glad I didn't have to tell them where I was going. Mrs Taylor agreed to look after Katie and Johnny and I wrapped Jeannie in my threadbare shawl and hugged her to me; then off I went on the two-mile walk into town. When I arrived at Corporation Street I was exhausted and I flopped down on the dirty wooden stairs to catch my breath. As I sat there Jeannie began to cry and I wished that I had brought some condensed milk with me. There was only one thing for me to do to quieten her cries. I unbuttoned my blouse and took out my breast, praying that she would find enough milk there to satisfy her. She tried her best, dear little thing. Then I happened to look up and found a small, well-dressed man gazing down at me. I felt a rush of embarrassment and fumbled to cover my nakedness but he put his hand gently on my shoulder.

'Dont cover yourself, mother. You both make a lovely picture.' And with that he pressed a ten-shilling note into my hand before he walked past me up the staircase. I could scarcely believe my good fortune; that money was a godsend. All thought of the X-ray vanished and I set off for home to buy some food. I made my first mistake by telling Mrs Taylor of my luck.

'That's all right dearie, yow goo an' get yerselves summat ter eat an' collect yer kids when yer get back.' I thanked her and asked if I could get her anything for looking after the children. 'Yer can get me twopenn'orth o' snuff,' was the predictable reply.

I bought sugar, tea, bacon, lard, bread, some stewing steak and milk for the baby. I still had change and I slipped it into my purse, which I carried between my breasts. I returned and spread my purchases out on the table, then I put Jeannie in her makeshift bed and went for Katie and Johnny. I went into the yard to find Mrs Taylor gossiping with some other old women. I ignored them and gave Mrs Taylor her snuff, and as I did so I noticed the others looking down their noses at me. I had nothing to be ashamed of although I could imagine how they would be speculating about how I got my ten shillings. I left Katie and Johnny with the other kids playing in the yard and went in to prepare a meal. I was so happy that afternoon that I even sang a tune as I waited for the kettle to boil. Just then Mum came bustling in. She looked in amazement at the food laid out on the table.

'Where yer got all this grub from?' she asked and I gladly told her.

'Yer a liar,' she exclaimed before I had hardly finished.

'It's the truth, Mum,' I protested.

'Men don't give yer ten bob fer just lookin' at yer breast,' she sneered. 'Yer sure yer dain't let 'im feel yer up a bit?' she asked slyly. That did it. I flared up in a fury at her suggestion.

'Yer disgustin'! Men don't bother me that way. I've got enough with Charlie. I ain't Liza yer know', I yelled at her.

'Yow leave Liza outa this!' she bawled at the top of her voice. 'An' close that bloody dower. I don't want all the neighbours ter 'ear!' I had touched a sensitive nerve because Liza had always been her favourite; in all the years I'd lived under her domination I'd never found the courage to retaliate until that moment. I had bottled my resentment up but now I let the cork out and my temper with it. Funnily enough, now that I had plucked up courage to speak my mind I felt no inhibitions whatsoever.

'No! I won't shut "the bloody dower" as you call it. Let the neighbours 'ear a few home truths for a change!' I had my dander up now all right.

Suddenly she lurched at me as if to strike me.

'Yow dare!' I screamed, grabbing the iron saucepan from the table. 'I'll bash yer brains out with this!' She could see that I meant it so she walked deliberately round the table and kicked the door to.

'Nosey lotta bastards!' she yelled through the closed door.

'One o' these days yer'll get summonsed fer yer language,' I told her.

''Ave yer finished?' She spoke more softly, sitting down on a chair.

'No! You've never loved me. Even before I was born yer never wanted me.' I was going to speak my mind now I'd started.

'Yer don't know what yo'er talkin' about,' she said, poking the fire with her back to me.

'I've bottled all yer secrets up fer years because I didn't want ter 'urt Dad while 'e was alive but now I'm goin' ter tell yer this. I know all about the 'ot baths you had an' the pikey pills and penny royal you took ter get rid of me.'

'That's a lie!' She shifted round to face me. 'Yer don't know nuthin',' she screamed.

'They're not lies. Mary told me when I was first married. You tried ter get rid of me an' you gave Mary the money ter give ter Mrs Taylor to get you all sorts of concoctions. My sister was only nine years old then an' she 'ad ter look after Jack an' Charlie an' the twins that died.'

''Ave yer done yet?' She subsided and resumed poking the ashes in the grate.

I continued with a few more home truths but I kept my distance because I wouldn't have put it past her to throw the poker at me.

'Mary told me the whole thing. I know Dad came home and found you in the bath with Mrs Taylor helping, and when he started to knock you about Mrs Taylor went for the police. He ran off an' didn't come back for a week.'

'Yer sister's got a lot ter answer for when I see 'er agen,' she yelled.

'I didn't want to talk about all this but now I 'ave I feel better. An' if you start on me again I'll let the neighbours know about how you an' Jack stole that pig!' I retorted. Then, just as she started up from the chair, Charlie walked in.

''Ave yer finished, you two?' he asked irritably.

'It's 'er,' Mum exclaimed.

'It's not all 'er Ma, I've 'eard every word,' he told her.

'Yoo bin listenin' at the dower then?' she asked sarcastically.

'I couldn't 'elp listenin'. I had to stand at the dower ter keep the neighbours from 'earin' what was goin' on.'

I started crying while he was speaking. I was drained by the effort of all this arguing.

'Wipe yer eyes luv an' collect up that food. We'll cook ours upstairs. I'll fetch the kids.'

I still hoped Mum and I could settle our differences and I turned on the stair and spoke to her.

'I'm sorry I 'ad to tell yer these things but yer asked for it.' But she just shrugged.

As I pottered about in the attic it occurred to me how like Mum I'd sounded when I lost my temper and I shuddered to think that I might become like her as I grew older. I just sat down and wept until I heard the children on the stairs. Then I pulled myself together and wiped my eyes. While I busied myself laying the table, Charlie lit the fire. As I waited for the kettle to boil I watched Charlie playing with the children on the floor. Katie had my old straw-filled golliwog, Topsey, that was made for me by Granny when I was a child. As she was doing so Charlie spoke to her.

'Katie, Daddy's goin' ter buy yer a real dolly one o' these days an' some lead soldiers for Johnny.'

I couldn't believe his thoughtlessness.

'There yow go again!' I flared up. 'Promising them things yow can't afford.'

'But we will when I start work tomorra,' he said smiling. I could hardly believe my ears as he added, 'I start at a factory an' there's a regular job if I keep good time. An' believe me, Katie, I'll keep it this time.'

I threw myself round his neck and as I kissed him I realised that it had been so long since I had done this that I'd almost forgotten how to do it. I couldn't remember being so happy as I was that teatime with a full table, my children, my husband and the prospect of a brighter tomorrow. Then when I'd put the children to bed and tucked Jeannie up in her drawer I sat down next to Charlie by the fire. He asked what we'd been quarrelling about and I told him about the ten-bob note.

'I already 'eard that,' he spoke softly.

'But you don't think I'd let a man do that to me, do yer?' I asked.

'No luv, but if it'd been Liza I would 'ave.' He chuckled. I had to stick up for my sister though, despite the fact that we didn't get on.

'Mum's to blame there. Liza'd have been a better woman today if Mum hadn't encouraged her in her wicked ways.'

'Well we won't talk about 'er. What I want ter know is, what's this about a pig?'

I satisfied his curiosity and told him about Jack stealing the pig and Mum and the hop-pickers and the comical court proceedings.*

* This incident is told in the first volume of Kathleen Dayus's autobiography, *Her People*.

He burst into laughter and so did I, for we could both see the funny side of the story.

'An' when did all this 'appen?' he asked.

'Oh, years ago when I was a small girl. Now come on, take yer shirt off so I can wash an' dry it for the morning.'

I felt so happy washing that shirt and putting it in front of the fire to dry. I was that pleased Charlie had a job and things seemed suddenly much brighter, like a black cloud had lifted. I turned down the lamp, undressed and lay in my place at the foot of the bed. Charlie lay down beside me and took me in his arms and we made love; the first time we had in twelve months.

Mum and I seldom spoke in the months after our showdown, but I didn't mind. I was happy being a housewife, looking after my husband and children. I no longer had to go and humiliate myself before pompous relief officers. With Charlie earning full wages I could pick and choose when I went to the shops. I bought second-hand woollens, unravelled them and knitted them up into clothes for the kids. They looked like Joseph's many-coloured coat. John was attending St Paul's school at the top of Legge Lane where I had gone myself. Katie went to Nelson Street school and I had more time to myself, and for a few brief months everything seemed rosy. I breathed a sigh of relief and thanked God for my blessings. Life, however, had taught me that it was just when things were going well that disaster struck. Existence was at the best of times precarious, and people like us never crossed our bridges before we came to them.

I was not so much surprised as resigned when Charlie was put on short time. I knew what I had to do. The two eldest were at school and Charlie could look after Jeannie while I went out to work. It had to be a part-time job that fitted in with with my husband's hours, but luckily I found one at Canning's jam factory. My job was topping and tailing goose-berries, and sometimes sorting out the over-ripe strawberries. Unfortunately the job lasted no more than a month. I was sacked for helping myself to the fruit. I suppose I should have expected this, but the kids loved them.

Troubles do not come singly and no sooner had I lost my job than Charlie, whose health had never been good, was brought home from work ill. Then I thought the bottom had fallen out of my world. I helped him up to bed and sent for the doctor. He took one look at Charlie and ordered him to go to Dudley Road Hospital. Charlie wouldn't hear of this and he prevailed upon the doctor to give him some medicine. He got his medicine but the doctor warned him that if he became worse he must send for him immediately.

The few shillings of savings we had soon dwindled away, but I refused to go on relief again and concentrated on nursing Charlie back to health. My efforts were rewarded. After a month he recovered sufficiently to return to work. He couldn't keep good time though, and soon he was given the sack. He went downhill after that. His spirit was being sapped away. He was irritable with the children and snapped at me. I used to take them on long walks and often visited my brother Frankie and his wife, Nellie, who were very kind to me. They had their own problems though, and I didn't like imposing on their generosity. I dreaded returning home, knowing that I would find Charlie raving drunk or snoring on the bed.

I had no choice. I had to get a job if Charlie could not or would not. I was fortunate I suppose. At least I was skilled enough to find work; there were plenty who were not. I was taken on at B. H. Collins in Frederic Street and I was happy there, enamelling metal badges of all kinds. We were able to survive and if I didn't see much of my family at least I was able to put food on the table.

Each Friday night after we'd been paid for the week the girls I worked with went for a drink in The Rose Villa, a local pub. They were forever urging me to join them and couldn't understand why I always refused. I was tempted but I couldn't spare the money I would spend on drink. Then one Friday Harry from the toolshop repeated the offer.

'Why don't yer stay an' 'ave one? 'It'll doo yer no 'arm,' he said, laughing.

'It's not the drink I'm worried about 'Arry,' I told him. 'It's my 'usband. If my 'usband comes home drunk and finds I'm not there, I don't know what will 'appen. Anyway,' I added, 'I have three children to see to.'

'Just 'ave the one then, it'll do yer good,' he persisted.

And I relented: where was the harm in just one drink, I thought. I joined them that payday and had a glass of stout before leaving. My mistake was making a habit of it. I went regularly and never thought that it was close enough to home for Charlie to get wind of it. He did and the next Friday night was waiting for me.

'So it's drinkin' in The Rose Villa now, is it? And with a married man as well!' He shouted so all the neighbours would hear. I tried to explain but he began raving, saying I'd been whoring, and he hit me several times. I don't know what he would have done if Mrs Taylor hadn't come running up the stairs to rescue me. When she appeared Charlie stamped off, still ranting.

I gave the job up. I was too ashamed to go back with my face bruised and my eyes blacked. Charlie was sorry when he'd sobered up; he promised to give up the drink, and he did for a time. He did his best to make it up to me and was kindness itself. I softened and forgave him that and other things.

I found another job the following week but this time it was not so pleasant. I was swinging a heavy press and it was heavy, dirty work, but the money was twice as good as I'd been getting. Now Charlie came to meet me from work and we walked home with the children. He was no healthier, however, and often complained about stomach pains. The doctor gave him tablets and they seemed to ease his pain for a while.

It was during this time that I noticed an advertisement in a shop window for a 'strong man to mend packing cases' at Gaunt & Sons, Warstone Parade. I was on my way to Frankie and Nellie's with the children and I hurried on my way. I was determined to get that job for Charlie, even if I had to beg. Strong man or not he needed a job and I had worked for this firm myself when I was sixteen. I left the children with their aunt and uncle and went along to inquire about the job and go down on my knees if necessary. I arrived breathless and pressed the bell hoping that the job hadn't already been taken. I didn't have to wait long. The forewoman I had known years before appeared. She recognised me at once.

'I seem to remember you, don't I? Didn't you work here before?'

'Yes, years ago. I'm married now, with a family,' I replied.

'Yes, I remember you. Your name was Katie Greenhill, wasn't it?' Nothing had ever escaped her beady eye. 'Well, if it's a job you've come for I'd be glad ter start yer,' she began, but I interrupted her.

'I'm sorry, Mrs Lane, it's not for me; I've come about the job for my husband,' I said in a rush. She looked surprised. 'Carn't 'e come 'imself?' she asked suspiciously, but I assured her.

'No, he's not, er, at home at the moment.' I nearly said he wasn't well, which would have lost him any chance of the job.

'Very well, you wait here an' I'll 'ave a word with Mr Booth. I'll do me best but remember, Katie, if you ever want a job yourself come an' see me.' With that she went away and I prayed she would succeed on her errand.

A minute or two later Mr Booth the manager appeared and asked how old my husband was and if he was strong.

'Oh yes, he's very strong,' I replied eagerly. I had to lie if he was to get the job.

'Very well, tell 'im to come and see me straight away, before five o'clock, and I'll see if he's suitable.' And with that he turned and went back into the workshop. I didn't wait around but made haste home, without collecting the children, I was so eager for Charlie to get that job. I fell into the kitchen and found Charlie talking to Mum.

'Charlie, I got you a job at Gaunt's, in the packing shop. You've got ter go an' see Mr Booth at once,' I told him, full of excitement. He didn't believe me at first until I'd spelled out the details.

'Now hurry yerself, before he changes his mind!' I was frantic at his apparent lack of concern. However, he had a quick shave and made himself presentable and went off without so much as a 'thank you' or a kiss.

'Come straight back an let me know 'ow you get on,' I shouted as he rushed out.

I returned for the children and after putting them to bed waited hours for Charlie to return with the news. I imagined all sorts of things had happened to him as it got later and later and still no sign of him. It was eleven o'clock when he eventually rolled in, drunk as a lord.

'I gotta start in the mornin',' he managed to say before I exploded with anger.

'An' a nice state you'll be in in the mornin'! An' where did yer get the money from for the drink?'

'I borrad it from me brother an' we've bin 'avin' a little celebration,' he mumbled.

'It's a pity 'e can't lend yer some food instead o' that lunatic soup you've bin drinkin.' I was furious by now.

I turned away in disgust as he fumbled to undress himself. Then he tried to put his arms round me and I pushed him away in a fury: I was not having him mauling me.

'Stay there yer drunken beast!' I screamed, pushing him over onto the foot of the bed where he collapsed in a heap and forthwith started snoring. I stood watching him sinking into his stupor then was about to go downstairs when I stopped and reflected that the last thing I wanted at that moment was a superior lecture from Mum so I returned to the bedroom. I was so bitter. He had to be up at seven o'clock in the morning and he had just selfishly gone out drinking with money he had yet to earn instead of thinking of me and the kids. Where would all this end, I thought, as I stripped off his shirt. I washed it and hung it over the chair to dry, then I undressed myself and lay down at the opposite end of the bed and hugged Katie and Johnny until I fell into a fitful sleep.

The next morning I was afraid to look at the foot of the bed in case he was still there but he must have got up early and left without disturbing us. He did keep the job for a few weeks too, and even brought part of his wages home to me but the rest he spent on drink. We quarrelled often and I refused to sleep with him.

'Yow'll be sorry one o' these days,' I remember Mum

saying. "E'll find another woman who will sleep with 'im,' she told me.

"E can sleep with a dozen bloody women! I don't care any more, as long as 'e brings 'is wages home instead of boozing 'em away!' I rounded on her.

Nevertheless we were both working now and I was able to put a little aside each week for the inevitable rainy day. And there were happier times. If Charlie was off the drink he could be very good company and although the first flush of love had passed long since we would go out together some Saturday nights visiting our old haunts around the Bull Ring markets. Mum even brightened up now she was receiving more rent money. Then a few months later I discovered that I was pregnant again and I was horrified. I didn't want another baby just as we were beginning to get on our feet. We still had no real home and were sleeping five in a bed. It was too much. I prayed to God for a miscarriage: an abortion was out of the question. I had to carry on for the children's sakes and couldn't risk anything that drastic. I continued working as long as I could but I knew that after the baby was born we would be back to square one and probably end up on parish relief again. I was more determined than ever that I would have no more children after this and that I would work as hard as I could to get us a place of our own, although I knew how difficult this would be when no landlord wanted to rent rooms to a couple with so many children.

As this pregnancy progressed Charlie became steadily more ill. I didn't appreciate it because he slept at the foot of the bed and I hadn't noticed how much stomach pain he suffered. Then one afternoon in April 1931 I became ill at work and two of the girls had to bring me home. We arrived to find Charlie being put into an ambulance and being rushed off to hospital. He'd been under the doctor and taking pills he had prescribed for about two weeks, but apparently one of the ignorant neighbours had tried an old wives' treatment on him that day. This consisted of putting a hot salt bag on his stomach and it had made him much worse. The doctor was called and after reprimanding the neighbour he'd sent for the ambulance.

When I heard from a neighbour what was happening I rushed upstairs just in time to see Charlie being laid on a stretcher. He was unconscious. With that I fainted and the next thing I remember was coming round to find that my labour had started. Mum and a friend of hers called Gert did what they could to make me comfortable and then went to call an ambulance to take me to Dudley Road Hospital where I had registered previously to have my baby. My pains were coming very fast by now and the ambulance was cancelled. I could hear the children downstairs crying for their Daddy and I felt totally lost.

Then Gert Wilcox stepped into the breach. She said she would take the children for a few days and come back later to see how I was. So she took them off to play with her kids and left Mum to look after me. I shall never forget that woman's kindness to me in that time of need. She lived nearby in Pope Street and her husband Harry, who was an old friend of Dad's, was a barman at The George and Dragon. She was 'a busy little body', always bustling about, cleaning and tidying. She always wore a starched white apron and although she was not a qualified midwife she was the next best thing. I decided to place my trust in her when she returned to help me. She'd telephoned the Hallam Street Hospital in West Bromwich where Charlie had been taken and they had told her he was comfortable. This eased my worries a bit but I was still in labour and experiencing very painful contractions. I didn't want this baby and that made it worse. Without doubt this was the most difficult birth I had ever undergone. I thought at one stage I was going to die and have never been so frightened in my whole life as I was then. I prayed that the child would be stillborn and that my mother or Gert would take it away and bury it somewhere, but that changed when it had been born and I'd seen Gert hold it up by the feet and slap it into life. When I heard those yells I knew my baby was alive and I breathed a sigh of relief.

'You've got a luvly baby daughter, Katie, and sure enough she's got a good pair of lungs,' she said smiling. She was as exhausted as I was and Mum had to do the tidying up. Gert washed the baby and put her on my breast. Then I knew she was here to stay. She was such a pretty little thing, with a mop of black hair, and as she sucked my breast I hugged her to me and thought how proud Charlie would have been to see her. But he never did see his daughter: three days later the news came that Charlie had passed away. That was 25 April 1931, our tenth wedding anniversary.

Thus, at the age of twenty-eight, I was left a widow with four young children to bring up now that Mary, two months premature, had arrived. I prayed for the Lord's guidance before and after Charlie's funeral. I had absolutely no idea how I would cope now. I wouldn't have had enough money for the funeral without my maternity money and the collection that the kind neighbours took up for me. I had no money and was too weak physically and emotionally to work. I applied for a widow's pension but was turned down because Charlie hadn't had enough insurance stamps for me to be eligible.

It seemed and still seems very cruel to me that I was forced back on the parish. There was, it goes without saying, no child allowance or supplementary benefit in those days. The good old days they may have been for some, but for me and plenty like me they were not good. It was pitiful to see the men and boys of all ages walking the streets looking for work or hanging around the yards idling away their time. Mum had had only her pension since Dad died and most of that went on drink. Now she said, 'If they won't pay yer a pension then the parish'll 'ave ter keep us.' So I went along to the Gospel Hall in Hockley Street where I had to queue outside for over an hour before being called in to state my case. I shall not forget easily the two stern-faced women who sat behind the table looking down their noses at everyone. While I waited to plead my case I remembered Mum's saying, 'God 'elps them as 'elps themselves but God's good but the devil ain't amiss'. I thought of the time I had considered gassing myself and the children but had had no money for the meter. I was sure that if I was refused help again I would start stealing or do something desperate. Then my name was called and I had to make myself humble. While I explained our plight to one of the women the other one shuffled through files.

'So you've had another child since you were here last?' She spoke coldly.

'Yes,' I replied, 'an' I've lost my husband too.'

'Have you applied for a pension?' she asked.

'I have but my application was turned down.'

'Turned down?' she asked in obvious disbelief. Then fixing me with her cold, emotionless eye she continued, 'But you say you were married or weren't you?'

'Of course I was,' I snapped. I explained the situation about the lack of insurance stamps and she wrote it all down.

'I see. So, you have four children and you are living with your mother? I see she is on our files too.'

'I 'aven't come about me mother,' I said, becoming angry. 'I've come for food for me children.' My impatience was showing now.

'I don't want any insolence. You sit over there and wait. I'll call you when we're ready.' She indicated a seat next to an old woman.

'That's tellin' 'er, but yer wanta watchit, luv, with that one or yow'l get nuthink,' she whispered to me.

I was past caring. I gazed blankly round the room at the drabs, old and young alike, resignedly waiting for their handouts. Then I silently said a prayer that if God gave me my strength back I would do something better for my children than sitting here being humiliated. Then I was called back to the table to be told they were sending a visitor to conduct a means test.

'But I'm desperate now! I want food for my children,' I insisted.

'You heard what she said,' the other woman chimed in. 'We can't give you anything until the visitor has called.' Then as I stood there dumbfounded, the other woman whispered, 'Some of these women shouldn't have children.'

'Are you married?' I demanded, losing my temper. 'No, I suppose you're a couple of old maids,' I continued when I received no reply. 'It looks as if it would do yer good ter 'ave a few ter keep yer occupied.' I turned and stamped out of the hall amid audible titters from the other women.

The visitor didn't call for two weeks, which I suppose was their way of punishing me for daring to speak out. In the meantime I'd pawned everything I had left of any value to buy food. Then when that was gone I went back to the relief office and threatened to leave my kids there with them if they didn't help me. There was a man there that time and he was more sympathetic. He asked me to sit quietly and he said he would try to help. Down came the files and we went through the same rigmarole again. It was all I could do to manage the children while I waited. Then he called me into an office. There he asked me about all the details of where Charlie had worked and about his illnesses and after he'd written every little detail down he eventually gave me a ration card to take to Baker's, the grocers. I thanked him. I was so happy to be getting anything. He told me to call once a week for food vouchers and in the meantime he said he would see about my pension although he couldn't promise anything. I thanked him again and told him I had every intention of starting back to work as soon as I was well enough. I might have saved my gratitude because when I found out what my ration was I discovered that it didn't amount to enough to feed me, let alone the children.

I wouldn't have survived at all if I hadn't taken the risk of trying to earn a few extra pennies doing odd jobs. I went into business making ginger pop for the kids. I worked with a neighbour, but after all the washing of bottles it was hardly worth it. Then I took in washing, but it was hopeless trying to get into the brewhouse because every day was somebody's washday. So when I heard about a job cleaning at Cullis's pawnshop I decided to investigate it.

I pushed the two youngest in a borrowed pram and set off. I went to the rear entrance and gave a girl who was hanging about a penny to look after the babies. I saw Mr Cullis in the back room where he lived and slept. It was filthy but I couldn't afford to turn my nose up at the money. It took me over an hour to scrub clean those bare old boards. When I told him the job was done he said I could clean the shop window. Before starting I popped out to see if the children were all right and found them fast asleep. Relieved, I fetched a bucket of soapy water and wet and dry rags and set to work. When I'd finished to my satisfaction I asked Mr Cullis when he wanted me again.

'Ye've done a very good job but I won't want it done agen for a long time now, so I'll let yer know.' And with that he handed me two shillings. I was livid and threw the bucket, dirty water and all, across the counter.

'Yer can do yer own cleanin' in future! Yer bloody skinny old Jew!' I shouted before leaving. As I stepped into the street I noticed an old woman collecting horse manure from the road with a bucket and shovel. I felt very inclined to daub that horseshit over his bright clean windows, but it was just as well I resisted the temptation because he would undoubtedly have called the police.

When I got back to the yard I couldn't find Johnny any-where. I was beginning to become worried when I spotted a policeman bringing him down the yard.

'What's 'e bin up to now?' I asked, half scared and half angry.

'I found 'im beggin' outside the factory gates an' I'm warnin' yoo now, if this 'appens again I'll 'ave ter take 'im ter the station.'

By now I was surrounded by our nosey neighbours and all I could do was meekly say 'I'm sorry'. I could see Johnny was frightened too; he had filled his trousers so I didn't scold him when I got him indoors. I scrubbed him in the bath and sent him off to bed without his comic.

'Oh God,' I moaned to myself as I was washing his soiled trousers through. 'Where is this all goin' to end?' I was desperate, friendless and almost at my wits' end. In the weeks that followed I tried my best to make ends meet and even asked my sister Mary if she would take one of the children until I could get back on my feet. But she'd hardened since her second marriage.

'Sorry Kate, but I've got me own three. Anyway, me and

Bill are thinking of selling up and going to try our luck in America.' That was that. It was a similar story when I went to Jack.

'Rosie's mother's livin' with us now an' we ain't got the room,' he said.

'But it's only for a few weeks while I get a job,' I pleaded but to no effect. I got nothing from him but a promise to try to help later; I saw neither hide nor hair of him for years after that.

Suicide was not far from my thoughts during that period, and I also considered becoming a prostitute. But I was too shy to talk to a stranger let alone lift up my frock for one. After all, I'd never undressed in front of Charlie even. I'd always insisted on blowing the candle out before going to bed. Charlie used to laugh at me but I didn't change my ways.

Then I was lucky enough to get a job cleaning at The George and Dragon. I had to start at six o'clock in the morning and work an hour lighting fires and scrubbing the bar. The ten bob the publican paid for this was very useful and the time was perfect for me. I could creep out before the children were awake and be back to get them off to school. I tried to keep this job quiet and told no one at all about it. The publican was well pleased with my work and gave me a cup of tea as well as bread and cheese and a bottle of stout to take home. It made me sad when I scrubbed that step. It was the same step I had sat on with my bum freezing while I waited for Dad to call for me to sing for the customers.

I might have realised that luck like this could not last. One morning when I'd finished the landlord called me into the smoke room.

'Mrs Flood, I've bin told you're on parish relief,' he began. 'Is this true?'

'Yes,' I admitted. It was no good lying.

'You should 'ave told me. I'm sorry, but I'll 'ave ter let yer go. We'll both be in serious trouble if they find out. But if you sign off, I'll take yer on again with pleasure.'

'I carn't do that,' I answered tearfully. 'What little they give and what I earn 'ere is the least we need. I'll 'ave ter find something else.'

I tidied away the brooms and brushes and was about to leave when he appeared with a parcel of bread and cheese and a bottle of stout as usual. I almost refused to take them but I thought twice. I could not afford pride in those days if it meant cutting off my nose to spite my face. I took the gifts and thanked him and he slipped a pound note in my apron pocket.

'I'm sorry,' he murmured as I opened the door to leave.

I realised that it was pointless trying to get a job on the quiet; there were plenty of wagging tongues to give the game away. However, I decided to try anyway. What could I do? I wasn't fit enough to work, and with four young children and no husband I couldn't have held down a full-time job. So it was back to chopping and selling firewood, and I found myself plodding round the streets till late at night touting my wares for a few pence.

Mum had a new drinking partner now. Her name was Bridget and she was short, fat and had three chins and beady eyes like boot buttons. She was Irish and very patriotic. She wore a long bright green dress, a green ribbon in her hair and usually sported a sprig of shamrock. This was her normal attire whether it was St Patrick's day or not, and when she'd had a few drinks she would sing the songs of her fathers. I remember her calling for Mum one evening at about this time.

As soon as they'd left I washed and fed the baby who was a few months old now and no longer being breastfed. She was another mouth to feed but I'm afraid the best I could do to fill it was to feed her stale crusts boiled to a mush with condensed milk. I made things easier for myself by lining her rag nappies with tissue paper before putting her down for the night in her drawer. I'd just done this and got Katie and Johnny to bed when Liza breezed in. She was the wild one in the family, was Liza. Although married with two children she was always gallivanting out to pubs and dance halls. Her men friends changed with the wind. As soon as I looked at her I could see she was out on the town.

Liza would have been a good-looker if she'd left the war-paint alone. She wouldn't have it though. She even shaved her eyebrows and pencilled them in with a thin line. She'd dyed her hair so many times it was multi-coloured.

'Where's Mum?' were her first words.

'Gone out with that Bridget woman,' I snapped. We'd never been close, now less than ever.

'Oh all right,' she snapped back, 'I'll find 'em. An' if Al asks yer if yow've seen me, tell 'im I'm workin' over,' she added.

'I'm not tellin' lies for yow.'E'll find out in any case,' I shouted after her as she disappeared into the yard with a shrug of her shoulders. Albert was a good, hard-working man and I felt sorry for him. But that didn't prevent me thinking how foolish he was to close his eyes and ears to what was going on. He was used to coming home from work and seeing to the children but I wondered why he didn't put his foot down with Liza. Despite what Liza had said, though, he was the last person I expected to call, so I was surprised when he walked in not long after my sister had left. I greeted him and offered him a cup of tea.

'No thanks Kate. I thought Betty' (he always called her that) 'might be here.'

'The kettle's boiled, it won't take long,' I stuttered, not knowing how to answer him.

'No thanks all the same, Kate. I carn't stay but if Betty calls, tell 'er I've put the kiddies to bed an' she'll find me at me mother's. Goodnight Kate.' So saying, he left.

I must have dozed off after that because the next thing I remember is the door slamming and my looking up to see Mum, Bridget, Liza and a scruffy-looking individual Liza called Joe. They were predictably drunk.

Bridget began to sing 'Danny Boy' and I shushed her because the children were asleep. At that Mum flared up.

''Er can sing when 'er like. Oo's bloody 'ouse is it anyway?' she demanded. I didn't reply; I knew it was useless arguing with her. I turned instead to Liza.

'Albert's been 'ere for yow,' I informed her coldly.

''Ow long ago was that?' she asked, apparently unconcerned.

'Just after yer left.' To which she replied, 'I'd betta be goin'

Mum. It's gettin' late. Yow comin' Bridget?' She didn't seem so cool now.

'Ah, twas a foine night we've 'ad Polly, but what about 'im?' she said, nodding at the still silent Joe.

'Yer betta goo with Liza, Bridget. I'll see ter Joe. 'E's missed the last tram an' it's rainin' now anyway.' I could see that the Irish woman was reluctant to leave but Liza took her arm and steered her out into the night, slamming the door behind her.

'An' where do yer think 'e's gooin' ter sleep?' I demanded when they'd gone.

'I'll mek 'im up a bed in my room.' I could guess what that meant. With that Joe heaved himself off the wooden sofa he was sprawled on and flopped in Dad's armchair. That was the final straw as far as I was concerned.

'Get yer bloody arse out of my Dad's chair. Yow ain't fit ter be 'ere,' I stormed, but he was either too stupid or too drunk to reply. Mum was neither, more's the pity.

'Yer forgettin' this is my 'ouse an' I'll 'ave ooever I want 'ere!' she bawled.

I knew argument was useless so I gathered up the children's clothes and went up to the attic to finish drying them by my small grate. I undressed and got into bed with the children and thought in despair of the pretty pass we'd come to. I wondered what Dad or Charlie would have done if they'd been alive. Next morning I knocked on Mum's door with her usual cup of tea but there was no answer, so I pushed the door open and to my surprise found the bed empty. In fact it hadn't been slept in at all and was just as I'd made it the previous afternoon. Mum didn't put in an appearance until the following day.

I didn't dare question her about where she'd been but I did wish sometimes that she would do a moonlight flit and never come back. People in the area often did a flit to avoid paying their rent arrears and the sight of chattels being loaded onto a handcart was not out of the ordinary. I would dearly have loved to leave the hovel we shared with Mum but there was no point simply moving to a similar house, and the idea of living in a better house in a pleasant district was a pipedream. I wanted above all to give the children a decent upbringing away from all the bad influences around them. They were always in and out of the neighbours' houses and came home repeating the bad language they'd heard. I hated having to correct them and it was a vain task trying to counter the combined force of the circumstances of our lives. Some children had been taken into homes and I came to believe that this was the best thing for them. Many times I'd considered allowing my own children to go into a home but I lacked the courage to go through with it, and as long as I could continue selling firewood we existed. I still hadn't notified the parish about this sideline but each week as I collected our ration I became more nervous.

Eventually the day of reckoning arrived. The visitor called one morning and told me I had to go to the office at once. I was terrified of what they would do to me but I had to go; if I didn't they would send someone to fetch me. When I arrived at the church hall I found there were several others there with equally worried expressions on their faces. I waited to be called to stand in front of the long wooden table behind which the inquisitors were seated. Finally my name was called and my heart sank to my boots.

'Come along, we have something to ask you.' The harsh voice echoed in the large hall and I crept slowly towards the speaker who sat there, hard faced and threatening. I have never felt so utterly humiliated and ashamed and defeated.

'It has come to our notice that you have been selling firewood,' the woman said loudly so that all could hear, and she wagged her finger at me so there could be no doubt to whom she was addressing her remarks.

'Yes,' I almost whispered, too scared to lie.

'And you haven't declared your earnings have you?' She did not look at me but glared round the room at the others. 'You know we can prosecute you for this deception, don't you?'

Then something inside me snapped and I forgot my fear in my frustration and anger.

181

'Earnings? You call it earnings! Sellin' a few sticks of fire-wood! What you lot dish out 'ere isn't enough to keep a sparra alive!' I shrieked at her.

'Stand back there, we'll deal with you later,' she said red-dening, indicating with an irritated gesture that I was to move to the back of the queue. But I was not budging. I was determined to say my piece now I'd summoned up the courage.

'You stand back there an' beg for crumbs an' see 'ow yow feel! Anybody'd think it was your money that paid for our chickenfeed! We're entitled to it an' a good deal more!' By now all eyes were on me and you could have heard a pin drop when I stopped, breathless.

'You'd better leave now,' she hissed, suppressing her obvious fury, 'or, I'll call the police.' But she could not outface me that easily.

'Yow can send for the whole bleedin' police force, yer bloody ol' cow!' There were murmurs of agreement from amongst the audience. Then a young man left his place in the queue and, taking my arm, led me outside.

'I'm glad you spoke up for all of us. I'd have liked to back you up but I've got my own family ter think about an' I can't afford to offend them,' he said gently.

'Neither can I but I'm glad now I've got that off me chest,' I replied.

Then I turned and walked slowly away from that miserable place. It was only then when I had calmed down that I realised what I'd said and done, and when I returned home I sat on the sofa and wept bitterly. I expected little sympathy from Mum and I got none.

'I warned yer they'd find out! Now what yer gooin' ter do?' she snapped after I'd told her about my confrontation at the relief office.

'I'm goin' ter do the best I can,' I said defiantly and went upstairs out of her way, but when I was in the bedroom I collapsed on the bed and realised how hopeless our situation was. And it was then that I decided to send the children to the only place where they would be well fed and cared for. I would put them into a home before they were taken from me, which they would be if I was sent to prison. I fretted and cried sleeplessly all that night and the next morning made my final decision. I went down to Mum's bedroom to tell her of my intentions, but her bed was unslept in so after I'd sent John and Kathleen to school, I called on Mrs Taylor to keep an eye on Jean and Mary while I went off to make the necessary arrangements. I had to confide in someone so, trusting her to say nothing, I told her of my intention to put the children into a home.

'I promise I won't say a word, but are yer sure yer want ter do this, Kate?' she asked.

'Yes, my mind is made up, Mrs Taylor.' I began to sob. 'I may 'ave ter go ter prison for what I've done an' I can't leave the kids not knowing where they'll be. I love them too much.'

'But whatever'll yer Mum say when she finds out?'

'I'm not tellin' 'er till it's done. In any case, she'll probably not be back for a few days an' by then we'll be gone.'

'Mary, Mother of God!' she gasped, crossing herself. 'Whatever's goin' ter become of us all?' she wailed. I left her in this state to look after the children and went to get it over with.

It was a cold, wet morning and although I had pieces of cardboard in my shoes my feet were still frozen. I pulled my coat closer round me and made my way to the tram stop. I walked along in a trance, still not finally decided. In my heart of hearts I knew there was no other course for me. I was in a corner from which there was no escape. We would get no more parish relief, I couldn't take a job without neglecting the children and I couldn't earn enough from the firewood to feed and clothe them. I knew where to go, and without being really conscious of how I got there I found myself outside the gates of the Dr Barnardo's home in Moseley Village, which was almost in the country then but has now been swallowed up by Birmingham.

Nervously I knocked at the door, which was opened almost at once by a middle-aged, kindly looking woman who had on a long grey dress covered by a white starched apron with a matching bonnet on her head.

I was too choked with emotion to speak but she put me at my ease and said she was the matron as she showed me into a large room and indicated that I could warm myself by the fire. The room we were in was almost bare: just four leather chairs and a large oak table laden with cakes, jam, bread and butter. In a corner stood a bookcase with books and ledgers. The floor was bare but brightly polished and above the fireplace was a large portrait of an elderly gentleman who I guessed was Dr Barnardo. As I looked up at this picture she spoke.

'Would you like a cup of tea, my dear?'

'Yes please,' I murmured. She offered me a cake but although I was hungry I couldn't have eaten a thing. I was overwhelmed by emotion and on the verge of tears. We sat on chairs, or at least I perched on the edge, and tried to explain why I'd come. After I'd completed my tale of woe I could see by the look on her face that it wasn't going to be plain sailing.

'I don't know whether we can help you. This is only a home for orphans,' she said quietly.

'But I must find somewhere for them, matron. It's only for a short time, till I get work an' find a proper home.'

'Well, perhaps if you tell me all about yourself we can do something to help.'

So saying, she reached for a large sheet of paper and began to note down everything I told her about myself from the time of my marriage. After this she offered me another cup of tea and told me she would send two visitors round the next day. As I was about to leave she asked if I'd walked from Birmingham and when I told her I had walked part of the way she pressed a half crown into my hand.

'I shouldn't do this,' she said, 'but maybe it will help.' I would have kissed that matron if I'd dared. I thanked her profusely as she showed me to the door. As I walked down the gravel path I could hear the sound of children's laughter.

I boarded the tram, tired and hungry, and as soon as I alighted I headed for the first butcher's shop where I bought sixpenn'orth of stewing steak. I spent the rest of the money on vegetables, bread, margarine, tea, sugar, jam, a tin of Nestle's milk and a few rusks for Mary instead of her usual sop. I busied myself preparing the meal until the children came home from school. I had to keep active to take my mind off my troubles. That day we had a meat dinner for a change and Mrs Taylor joined us. After the children had returned to school I put Mary to sleep on the sofa, and while Jeannie played in the yard Mrs Taylor and I set to work to scrub and clean the attic ready for the visitors' inspection the following day. I was glad Mum wasn't about because it would have been 'don't move that', 'leave that there', and 'I want my things where I can lay me 'ands on 'em'. When we'd finished, Mrs Taylor left.

A little later there was a loud knock on the door and when I peered through the curtain I saw a tall man and a woman standing there. My first thought was that it was the police come for me. I didn't know whether to hide or not, so I called out that Mum was out.

'We haven't come to see your mother. We've come to see you, Mrs Flood. We're from Dr Barnardo's,' the man's voice replied. I opened the door slowly to let them in and as I glanced round the yard I noticed the neighbours' nosy faces peering out of their windows.

'I'm Mrs Flood but the matron said I wouldn't have any visitors till tomorrow.'

'Yes, but the matron thought we had better call as soon as possible. May we look around and see the children?' the woman answered my question.

I picked Mary up off the sofa and hugged her to me and managed to say, choked with emotion, 'This is my baby; Jeannie is playing in the yard, and John and Kathleen haven't come home from school yet.' They inspected my two youngest and then went up to inspect the attic. Then they asked me all the same questions that I had already answered for the matron. Finally the woman asked if I really wanted to let the children go into the home.

'No, of course I don't, but there's no alternative for me, is there? We're living 'ere with my mother who don't really want us, we've no money for food, an' all I've got is what I earn sellin' firewood,' I answered in exasperation.

185

'Are you sure you can't get help from the parish?' the man asked again.

'Not now. They're goin' to prosecute me for not tellin' them I'd bin sellin' firewood,' I explained patiently. 'An' now if you refuse ter 'elp us I might end up doin' something desperate.'

'I'm sorry to have upset you, Mrs Flood. If you bring the children to the home tomorrow we can talk some more and make the necessary arrangements,' he said.

A weak 'thank you' was all I could say as I showed them out. Then as soon as they'd gone I collected all the children's clothes which, although well worn, I was determined would be clean. While I was hanging them on the line across the yard, Mrs Phillips came over to speak to me.

'I see yow 'ad a couple o' visitors, Kate. An' I can see yer 'avin' a good wash day' she said, inviting a reply.

'Yes!' I snapped at her. 'Do yer good, an' some o' yer kids, if yer'd do the same.' As she turned to go indoors I called after her, 'Yer nosy old sod.' She slammed her door and I continued with my task, wondering when I would wash my children's clothes again. I knew Mrs Phillips would tell Mum what I'd said and I hoped that we'd be gone by the time she returned. That night I gave the children a good wash ready for the morning.

'But Mum,' Johnny said when I fetched in the zinc bath, 'it ain't Friday night.'

'No, I know, but yer 'avin' a bath tonight anyway.'

'But why?' He was like all small boys, reluctant where washing was concerned.

'I'll tell yer in the mornin'.' I could hardly speak, I was on the verge of tears.

'But why carn't yer tell me now?' he persisted.

'All right I'll tell yer later then. Now get in that bath before the water's cold. An' don't ask questions.'

I helped him give himself a good scrub, then he took himself up to bed. Later when I went up to turn in, Jeannie was asleep but Katie and Johnny were sitting up waiting for me to read them the 'funnies' from the newspaper. I thought to myself, this is as good a time as any, so I steeled myself to get my secret off my chest. I settled down to explain where I was going to take them the next day. I didn't know where to begin until Johnny spoke.

'Mum, what yer tryin' ter tell us?'

'Well,' I began, 'you and Katie aren't goin' ter school tomorra, I'm takin' yer on a kind of holiday to a place where where there's lots of trees and flowers and a big lawn ter play on with other little children. There's a kind lady there too who'll look after yer an' give you cakes and nice things to eat.' I struggled to make it sound inviting but I really had no idea what life in the Barnardo homes was like; all I had to go on was their reputation and the few brief impressions of my visit.

'Are yoo comin' too?' they chorused.

'Yes, I'm takin' yer in the mornin' but then I'll 'ave ter leave yer but I'll come an' visit yer and bring yer treats ter eat too.' I soothed them as well as I could. 'Now lie down an' I'll read the funnies.' But as I tried to read to them I had to turn my face away to hide my tears. Bless them, they didn't seem to notice or to question that they were going on holiday but simply accepted what I had told them and soon they were fast asleep. Then I kissed their cheeks and tucked them in. I busied myself putting the bath away and eventually went back upstairs, undressed and climbed into bed beside them and quietly cried myself to sleep.

The children were up bright and early next morning, excited at the unexpected prospect of going on a long tram ride and having a holiday from school. I dressed them in their clean rags and after a breakfast of porridge we started on our journey.

The trams in those days had two long wooden benches facing each other on which the passengers sat. When we got on, there were only three vacant seats so I had to sit down with Mary and Jeannie on my lap. The people on the opposite seat seemed to stare at us as if they knew where I was taking the children. On the next tram it was the same. I imagined they must be thinking what a heartless mother I was to be parting with my children in this way, but I put these thoughts out of my mind with the thought that it would be for the best in the long run and at least the children were enjoying the ride, even if I was not.

When we arrived at the home the matron was ready waiting for us with warm milk for the little ones and a cup of hot cocoa for me. Then she sent the children out to play while she talked to me. She said they'd decided to take the children into the protection of the home until such time as I was in better circumstances and was able to provide a better home for them. When I thought that this time had come I would be visited by their inspectors who would, if they saw fit, recommend that I could have my children back. I remember thanking the matron and promising that I would work night and day to get back on my feet, and I really meant it. But I had no idea then how long this would take or how difficult it would be to get your children away from Dr Barnardo's once you had allowed them to take your children.

When we had talked for a while the matron got up and showed me through a glass door which led onto a large lawn where I could see Johnny and Katie playing and laughing with the other children. They didn't notice me; they were too absorbed in their game to see me standing there, but as I watched them I began to feel easier in my mind, seeing them settled down so quickly to their new surroundings. So despite my continued reluctance to part with them I was happier thinking that they were in good hands and would be well cared for until I reclaimed them. How they felt when it dawned on them that this was their home I do not know, but I can imagine. I hoped then and later that they wouldn't feel that they'd been abandoned by their mother, and indeed I was determined to visit them every Saturday afternoon as the matron had informed me I could. She also told me to tell the home immediately I had a change of address, and with that I thanked her and she called the children over for us to say our 'goodbyes'. I was choked with emotion and sorrow when I kissed them but they didn't seem to notice and ran off, eager to rejoin their new chums.

I returned in a trance to my mother's house, overwhelmed

by feelings of loss and loneliness. Just how much I'd given up I realised when I went into the kitchen, empty now with no grubby little faces to greet me and none to greet for I had no idea how many months or years. It was then that I knew how lonely and single minded would be the furrow I must plough if I was to achieve my goal, a goal I was determined to reach at any sacrifice.

'Oh God, what 'ave I done ter deserve this?' I moaned self-pityingly, hunched in Dad's old armchair, but the mood passed and I pulled myself together. I must get away from this unlucky house and my mother as soon as possible, I thought. The warning from the parish inquisitors about setting the law on me was also in my mind. Suddenly I was galvanised into action. I crammed a few clothes into a shopping bag and went downstairs to leave, vowing that I would never return. I closed the door behind me and looked round the yard for what I thought was the last time.

These were the familiar sights and sounds of my entire lifetime, stretching back to before I could remember anything, but I was not sorry to be cutting myself off from them. All my troubles resulted from this poverty and degradation. Anything would be better than this. I saw the twin three-year old daughters of a neighbour sitting on a cold, wet step, frocks up over their knees so you could see they had no underclothes on and sucking grubby dummies. There were other girls and boys fighting and swearing while their mothers gossiped, oblivious. I was sad but also angry to think that these young drabs were fellow creatures who'd been worn out by the struggle, day in, day out, year in, year out, simply to survive in the web of penury and squalor that had trapped them. Chin up, I thought. You're young and still healthy and with luck and hard work you can make a better future for yourself and the children. As I struggled with my wordly possessions up the hill I was thankful that the Lord had given me the strength to go through with my resolve.

I might have known that I wouldn't escape so lightly. My mother must have heard on the grapevine about what I had done because as I neared the corner I heard her shout, 'Katie', in her too-familiar bray and I turned to see her and several neighbours bearing down on me.

'Yer oughta be ashamed o' yerself,' she started, 'tekin' me gran'chillun away. An' where d'yer think yer gooin' now?' She could see what I had in the bag.

'Away from this unlucky hole! An' yoo! An' I ain't ever comin' back either!' I yelled, near to tears.

'Yow'll be back, yow'll see,' she said triumphantly, looking around at her cronies for support; I didn't answer her. Instead I went on my way, but I could hear them muttering about how I was 'a terrible woman', 'the wust woman in the district', for putting my children into a home. It mattered not to them that I couldn't properly care for them. As far as they were concerned any kind of inadequate dragging up was better than allowing your children to be taken care of in an institution. I hurried away tearfully, cursing them for their ignorant prejudice and me for the terrible fortune fate had dealt me.

There was only one person in the whole world I could turn to now: my brother Frank. And, bless their memory, he and his wife Nellie welcomed me with open arms when I reached their door. I broke down and wept bitter tears as I tried to tell them what I'd done but they comforted me and told me I needn't explain to them. They understood, and in any case Mum had been there already. Nellie put her arm round me and sat me by the fire to warm up, and soon I had a cup of tea in my hand and we talked while she prepared the supper. I had no appetite for food but I drank two cups of tea. Then Frankie came back in and asked me why I'd let the children go and I found myself trying to explain again, but he cut me short.

'Yoo know if yer'd asked Nellie an' me, we'd 'ave taken two of 'em until yer got back on yer feet,' he said with regret in his voice.

'No, Frank, it wouldn't 'ave worked out. Yow an' Nellie 'ave enough on yer plate, what with two daughters an' another babby on the way. An' yoo on short time as well. No, I couldn't think of that.' I didn't want him to feel hurt that I hadn't turned to him in my hour of need.

'Did yer ask Mary or Jack?' he asked after a pause.

'Yes, Mary ses she's gooin' ter America soon, an' Jack ain't got the room.'

'Did yer ask Liza?' he continued, shaking his head in apparent disbelief.

'No Frank. She offered, but yow know as well as I do she's the last one I'd leave 'em with. She ain't got time ter look after 'er own or 'erself, let alone any of mine.' This was the truth.

'I understand, Kate,' Nellie chipped in sympathetically.

'I know I've done the right thing, Nellie.' I turned to her. 'The matron ses I can visit them an' as soon as I can get a house of my own, I can 'ave them back with me again.' I tried to sound positive and confident although the reader will appreciate how daunting the task seemed to me.

'That's all very well, but where are yer gooin' now?' she asked.

'I don't know, but I'm not goin' back there again if I 'ave ter walk the streets all night.' And I would have, too; nothing would have induced me to go back there to defeat. But I didn't have to.

'Yow can stay 'ere.' Frankie volunteered at once. 'I'll mek do on the sofa an' yow can sleep with Nellie. Then we'll sort summat out in the mornin'.' And that is what I did.

It was wonderful to sleep between clean, crisp, white sheets after my makeshifts, but I lay awake long after my sister-in-law had dropped off to sleep, thinking and planning what I was going to do to make a brighter future. As I turned my prospects over in my mind it occurred to me that I had only one asset, the notebook which contained the list of names of people who still owed me for the bundles of firewood they'd had. Further reflection convinced me I could never bear the humiliation of begging them to give me what they owed me. I fretted in this way until tiredness eventually overcame me and I fell asleep.

10

My Struggles Really Begin

Next morning I came down to find Nellie, Frank and my two nieces sitting down to Sunday breakfast.

'We thought we'd let yer sleep in a bit longer, Kate,' Nellie greeted me.

'Thanks, Nellie,' was all I could bring myself to say although I was grateful for the extra rest: the last few days had been exhausting and now the immediate pressure was off, fatigue had hit me. I pulled a chair up to the table and joined them. When I saw the delicious-smelling bacon, egg and tomatoes on the plate I realised how hungry I was as well, and I tucked in with a will. I hadn't eaten for nearly two days.

'Thanks Nellie, this is really good of yer,' I thanked her between mouthfuls.

After breakfast was over and the breakfast crocks cleared away I gave Nellie a hand with the housework. While I was busy sweeping and dusting I found myself glancing up at my brother sitting in his armchair, smoking his pipe. It was then that it dawned on me how very like our father he was and tears welled up into my eyes.

A little later when the girls had left for Sunday school Frank asked me what I planned to do and where I was going to go.

'I'm gooin' ter look for a job first, Frank. Then I'll have ter look for lodgin's,' I replied. His immediate response was to ask me if I had any money. I had to admit that apart from the list of names I had no more than a few pence.

'But I'll 'ave ter let that goo, Frank. I carn't face them people any more.' At that he jumped up.

'Yoo give me that book, I'll soon get it for yer,' he volunteered.

I was in two minds but I still went upstairs and brought it down for him. I handed it to him and after a quick glance he donned his cap and jacket and was off with a cheery 'see yer soon'. And, as good as his word, he was back in hour or two and, with the exception of a handful, they'd all paid up. When we counted it all up we found I was better off by over two pounds. My first thought was to offer to pay them for the food I was eating but Nellie wouldn't hear of it and told me to put it in my pocket. She looked offended.

'Yow don't 'ave ter pay us for anything. Me and Frankie'd loike ter 'elp yer more but yer know times are bad an' we ain't got much but while yer under ower roof yer welcome ter share what we've got,' Nellie said firmly.

'Thank yer both, very much. I've got ter find a job an' a place so's I can get the children back,' I replied.

'Well, yer welcome ter stay 'ere till yer find summat suit-able,' Frank assured me.

When I thought it over I was grateful to stay where I was wanted although I decided that I couldn't let my brother give up his bed for me. I told him I would swap and take the sofa. Although he was on short time, on the days he was working he had to be up at five in the morning before leaving for a ten-hour day in the brass-casting shop where he worked. He needed his sleep and in any case I had no intention of letting the grass grow under my feet now my mind was made up. I wanted to get away from the district with its myriad of mostly sad memories. I confided my plans to Nellie in case she thought I wasn't grateful for their help and she understood my feelings perfectly. So it was decided that my stay with them would be as short as possible.

Escaping completely from the Jewellery Quarter was of course impossible. I would keep clear of the Camden Street area but this was the only place I knew, and more important the only place I could find work as an enameller. I was soon out tramping about on the lookout for something. I could have returned to Collins's in Frederic Street but I was well known to all the girls there and I didn't want to have explain to them what I had done. They would have been sympathetic, of that I had no doubt, but it was sympathy I could do without: I wanted to put that behind me and square up to the task I'd set myself. In any case, it was too near the streets I wanted to avoid.

After I'd been walking for what seemed like hours, I spotted a notice in the window of Canning's for 'a young woman to work press', and I hurried in to inquire how long the notice had been there. The lad who was serving said it had just gone in, and hearing that I dashed to the address he'd given me as quickly as I could in case anybody had got there before me. When I arrived at the factory in Vittoria Street I spoke through the trap to the boss, a Mr Gibbons, who told me that the job was still vacant. He asked me my name and age and then, asking me to wait, went to fetch the foreman who turned out to be a pleasant little fellow named Bingham.

'Well,' he said, looking me up and down, 'you don't look strong enough to work a press.'

'Oh, but I am,' I told him eagerly, 'I've worked a hand press before.'

'All right, if yer like ter give it a try, the wages are two pounds ten shillings a week, eight o'clock till six, an' one o'clock Saturday. Bring yer unemployment card and your insurance card an' yer can start next Monday.'

'But that's a week away. Could I start tomorra? I need the money, yer see.'

After a pause he said, 'Very well. Don't forget eight o'clock in the mornin'.'

I ran nearly all the way to Frank's to tell them the good news. They were as pleased as I was, and had also found me lodgings with a middle-aged widow who lived in Warstone Lane. Frank told me her name was Knight and the rent was a pound a week for my bed, which turned out to be poor, and my food. I moved into Mrs Knight's as soon as I could and started work at the foundry. During this period I was able to begin to sort myself out. I saved some money and got myself some new second-hand clothes. I treated myself to a hairdo as well: a Marcel wave which was all the rage then. The hair was curled tightly to the head with heated irons which waved the hair like corrugated cardboard.

Despite my change of fortune the job on the press was

getting me down: I still aspired to something better, and when I asked the boss for a change he put me on an even heavier job. On that I had to use both hands and duck each time I swung the press handle round otherwise it would have laid me out. The grease and oil got in my hair and on my clothes and each night when I returned to my digs I had to have a thorough wash down. By the time I'd followed this with my supper I was too exhausted to do anything but drag myself off to bed.

Further up Vittoria Street, however, was an enamelling firm, J. A. Butler's, and when I saw they were advertising for learners and experienced girls I gave my notice at the brass foundry and went to work there. This time I was determined to learn everything there was to know about the business and complete my training. The job was a vast improvement on my previous one: it was clean work and so was the workshop, and after working there only a few days I went onto piecework and was able to earn four to five pounds a week with all the overtime I did. Naively I thought that if I could keep this up for a few weeks I would soon have saved enough to be able to afford to rent a house, buy some second-hand furniture and have the children back with me. At that stage I had still to discover how tenaciously Dr Barnardo's clung on to your children once they had their claws in them.

When my wages improved I offered Mrs Knight another five shillings a week, but she didn't need it because she'd taken in a gentleman lodger since I had taken up residence with her. Still, I made her accept it. I kept out of the way of the man and avoided meeting him, but one night when I returned he was already seated at the table eating his supper.

'This is Fred,' Mrs Knight introduced us, 'he's come fer a few weeks.'

'Good evening.' I greeted him formally and shook his hand. He turned out to be a rather nice-looking fellow, dressed in a dark suit, clean white shirt and dark blue tie. His dark, thick hair was brushed back from his open face and I noticed what a personable manner he had.

'So you're Katie. Very pleased ter meet you.' He spoke gently and all through supper I could hardly keep my eyes off him, but when he looked up and caught me looking at him I became embarrassed and, making excuses, left him talking to the landlady and went off to my bedroom to write a letter to the children.

A few days after this he asked me if he could take me to the pictures.

'Make a nice change for yer Katie, instead of stayin' up in yer room each night,' he said persuasively, but I was too tired to go anywhere and refused his offer. 'Some other night then, Katie?' her replied, taking my refusal well. 'Perhaps I will, one night,' I assured him, and after thinking it over on the tram to visit the children I made up my mind to accept his offer.

We went to the cinema, and after dropped in at The Vine in Carver Street for a drink. He was quite the gentleman and showed me the sort of consideration I had not experienced for years, and when we got to our digs he wished me 'good night' with not so much as an attempt to kiss me. Although he was kind, he was also persistent, and took it for granted that I would go out with him again. When I refused he told me he would like to be more than a friend. I knew what he meant but feigned obtuseness, but then he came out with it and asked me to marry him.

'I'm sorry Fred,' I replied with difficulty, 'I like you very much but marriage no.'

'Well, at least say yer'll sleep on it an' think it over,' he insisted and held my hands tightly so that I couldn't turn away from him.

'I will Fred, but now let go of my hands an' I'll give yer my answer in the mornin'. Good night,' I added as I made my way up to bed. But I had no intention of reconsidering: my mind was made up. I was glad the landlady was out when I came downstairs the following day. I could face him alone and give him my answer.

'Good mornin' Kate,' he said, advancing towards me eagerly. 'Have you considered my proposal, dear?'

'Yes, I have Fred, and I'm afraid I don't want ter marry again. All I want ter do now is ter work 'ard an' get a home of me own,' I said firmly.

'You will, dear, if yer'll marry me, an' if yer want, I'll even take yer away from 'ere as soon as yer like.' He pleaded, trying to put his arm round me, but I brushed him aside.

'No. I won't go without my children. Anyway, if I did marry yer an' we went away I'd be startin' another family an' I don't want marriage or any more kids.' I began to weep and although he tried to comfort me I pushed him gently away and told him as well as I could between sobs, 'No, Fred, that's my final answer.'

I was relieved when at that moment the landlady walked into the room and I was saved from further difficult explanations. She wanted to know why I was upset, of course, but I left Fred to tell her and sat down to recover myself.

'Well, Katie, yer could doo worse,' was her first reaction. This was more than I could stand and I went straight up to my room without saying a word and waited for him to go out. I kept out of their way until I returned from work the following evening to find Mrs Knight in tears. When I inquired what was wrong she turned on me.

'He's gone!' she yelled.

'Who's gone?' I asked, perplexed at her behaviour, which was normally so polite.

'Fred, who do yer think? 'E's taken 'is clothes an' left. I put 'is supper in the oven an' while I was out he must 'ave took 'is things an' gone,' she wailed, upset more about her reduced income than anything else as far as I could see.

'Maybe 'e'll come in later an' explain,' I ventured weakly but I could sense that she blamed me for this unexpected turn of events. I had no desire to argue with her, so I washed and changed and took a walk to visit Frank and Nellie. I talked things over with them and Nellie advised, 'Yer know yer own mind best. Yer an attractive young woman but I know yer'll be careful.' I stayed a while with them, then wished them 'good night' and returned to my lodgings. When I got to the step the door opened and Mrs Knight dragged me inside and slammed the door.

'That bugger was married! An' 'is wife's lookin' for 'im fer maintenance!' she gasped breathlessly.

'Who?' I was thorougly confused.

'That plausible bugger Fred, that's who!'

'How do yer know?' I could not believe this.

'The police 'ave bin 'ere asking questions. I knew he sounded too good ter be true,' she said, as if she'd known all along that her lodger was a conman. To me it was a complete shock when I realised how close I had been to being duped.

'Come an' sit down, Kate, an' I'll get 'is supper outta the oven. It'll still be all right an' we can 'ave a double 'elpin'. Open that bottla stout an' we'll 'ave that an all.'

I could think of nothing to say. I was still getting used to the idea of Fred being a total fraud and an attempted bigamist to boot.

'Yow was lucky to turn 'im down,' Mrs Knight confided in me when we sat down to our supper.

'Yes, an' ter think I might 'ave weakened when you said, "yer could do worse",' I said, mimicking her, and we both burst out laughing and continued until our sides hurt. When we'd calmed down sufficiently she said she'd try to get a proper gentleman lodger next and at that point I decided that before that happened I too would leave for a quieter berth.

The same weekend I began answering adverts for rooms but they were all too expensive; some landladies wanted almost as much per week as I was earning. However, I was determined not to admit **def**eat but to keep on until I found some respectable digs in a better class of area than I was living in in the Jewellery Quarter.

Finally I found what I was looking for in the small-ads columns of the local evening paper, the *Evening Mail*. It was a notice for 'a young respectable woman' and the address was Soho Road, Handsworth. Handsworth was then a solidly middle-class district of quiet streets of large terraced houses. The houses had double bay windows and neat little gardens and it was a pleasure to walk along the streets. Unfortunately, this is no longer the case today and the area has steadily slid downhill and the appearance of the place has suffered, although I noticed recently that the urban renewal schemes have improved some of the streets. Be that as it may, it was a pleasant area when I first went there, *Evening Mail* clutched in hand, to find lodgings. I found the house and from its size and appearance I anticipated another disappointment, but since I'd walked all the way there I decided to inquire anyway; so I lifted the brass knocker and waited for my knocks to be answered.

I waited for several minutes but, becoming impatient, I eventually turned to walk away. It was then that I heard a woman's voice behind me say, 'Did you knock, dear?' When I turned round I found myself facing a neatly dressed middle-aged woman. She wore a white blouse, long black shirt and had pearl drop earrings in each ear, with a matching string of pearls around her neck. She was slim and about five foot six in height, and although she was an imposing figure she had a pleasant smile on her face. 'Y-yes', was all I managed to say in reply.

As she opened the door wider I saw how highly polished the hall was and caught sight of the richly patterned carpet. My heart sank: I was not going to ask about the room because I knew I'd be disappointed.

'I'm sorry, I must have come to the wrong house,' I apologised, but I noticed her eyes light on my newspaper.

'Have you come about the room?' she asked, and I had to admit that I had. 'But I'm afraid it'll be more than I can afford.' But she put me at ease immediately and brushed aside my protests and I agreed to look at the room, more out of curiosity than any serious hope that I would be able to take it. I followed my hostess into a beautiful room she called 'the parlour'.

'Sit down by the fire, dear, and I'll put the kettle on. Then while we're having a cup of tea I'll tell you about the room and you can decide if you want to see it or not.'

'Thank you,' I replied, making myself comfortable in a chair by the fireplace. When she'd gone to the kitchen I looked at the wonderful things the room contained. The round table was covered with a lace tablecloth. On it were three china cups and saucers – not the odd crocks I was used to at Mrs Knight's – places to match, a cut-glass jam dish and a cakestand laden with homemade scones. Against the wall stood a large oak dresser with several shelves full of china dishes and plates and glassware of every description. Against the opposite wall was a highly polished leather couch which matched four high-backed chairs. Around the fireplace were a low brass fireguard, brass fender, brass fire irons and a small bellows, all of which shone as if they'd just been polished. On the mantel stood silver-framed photographs. The whole room was spotlessly clean and all in all I was extremely impressed, never having set foot in such a palace of a house before. I was still trying to take it all in when the lady of the house returned with the tea. I made a mental note that I would have a room like this myself when I'd sorted my affairs out. Then I took the proffered cup of tea and in answer to her question told the lady my name was Mrs Flood.

'Oh,' she said, 'but I didn't see you wearing a wedding ring. I thought you were single.'

'I'm a widow,' I replied.

'Do you have any children?' was her next question.

I hesitated before answering, but I could see no harm in telling her, particularly since I wouldn't be taking the room in any case. She looked disappointed when I told her I had four children and said she was sorry that she had no room for them. This annoyed me. I was still very upset about their fate and I flew off the handle.

'I didn't ask yer to!' I made to get up, tears welling into my eyes. 'I only wanted the room for myself until I can get a home of my own and have them with me,' I blurted out.

'I'm sorry, I didn't mean to upset you, dear. Now sit down and have another cup of tea.' And while I drank my second cup I told her a bit of my story. Then I noticed the time and made my excuses and made to leave.

'But you haven't seen the room,' she said. 'Would you like to?'

I was curious to see the room so I agreed and I followed her up the red-carpeted stairs and into a well-furnished bedroom off a small landing. I was amazed at how sumptuous it was, right down to the rose-patterned bedspread. There was a bedside electric lamp that could be switched on and off. It was simply luxurious and I was glad to have seen it because it gave me ideas about what I wanted to do when I could afford a house of my own. As I was musing like this and absent-mindedly looking under the bed the lady startled me.

'We have a bathroom down the corridor,' she smiled and I reddened.

'Well,' she said finally, 'do you like it, my dear?'

'It's lovely, but I couldn't afford to rent a room like this. But I would like to know how much it is. Just for curiosity's sake,' I replied.

'It's only twenty-five shillings a week all found,' she told me to my amazement. There must be a catch somewhere I thought.

'Did I 'ear you right?' I asked.

'Yes, Mrs Flood. You see, it's not the money I need. It's someone to keep me company, to talk to. I'm afraid I get very lonely by myself at night and I've got this spare room, so rather than keeping it empty I thought I'd let it. I've had several young women call to see it but I'm going to let you have it, if you wish.' She told me she'd taken to me at once and said I had an honest face and that I could move in as soon as I wished. I was still suspicious: it seemed too good to be true and besides if she lived alone, as she had said, why were there three places laid for tea.

'You say you live alone,' I said, and she nodded. 'Then who was the table laid for, then?' At this she smiled broadly.

'I was expecting George, my gentleman friend, but he can't come until next weekend. I have an old chap, too, who tidies up the garden once a week.'

'Oh, I'm sorry. I didn't mean to pry.' I was embarrassed by her forthrightness. Then to change the subject I told her about Mrs Knight's and why I had to find new lodgings.

'I understand your reasons,' she said kindly. 'But you're an attractive young woman. Do you think you'll ever marry again?' she asked.

'No. All I want is to work hard and save enough to rent a house with a garden and get my children back.'

'Well, I wish you good luck in your ambition. In the meantime I'll do my best to help, but be on your guard in case any more Freds come along.' She smiled and we shook hands and it was arranged that I should move in on Monday evening.

As I walked back down Soho Road I seemed to be floating on air. I thanked my lucky stars I'd found such a delightful berth and such a sympathetic confidante. Although I went straight back to work my boss reprimanded me for lateness so I had to tell him where I'd been. But all he said was, 'Well, yer betta keep regular hours or yow'll 'ave yer cards. Now get on with that job yer left 'alf finished.' My workmates were more pleased when I told them about my good fortune after knocking-off time. I felt as if a great weight had been lifted from my mind and that I could settle down and plan my future and the children's.

When I returned to Mrs Knight's I was surprised to see her two new lodgers sitting down to their meal.

'I see yer 'aven't wasted much time.' I spoke sharply and she started up from the table and tried to introduce me. I must have seemed very rude when I snapped at her.

'There's no need for introductions now, Mrs Knight. I'm leaving on Monday.'

'Where yer goin'?' she asked, obviously taken by surprise.

'I'm going ter see my brother. I'll tell yer when I get back.' And I hurried out without another glance at the startled company.

Nellie and Frank were pleased to hear I had better digs. Then as I was telling them about the house, Frank interrupted to tell me Mum had been by and left a letter, which he handed to me.

'But it's bin opened,' I said at once.

'Yes, she said she opened it, thinking it was summat important,' he replied.

'But she can't read.'

'I know. She probably got one of the neighbours ter read it,' said Frank, stating the obvious.

'Bloody cheek. She thought there was money in it.' I was furious.

'Most likely,' Nellie agreed.

I looked at it and saw that it was a week old and had come from Barnardo's. I was to call to see the matron as soon as possible to discuss my children's welfare. This was worrying and my anger at Mum's lack of concern for the urgency of the matter increased. I decided that I must go first thing in the morning. It was Saturday, the day of my weekly visit anyway.

I stayed with Frank and Nellie and joined them in a bite of supper. I was famished for I'd not eaten all day, and after the meal, over a glass of stout, we chatted and Frankie told me Mum had reapplied for relief now I'd left her.

'But I thought she had a couple living with her.' I didn't see that it was my fault.

'She did, but they left after a row last week, so I was told. So the visitor asked her how many sons she had working and now Jack, Charlie and me have ter allow her two an' six each per week to 'elp maintain her,' Frankie continued.

This was typical of the meanness of the parish officers, but as Nellie pointed out it was better than having her there to live with them.

'She's got money hid away, if I know my mother.' I knew she wouldn't go short if she could help it. But by this time it was late and I had to leave to face Mrs Knight and postpone further discussion of Mum's plight until another day. I said good night and left, promising to let them know what happened when I visited the home the next day.

I was glad to find Mrs Knight alone when I entered but I could see at a glance that she was angry. She was taking it out on the fire with the poker as I explained about my new lodgings.

'That's the thanks I get fer tekin' you in, she snapped.

'But I told yer I wasn't settled when that Fred was 'ere. Surely you don't expect me to stay now yer've got another two lodgers? Anway where am I goin' ter sleep now?' I added.

'I thought being you're leavin' on Monday, yer could sleep with me,' she said slyly. But I couldn't bring myself to accept this offer, for although she was a kind woman in many ways she was not very particular in her personal habits. In fact I wondered if she were not deaf, she broke wind so thunderously on occasion.

'No,' I said simply.

'Why not?' she asked and I could only make the excuse that I'd arranged to stay with Frank and Nellie.

She didn't seem disappointed as I paid her what I owed. Then I went up to my room and found to my disgust that the lodger's suitcases were already there at the foot of the bed. I hastily stuffed my clothes into my case and returned downstairs, hopping mad, to find Mrs Knight sitting staring glumly into the fire.

'You crafty old cow!' I screamed at her. 'You'd already planned this.' I didn't wait for her to reply but swept out, slamming the door behind me.

Now I had to rely on Frank and Nellie to let me stay for a couple of days, but I needn't have worried because they quickly offered me their sofa. Next morning I took Nellie up a cup of tea – Frank had left for work – and later I helped with the housework before leaving for the children's home and my interview with the matron. On the way I bought the usual basket of fruit and made for the tram. I was half an hour early, so I called in at a teashop for a snack and soon it was time to be on my way.

As I walked up the gravel path to the front door of the big house I was surprised that it was so quiet. There were no children's voices screeching in the background. I assumed they had been taken out for walks and thought no more of it as I lifted the knocker. Then, almost at once, it opened and I was confronted by a tall, elderly, stern-faced woman, dressed in the same uniform as matron.

'Well?' she asked sharply. 'What do you want?' I was very nervous but managed to stutter that I had come to see matron.

'Matron is not here anymore but you may leave a message,' she informed me snootily.

'But I've come ter visit me children,' I blurted out.

'Oh, I see. Matron and all the children have been transferred to the homes at Barkingside. Weren't you notified? This is only a receiving home for a few weeks.'

'But why wasn't I told? An' when will they be back?' I asked, unable to grasp the situation until she told me where Barkingside was. Barkingside, Ilford, Essex meant nothing to me until she explained. Then I was shattered. I couldn't understand why they'd taken the children away without my consent and I received little in the way of explanation from this cold-faced woman. Soon I found myself facing a closed door and all I could do was turn and retrace my steps down the gravel path to the street.

How I got back to my brother's house I cannot remember. I was broken-hearted. I imagined I would never see them again. I had only a few shillings in the world, but the next day I boarded a train bound for Essex. When I got off the train at my destination I found a policeman and asked directions to the homes, then after jumping on and off several buses I found myself outside an imposing institutional building that made me feel scared. But I'd come this far and was determined to see my children. I'd walked only a few steps towards the house when I was stopped by one of the 'mothers', as the women in charge were called, who asked me who I was looking for. I told her I had come from Birmingham to visit my children, and I was surprised that this seemed to displease her. She told me that all the children had gone to church, it being Sunday of course, and that I couldn't see them anyway without a pass, and then only once a month on Saturday afternoons. This was too much for me and I collapsed in tears.

'Please let me wait an' see them. I've come such a long way,' I pleaded.

All she said was, 'Wait here,' before turning on her heel and disappearing into the house. While I waited I kept a lookout, hoping to catch sight of the children but all I saw were a few older girls going from house to house. They were dressed in uniform grey, with white, lace-trimmed pinafores. Just then the house mother reappeared and beckoned for me to follow her and we made our way to an almost bare office where without another word she handed me a pass with the rules and regulations. I handed over the basket of fruit and sweets I had brought and read the paper through my tears. I pleaded with that woman to let me see the children but I could see that there was no melting her hard heart, and eventually I left. But I hung around for a long time in the hope of catching a glimpse of them until I was spotted and ordered off the premises with a warning not to return. I know if I'd seen them that day I would have run off with them. Anything to get them away from the prison I had inadvertantly handed them over to.

I was only just in time to catch the late train for Birmingham. I flopped into a seat and took a closer look at the pass and saw that it was only three weeks until the next visiting day, and that cheered me slightly. During that three weeks I had to work very hard to save the extra for the fare and the basket of treats. It was years later that I found out that my children received none of the presents I had taken for them. Whether the staff had them or they were added to the general food supply I do not know: all I know is that it was very cruel to leave my children thinking that their heartless mother never took them even the smallest gift. But then there was more heartlessness in the administration of Barnardo's than the public would have suspected if they'd judged by the favourable publicity the homes usually generated. I suppose that to the people at Barnardo's I was an inadequate mother who was incapable of looking after her children. But I felt that I was being treated like a criminal and I can't say they showed much sympathy for me and my circumstances. My efforts to improve my life were not regarded with much interest by Barnardo's, because in the eight years the children were with them they sent somebody to visit me only once.

Those three weeks seemed like years and when the time eventually came the train seemed to crawl. But at last I arrived outside the main gate where I found two elderly women and a young man waiting for it to be opened. We fell into conversation and I found that they had children there too. Some children were orphans and had no visitors at all. The man was of the opinion that it was good that such a place as this existed to cater for orphans but the women did not agree.

'It's a 'ard an' cruel place,' one insisted, 'an' if my ol' man 'ad bin alive mine wouldn't be 'ere now.' But I was hardly listening and it was years before I discovered how true that woman's words were.

I was led into an office where a stern-faced 'mother' faced us from behind a large oak desk strewn with files. She asked me whom I had come to visit and when I gave my children's names she reached for a hand bell and rang it loudly. In no time at all a young girl, aged, I would think, about twelve, appeared at the door. The child was thin and pale and dressed in the uniform grey and white pinafore of Barnardo's. She had thick stockings and heavy boots and her hair was cropped as if someone had put a basin over her head and cut round the edge. She bowed to the mother and stood waiting for her orders.

'Bring in the Flood children,' she snapped at the timid-looking girl.

I didn't have long to wait when Kate and Jean appeared, curtsied as well and stood there awaiting their instructions. They too were clad in grey and had the same prison-cut hairstyle. I went towards them and as I bent down to kiss them they forgot their drill and threw their arms round me and we embraced. Mary was only a babe in arms and too young to understand, and when I held her to me she seemed unused to affection and didn't respond. Soon we were all in tears, but this only provoked the mother to reprimand me for this show of emotion. But I kissed and hugged them and told them that they would only be there a few weeks while I got a home for them. I had no idea that it would take me eight years before I had them back with me. Then after a few minutes they were led away and I was informed in cold tones that if I upset them again I would have my pass revoked and would be prevented from seeing them. I had no time to reflect on the injustice of this and had no idea that any of this harsh regime could be challenged then or later. Today this kind of institution would be exposed publicly in the media but before the war nobody thought that the parents of Barnardo's children had any more rights than the poor children did themselves.

I asked where my son John was and I was told he'd been

transferred to the boys' home in Kingston-upon-Thames. I visited him there later. He was there for nine months until he was eleven years of age, when he was sent to Watts Naval Training School at Elmham, Norfolk, and later, while still only eleven, was put on HMS *Ganges* at Shotley, where he was trained for warships and practised with live explosives and firearms and did bayonet practice. It is horrifying to think that Barnardo's had the right to force the youngsters in their care into the armed forces at such a tender age. Needless to say the life at HMS *Ganges* was even more strictly disciplined than in the homes and the men who were in charge were all hardened naval men. It seems clear to me that the Navy used Barnardo's to ensure a supply of young recruits who had no choice at all about whether they were pressed into service or not. When John was barely fifteen he was put aboard the HMS *Hood*, a battle-cruiser. When I found out I wrote to the Admiralty and to his captain explaining that I was a widow and that he was too young for active service, but they brushed my protests aside because he had signed on for the duration of the war. After that my letters went unacknowledged and I became very bitter. If I had had the right contacts I could have got him out but what could a poor widow like me accomplish when it came to the Navy's need for cannon fodder?

After he joined the *Hood* all I could do was pray that the Lord would watch over him and keep him safe from harm. He broke his arm while doing PT, however, and was given leave while his arm healed. It was during that period, in 1941, that the unfortunate ship was sunk with all bar two or three hands, so I suppose my prayers were answered. John was next sent to the HMS *Dorsetshire* where he was the youngest leading seaman as well as a torpedo man. He was aboard during the engagement with the *Bismarck* as well as seeing service against the Vichy French fleet off West Africa. The *Dorsetshire* engaged the battleship *Richelieu* which was fortunately out of ammunition. Later John saw service in the HMS *King George V* on Russian convoys before being based at Simonstown, South Africa, where his ship engaged in escort duties. Those war years were the most worrying of all my life.

While I was visiting the children regularly all my money was going on travel and I was unable to save enough to have any realistic hope of ever getting my own home. I used to lay awake nights thinking about the children and wishing I at least had Mary with me. Then one day on my way to the station I bumped into Liza who offered to go with me. I agreed; I could do with the company, I thought.

'I'd like ter see 'em too,' I remember her saying and when I told her I was going to try to take Mary back she replied, 'The best thing yow can do anyway.' Then she added with a wink, 'Just leave it ter me.'

I thought if we both pleaded the authorities would allow me to have my youngest child back, but it was a terrible mistake. For a start it was Sunday and when we arrived we were told we couldn't see the children on Sunday, only Saturday. I began to weep at this, but we were turned away.

'If they were my kids bloody 'ell an' 'igh water wouldn't stop me from takin' them away from this cold-lookin' prison,' Liza exclaimed angrily. 'Would yer like me ter try an' get Mary?' she added.

'Yes, Liza,' I said tearfully, not really thinking about what she intended.

'Well, you leave this ter me. Yow 'ide be'ind this wall an'as soon as I see 'er I'll call out, then you grab 'er quick an' run.'

We didn't have long to wait. All the older children were at church and the place was almost deserted when a few minutes later we spotted one of the housemaids coming across the yard with my daughter in her arms. Liza went over to her casually and engaged her in conversation, then I grabbed my baby and made for the gate. But Mary didn't know what it was all about and probably didn't recognise me, and she began to scream. Before I realised what was happening she was roughly snatched back from me by one of the staff whose attention had been attracted by the screaming and I was caught. I tried to explain but it was no good. I knew I should never have taken Liza's advice but I was desperate and hadn't stopped to think of the consequences. Now it was too late. We were ordered off the premises and were warned that if we were seen around the grounds again we would be dealt with severely. We left crestfallen and later that week I received the inevitable letter informing me that I would not be able to visit my children until further notice and should I attempt to contact them I would be dealt with by the law. My sister and I quarrelled before we parted that Sunday, and I didn't see her for many years after that.

11

My Dreams Are Realised

After my ill-fated attempt to snatch Mary away from Barnardo's I could do nothing except wait for replies to my letters and work at my one aim of saving as much money as I could, living in hope of my dreams being realised one day. However I seemed to be dogged by bad luck: often I was unwell and had to have time off work, and after three warnings I was given my cards and left Butler's. Then I had to take a job on a power press at Joseph Lucas's in Great King Street. I had had plenty of experience on a hand press but none on a power press, so when I applied I lied. The money was attractive so I had to try and I clocked on and the following Monday morning, received my brown overall and cap and, nervous as a kitten, made my way to the block where the power presses were. Then as luck would have it a young woman spoke to me.

'Don't be nervous,' she said, 'I'll show yer the ropes.' She was a real chatterbox and a jolly girl. I soon found out her name was Ada.

'I've only worked a 'and press before, Ada. I shouldn't 'ave started really, but I need the money.'

'Don't we all?' she smiled. 'But there's nothin' ter be afraid of. The noise from the presses gets on yer nerves but yer'll get used to it in time.'

Then the hooter sounded for everyone to get to their places. I took a three-legged stool like the other women and sat in front of the machine. When the motor started I nearly jumped out of my skin. Ada pushed me down onto the stool and showed me how the press was operated before the foreman had time to come down the block. Fortunately, I picked the job up in a minute or two.

'Yer OK now, Katie?' Ada shouted above the din. I stuck

my thumb up and nodded. Ada was cutting out blanks which were passed to me to have holes pierced through them by the press. Then they were sent to the assembly shop where wires were threaded through them before they were sent to car plants to be fitted to dashboards. Ada and I could talk only in the canteen during breaks because talking was forbidden while the presses were in operation to cut the risk of accidents. She told me she'd only been there a month and I was sorry to hear that she was leaving soon to join a friend who was learning to be a dressmaker.

'Don't yer like it here, then?' I asked.

'Well, the money's good, but the bloody job's too dirty and greasy for my liking,' she replied and I had to agree. We chatted like this whenever we had the chance and became quite friendly. She promised to introduce me to her friend, which I looked forward to.

The following week everyone on the power presses had to go over to piecework. The rate fixers came with their stopwatches and stood over us. Every job was timed according to the Beddow system, the name of the organisation expert who dreamed the method up. As the reader might appreciate, this system was not devised for the benefit of the workers. It was real sweated labour and there was scarcely time to go to the lavatory. There was great pressure to cut corners to make sufficient money and one day my friend Ada did a very foolish thing. She tied back the safety guard to work more quickly. Suddenly I was startled by a scream which pierced the hubbub of the workshop. It came from the direction of Ada's machine and I went over immediately to see what had happened. I bent over Ada who was on the floor and blood spurted over me. I'm afraid I fainted at the sight of blood and when I came round I found myself lying beside my friend in an ambulance. She was unconscious and when I looked I saw she had lost several fingers; I vomited and passed out again.

The next thing I recall is coming round in bed in a hospital ward. I'd been washed and was lying between clean sheets. I enjoyed being waited on but I couldn't see why I had been kept in. I inquired of one of the nurses but all she could tell me was that I would have to wait until the doctor had seen me the following day. I didn't think there was anything wrong with me but I was enjoying the service, particularly when a boiled chicken dinner arrived followed by a mug of Ovaltine for supper. Later, in the middle of the night, I got up to use the toilet. I tiptoed down the ward to the lavatory but before I could switch on the light I felt something squelch under my bare foot. I was horrified when I flicked the switch and looked at the floor. There were dozens of cockroaches scuttling for the skirting. I screamed and fled back to my bed. This awakened some of the patients and brought the nurse running. She smiled when I told her what had happened and explained that although they 'tried to keep them down, the building was old.' I still wanted to go to the toilet though so I asked the nurse for a bedpan.

'You are a nuisance, aren't you?' she replied. 'You'll have to wait. Didn't you go when you went to the bathroom?'

'No. Not with them things running around me feet. An' I'm cold now,' I added.

She went away and returned in a few minutes with a hot-water bottle and a warm bedpan. Such kindness, despite my troublesomeness, was more than I had experienced for some time and I revelled in it. When the doctor examined me all over he gave it as his opinion that there was nothing wrong with me, simply that I was undernourished. I was told I was to be discharged the next morning and to call at the dispensary where I received tablets and Parish's Food. This brought back memories of the children.

I returned to Lucas's the following afternoon and gave in my notice, having decided to have another try at enamelling. I was determined to leave the heavy factory work alone; indeed, just the mention of a power press made me nervous. I often thought about Ada and wondered how she was. She would never be a dressmaker after her accident. I wished many times I had taken her address so I could have kept in touch.

My next job was in a small shop; 'Hart's, enamellers to the trade' it said above the door. I told Mr Hart I was fully experienced although I still wanted a lot of knowledge in the trade. There were ten other women beside myself, one of whom, a young woman called Rose, was in charge. She was a bit of a snob and very stern. She wasn't liked because she lorded it when the boss was not around. Sometimes he would be away for days 'on business', that is to say, at the races. We could tell when he'd lost and then we dared not say a word, but when he'd been lucky he would bring in cakes, strawberries sometimes, and then ask us to work over.

One day Mr Hart gave me a special job. I had to enamel a little white dog on a brooch. This was to be the sample for an order. I tried hard to get it right and the boss was pleased, as was the customer. It was to be a big order which would last for weeks, but when Rose found out I was in Mr Hart's good books she became very jealous. This was compounded when Mr Hart commented that I was turning out more than she was. Inevitably she had to have revenge.

A few days later I found I was having difficulty with the white enamel which kept bubbling up. I kept swilling the colour and used a clean cloth, but to no effect. Then Mr Hart saw what was happening. It must have been one of the losing days because he flared up a temper and started to rave. Then I noticed the smirk on Rose's face and realised something was wrong. So did he; he sat down and examined the frit. Then he exclaimed:

'I knew as much! There's salt in here.'

He sent for Rose in the little back room he called his 'office' and after a few minutes she emerged in tears. She'd been given the sack on the spot. This I thought a bit unfair, but later the girls explained that this had happened before when she'd taken a dislike to somebody. I felt a little less guilty when I heard them say 'good riddance'.

After this Mr Hart joined us in the work for a bit until a couple of weeks after Rose's departure he called me into his office and asked me to take charge and inspect the finished work. Then he went out 'on business'. He couldn't have taken so much time off if he hadn't had a reliable manager in the shop all the time.

I was able to get to know much more about the business side of the trade in my new position: the prices of every kind of enamel badge, invoicing and accounts. Then a few days later I ran out of paper to wrap an order so I tried the door to his private room off the office and found it was open. I went in and found a small room like a living room with carpeted floor, two red plush chairs, pictures on the wall and a table in the middle of the floor strewn with racing papers. Thinking he would not miss a couple I took them to wrap the work and closed the door behind me. When Mr Hart returned two days later we all went quiet: we could tell at once by his manner that he had lost. He stormed through the shop to his office and into his private room. Then all at once he came storming out.

'Who's been in my room?' he demanded.

'I did,' I told him. 'The door wasn't locked an' I wanted some newspaper to wrap some work in.'

'I never leave that door open!' he shouted.

'But it was open.' I was indignant. 'An' a customer's got yer racing paper now.'

He calmed down after this and replied more quietly, 'Very well, next time I'll leave you the key.' But he never did.

I was now chargehand enameller, viewer and office worker all rolled into one. However, I was not complaining; I knew the trade inside out and I was getting top wages with a promise of a bonus on our turnover. Some of the girls worked faster than others so we worked as a team and got on well, especially when Mr Hart was out. However, his unpredictable moods could be extremely trying, and in the end too much.

Late one afternoon he came bounding in, picked up a handful of badges, glanced at one and then threw them onto the floor in a temper.

'These are the wrong colour!' he bawled.

'But that's the colour we always do them,' I replied.

'You should have asked for the sample,' he yelled at me and before I could reply he'd disappeared into the office. When he came back he almost threw the badge at me.

'Now that's the one! Pick it up, I want you in the office!'

This was the final straw for me: I couldn't tolerate his tantrums any longer.

'Pick it up yourself. You should be 'ere to run yer own business instead of 'avin' it out of me when yer lose on the 'orses!' The girls stared at me, mouths open. So did he when I added, 'See if yer can get somebody else ter do the work I do. I'm leaving right now!' And with that I put my coat and hat on and left.

On the following Friday I had to fetch my pay and my unemployment card. Hoping he was not at a race meeting, I rang the bell and waited. I was ready with an answer if he started on me again. Almost at once the door opened and he asked me in. It must have been one of his good days.

'I've come for the few days' pay that's due to me and me cards,' I said before he could say anything.

'Won't you think it over and come back?' he asked very pleasantly.

'No, Mr Hart, I've got my old job back,' I told him.

'Enamelling?'

'Yes, just enamelling and more money.'

'Well, I can give you a rise.'

'No, I've made up my mind.' And so I had.

'Well, if you should change yer mind, you've only to ask,' he said. Never, I thought.

As he handed over what was due to me he said how sorry he was to lose me. I nearly told him he should have thought of that before now, but I buttoned my lip, seeing no further point in arguing with him.

I started back at T. A. Butler's the following Monday morning. I didn't intend to let the grass grow under my feet now I was saving hard and fast. I was still lodging with Mrs Green in Soho Road and enjoying being there. Each night we would chat about our respective days and we were on Christian-name terms.

Then one day the tide turned for me. My opportunity arrived at last. It happened that Mr Butler – Tom, we all called him – had a large order for different kinds of badges and motor plates but he couldn't employ enough experienced

216

workers to cope. So one night I asked Nell, my landlady, if she would rent me her small empty back room to do some work at home. She agreed willingly and offered to help, to learn herself. It was easy to talk to Tom; he was like one of the workers, who would always find time for a friendly chat with his employees. My chance came to raise the subject with him and I offered to do some of the filing, a process prior to firing, at home. He agreed at once and let me take some Castrol badges and return them the next day. I laid the enamel on during the day and took three or four gross of the red and green badges home in the evening. Nell and I would sit up in her little back room after supper singing to the gramophone as we filed the badges with carborundum stones.

For me this extra work was worthwhile because I wanted to earn more and more and one day start my own business. In normal circumstances you had to work much harder then than today. There were no paid holidays except for Bank Holidays, and normal working hours were long – 8 a.m. to 6 p.m. – and included Saturday mornings as a rule. In the two years after I started doing homework I worked through, only taking off Christmas Day, Boxing Day and Good Friday. The only recreation I had was when George and Nell took me for a drink on Saturday nights or occasionally to the pictures. During those two long years I managed to save over a hundred pounds which in the 1930s was a considerable sum of money. However, it still was not sufficient to buy or rent a house and obtain furniture and all the things I needed for the children. I thought about what I was to do and decided to ask Tom Butler if he would supply outwork if I could find suitable premises and, bless him, he agreed.

After that I kept my eyes peeled for a workshop and it was on Good Friday 1937 that I happened to be walking along Spencer Street and paused outside a cake shop, in the window of which were hot cross buns. I went in and bought some to take back to Nell's. As I came down the steps with my purchase I glanced across the street and saw a notice which read, 'Top Floor Shop to Let. Apply Within'. Everything was closed for the Easter holiday so it was the following Tuesday when, hair newly Marcel-waved, in my Sunday-best hat, coat and gloves, I went to try my luck. The name of the principal occupier of the premises was 'F. Marson, makers of diamond rings, 90 Spencer Street'. I was interviewed by Mr Marson himself. His questions concerning my age, marital status and so on made me nervous, but I told him what I wanted the rooms for, who I worked for and what my boss's name was; but Mr Marson still said he needed references. I told him that Mr Butler would vouch for me and he said he would ring him and that I should hear from him in a few days.

Later in the week Tom Butler called me into his office to tell me he had given me a good reference, and when he handed me my wages that Friday I could've thrown my arms round his neck and kissed him. I didn't, though, because he had a reputation as a lady's man and I didn't wish to encourage him. But I thanked him sincerely. He told me to let him know when everything was fixed, and when I was ready to start he would send his errand boy round with badges and motor plates.

That weekend I was so excited I couldn't sleep in anticipation of going round the following Monday to see the rooms. Mr Marson took me up to the top floor and when I looked round I could see that it hadn't been used for years. There was rubbish everywhere and it was thick with dust, but I didn't mind the filth. That could soon be cleaned away and I was eager to start. Against one wall there was an old roll-top desk and there was some old machinery including a rusty old motor which was nevertheless in working order. In the corner was a cupboard that was supposed to be an office. All in all it was scarcely believable that such a place could exist, but when Mr Marson told me the rent was twelve shillings and sixpence a week I could have jumped for joy. I sealed the bargain by giving him a month's rent in advance and said I would be cleaning it out that week. He gave me the key and we shook hands.

When I got back I told Nell all about it. It had been a glue factory at one point, but with a little elbow grease would be just right. We set to and used just that. Frankie and a mate of his whitewashed it for me the following weekend. Then I went to the bank and withdrew fifty pounds to buy materials. I purchased enamel from Hutton's in Great Hampton Row, carborundum files and wire panning from Harry Smith's, Key Hill, and several second hand three-legged stools and tables as well as pestles and mortars. Nell came the first week to help but when she found we had rats refused to come again. Frank had warned me that we had them but I was used to rats from childhood and carried on working alone until the council workmen arrived to poison them. However, they were tenacious creatures and the council men had to come back every few weeks.

When everything was cleaned and scrubbed I put a notice for experienced enamellers and learners on the wall outside and I was in business. During the next month I employed four experienced women and two learners. Later I took more girls on and a mixed bunch they were, but I worked beside them and we were quite a happy family. I was always first to arrive at seven thirty in the morning and last to leave after seven o'clock most nights. I'd always been a jack of all trades but now I had my own business and I was independent for the first time in my life.

The girls knew about the rats although they didn't come out during daytime, but each night before I left I would set a trap, baited with half a kipper, and in the morning there would be a rat, sometimes two, to be drowned in the bucket. The girls never knew about this.

I was still at Nell's in 1937, and weekends would sit with her and George who was very interested in what I was doing. It was during one of these evenings that they told me that they were getting married in a few months and that they would sell up and go abroad. I was not surprised: I knew they slept together at weekends. I didn't comment: they'd been good to me and it was none of my business what they did. I would have loved that house and the furniture it contained but I couldn't afford to buy it, so I had to start looking for a house to rent.

I was extremely busy now. After paying the girls and taking

care of all the overheads I was able to bank money each week. I was still able to visit the children more than I had when I was working all hours God made doing homework. Kathleen was still at Barkingside but Mary and Jean were fostered out to two maiden ladies they called 'aunties'. When Nell and George had sold up I rented a house in Albert Road near Handsworth Park. I was in seventh heaven furnishing the front room, sitting room, the kitchen and the three bedrooms. What was best was the large garden at the rear where the children could play. As soon as everything was ready I wrote to the offices at Ilford and told them about my business and the house and that I was now in a position to have my children back with me. Two weeks later I received a letter informing me they would be sending a visitor to inspect my business premises and my house as soon as they could. In the meantime the work from Butler's went slack and I had to look round for other customers. First of all I took down the sign outside and replaced it with one which read, 'K. FLOOD, ART, ENAMELLER TO THE TRADE, TOP FLOOR'. My first customer, the next day, was R. Gomm. He gave me a good price for the work I did and he supplied me with orders for years, and after I had retired I continued to do outwork for him. I obtained work from Munster's in Hockley Street as well. Often Mr Munster himself would bring the work. He was a well-dressed, elderly gentleman and rather thickset. He had silver-grey hair and I thought him very distinguished-looking. He was German but spoke very good English. He was quite the gentleman and had beautiful manners. So one day when he invited me out to lunch, I accepted even though he was old enough to be my father.

I had some happy times with him; he was wonderful company, very considerate and not an emotionally demanding man: each time we parted he would just kiss me on the cheek and say, 'good night'. Then one night after dining out he took me in his arms gently and asked me to marry him. This was both flattering and upsetting because I had to tell him that I could not marry him, not until I had my children with me. He knew about them and how they came to be at

Barnardo's. He was obviously disappointed but said if I changed my mind he would take me to Germany and make a future for the children there. In the meantime he was going abroad on business. But, he said, he hoped I would say yes when he returned. Next day I saw him off on the train and when we embraced and kissed he said, 'Goodbye my dear, don't forget your promise.' However, I never saw Mr Munster again although sadly I heard some years later that he'd been interned for the duration of the war. If I had not had the children to think about and the business to pursue I believe I might have married him. I might have married several times in those years before the war; I had several proposals, but when I told them I had four children their ardour seemed to subside for some reason.

During these years I lost touch with most of my family – Frank and Nellie excepted, of course. Then one day when I was picking up some work from a customer in Albion Street I saw my brother, Jack. I tried to avoid him but he spotted me and approached.

''Ello Kate,' he called out. 'I dain't know yer in yer smart get up. An' 'ow's the kids?' he inquired cheerfully.

'No thanks ter you that they're all right!' I snapped, and made to walk away. But he grabbed me by the arm.

'Don't yer wantta know 'ow yer Mum is?' he asked.

'No! Nor yow! An' yer know why.' I'm afraid I was still very bitter about how they had failed to help me when I needed them. Then he changed the subject.

'Yer know Mary's back from America, don't yer?' And I was willing to listen to what he had to say about my older sister who I hadn't seen for years.

'No, I didn't,' I answered more calmly. 'Where's she living now?'

'She's livin' in the Drive, in the top yard for the time bein'.'

'Oh, my God!' I exclaimed. 'What a comedown for her. If you see her will you tell her I'll come an' see her in a day or two. Thanks for telling me, I've got to be off now.'

As I turned away he said, 'I'm just goin' in The George an' Dragon to 'ave a drink. I'll buy yer one . . .'

'Don't bother, I don't drink!' I snapped in bitterness at him.

I decided I would look Mary up, and a few days later I was on my way there when by coincidence I bumped into Mrs Taylor's twin boys. They were in their mid-twenties now but unmistakable as the little tots I used to drag along in my go-cart to Titty-Bottle Park all those years before. Joey was still bandy and Harry hadn't lost his squint. I still had a soft spot for them. Joey was pushing a basket carriage full of firewood and Harry was walking beside. I tapped Joey on the shoulder.

'Don't yer know me Joey?' I inquired jokingly.

''Ello Tatie,' they both replied in unison: they always called me 'Tatie'. 'Where'd yer spring from? An' where're yer gooin'?'

'To see my sister Mary, but I'm glad I've seen yer both. An' what are you two up to these days?'

Then they both looked sheepish and Harry replied, 'I 'ope yer don't mind but when yer went away an' yer told ower Mum yer wasn't comin' back, we thought we'd take over yer customers, an' now we've got a good little business goin'. One day we 'ope ter buy an 'orse an' cart, don't we Joey?' he added and gave a broad grin.

'Of course I don't mind Harry. I'm glad yer both doing well, but don't trust anybody on the slate.'

'No fear. We only sell for cash an' we put money in the post office every week.'

'Harry, will yer do me a favour?' I asked.

'Yes Tatie, anything fer yoo,' came the prompt reply.

'Would you go down the Drive an' see if my mother is about? I don't want ter see 'er if I can 'elp it.'

'Don't worry. I'll go. You mind the basket, 'arry,' said Joey before running off in the direction of the Drive. While he was gone I asked Harry how his mother was.

'She died a few weeks after yow left,' he answered sadly.

'Oh, I am sorry to hear that,' I replied shocked. 'I loved your Mum, she was good to me.'

'Yes, she always said 'ow kind you were to 'er an' us when we were little lads,' he said with a tear in his eye.

222

'Never mind, wipe your eyes, Joey's coming.'

Joey came hurrying back, all smiles. 'Yow don't 'ave ter worry, Tatie. The ol' battleaxe 'as gone away agen an' the door's locked.' He grinned. 'Yer know,' he added, 'when yer left she took in a coupla lodgers who 'ad a little lad. Poor little bugger was all skin an' bone. 'Is Dad was always beatin' 'im with 'is belt an' one night ower Mum 'eard 'im cryin' down the cellar among the bleedin' rats. Well, she sent for the cruelty man an' when 'e see the bleedin' red weals on 'is arse 'e tuk 'im away. Then when yer Mum found out, she threw 'em out with all their things in the yard.'

'What 'appened then?' I'd not heard this before.

'They both scarpered cos the neighbours threatened ter beat them up.'

'An' yer know summat else,' put in Harry. 'We admired what yer did, an' some o' the neighbours said they wished they 'ad girls ter do what yow did.'

'Well, the children should be coming home soon an' when they do I'll bring 'em down ter see you.' I was pleased that I was not universally condemned for sending the children into a home. 'An' now I'll 'ave ter be on me way.' And I turned to go. Then Joey spoke shyly.

'Doo yer mind, Tatie, if we give yer a kiss?' he asked.

'No, course not. But hurry up; I don't want the people round 'ere to get the wrong idea.' And they each pecked my cheek and blushed. Then they hurried off.

I continued towards my sister's yard where I asked a small girl which house Mrs White lived in.

'In that one,' she told me, pointing to the fourth house. As I approached it I saw a tray of steaming doughnuts on the windowsill which made my mouth water. The door stood wide open. My sister was nowhere to be seen and when I looked round the place, I was surprised to see it was almost bare. It was clean enough, apart from flour all over the floor, but the only furniture was two wooden chairs and a deal table. There was a fire in the grate and on the green-mottled gas stove stood a bubbling pan of fat. As I stood taking this in my sister came bounding down the stairs with a large bag of flour in her arms. I could hardly believe my eyes; she'd put on so much weight. Round her ample waist she wore a hessian apron and she had men's boots on her feet and was covered from head to toe with flour. She gave an exclamation of surprise, dropped the bag on the table and flung her arms round me. We kissed and wept as you might imagine after such a long break.

'Oh Mary, I can't believe you've come down 'ere to live.' I was genuinely shocked because as the reader will remember Mary was always so disdainful of the yards. 'What a hole!'

'Oh, don't let that worry yer; this is only temporary,' she assured me.

'But I thought you were doing well in America,' I said.

'I was, at least at first, but the Americans don't live like we do an' ower money didn't last. But when I was there I did learn to make doughnuts an' now I've got a little business selling to neighbours an' supplying the shops. Carn't make 'em quick enough in fact.' She sounded cheerful enough.

'Does it pay?' I was unconvinced, having engaged in similar enterprises myself without much success.

'W-e-ll.' She hesitated. 'I'll let yer into my little secret; I know you'll keep it. I don't want Bill to know yet, but I've got quite a little nest egg now and Mrs Charles, 'er who 'as the draper's shop in Albion Street, is thinking of leaving soon an' she's given me the first chance to buy it.' She spoke confidentially.

'I wish you all the luck in the world, Mary. I'll keep yer secret, but mind 'e don't find out,' I replied.

'I'm past carin' about him now, Kate,' she said bitterly. I wondered at this because although Bill was a Casanova, a liar and a drunkard, I remember Mary would never have a word said against him. Anyway, we sat talking for a long time and I told her about my business and the house in Albert Road. She was pleased to hear that I was expecting a visitor to decide whether I could have the children back. She made tea and I sampled her doughnuts, which were delicious, and I bought two dozen for my workers. Then we kissed and I gave her my address.

'But don't bring 'im,' I warned her and she knew what I meant.

'I won't,' she replied, and as I hurried down the yard I noticed several customers arriving with bags ready for Mary's doughnuts.

I returned the next week to see how she was getting on and to purchase more doughnuts, but when I got near Mary's I saw several women eyeing me up and down. I gritted my teeth and ignored them. Mary was still the same, sleeves rolled up, perspiring as she dipped her doughnuts into the boiling fat and rolled the cooked cakes in sugar. Like me Mary wanted to better herself and neither of us had any reason to be ashamed of wanting to join the ranks of the employers. We'd been downtrodden, starving even, ourselves, and there was little chance that we would forget that in our dealings with our people. There were plenty of Brummies, born in poverty, who pulled themselves up by their own bootstraps. One, now a scrap-metal millionaire, had been sweet on Mary in the old days. Perhaps she should have encouraged him. There was Joe Lucas, who founded the famous engineering firm, who still lived in Carver Street in those days and who my Dad could remember selling tin bowls and kettles from a wheelbarrow. There were plenty more like these. I knew many like them. We didn't have parents who could give us a start in life, nor government grants, nor even social security when we were at rock bottom; just hard work and sink or swim. Unfortunately, Mary never really made it but it was not for want of trying. I haven't got any answers, but the grinding poverty of the old slums did breed some very determined people.

I was doing well enough now to think about getting a small car. Then as luck would have it I bumped into Freddy Jones, an old mate of Frank's, and he happened to mention he had an Austin Seven he wanted to sell.

'Why ask me?' I asked, my suspicions roused.

'Yower Frank ses yer might be interested. It's me own car, an' paid for,' he added in his salesman's patter.

'How much do yer want fer it?' I asked him, still not convinced by a long way.

'Well, I 'ave bin askin' thirty poun' but I'll let yow 'ave it for twenty-five.

'Why do yer want to get rid of it?' I thought it sounded too cheap to be any good.

'It's like this, yer see. I've bin put on the labour an' the kids ain't got any boots on their feet,' he explained.

'All right. When can I see it?' I asked, my doubts answered to some extent.

'I'll bring it round,' he said eagerly. As good as his word, five minutes later he appeared in a black Austin Seven. It was mud-splattered and full of junk but when Freddy saw the look on my face he cried out cheerfully, 'It only wants a good clean out an' it runs like a bird. Jump in an' I'll show yer 'ow ter drive it.'

There was no harm in having a demonstration drive, I thought, and if Frank had recommended him he must be all right. I climbed into the driver's seat full of trepidation. I listened carefully to the instructions and amazingly I set off successfully and did three circuits of the block. When I arrived at the starting point, excited after my first drive, I stopped to exchange a word and then made to set off again.

''Old on! Yow'll be usin' all me petrol an' yoo 'aven't said if yer'll 'ave it yet,' Freddy exclaimed.

'Right. Bring it round to 90 Spencer Street – you'll see my name on the door – an' I'll give you the money.' I had decided to take this opportunity to become mobile and I must admit that the thought of driving about in my own car had me in quite a state of anticipation.

'Thanks Mrs Flood. I'll get the missus ter gi' it a good clean out,' Freddy shouted as he drove off.

That night whan I got home I wondered if I'd done the right thing. It was a battered old banger and I knew nothing at all about motorcars. But it was too late to change my mind now I'd accepted his price, so I put any lingering doubts out of my mind. Freddy kept his promise and arrived with the car the following afternoon and when I went downstairs, there it was, shining black and well cleaned inside and out.

'I've filled 'er up with petrol, Mrs Flood,' he assured me as I climbed into the driver's seat and clutched the wheel again to savour that feeling of having made it that sitting there gives a new car owner.

'Yoo are gooin' ter 'ave it, ain't yer?' he asked.

'Yes, Fred. Stay 'ere while I slip up an' get yer the money,' I said finally.

I didn't have enough cash on hand so I wrote out a cheque to bearer. However, when Freddy saw this he wasn't pleased.

'I carn't tek that. I'll 'ave ter tek the car back if yow ain't got cash.' He sounded annoyed. He needn't have done though, because I'd fallen in love with the car.

'Jump in then,' I smiled, 'an' I'll draw some out of the bank.' We drove round to my branch and I took out twenty-seven pounds and I gave him a pound extra for the petrol and a pound for his wife for cleaning it up for me. He was pleased as punch with this and thanked me. He wanted a lift home so we set off, me needing no excuse to experience the thrill of being behind the steering wheel. On the way I asked what he was going to do with the money.

'First of all I'm goin' ter buy the kids some boots an' things an' then I'm gooin' ter buy vegetables with the rest so's me missus can open up the front room as a shop.' I was pleased to hear that he didn't intend to fritter it away on the horses, because I knew he liked a flutter. He kept his word too; a few weeks later I happened to pass that way and I saw the Joneses' front window full of fruit and vegetables. I stopped and parked and popped in more out of curiosity than anything else. There were several women waiting to be served but when Fred saw me he called his wife to serve me. Then someone piped up, ''Er's gotta tek 'er turn, same as us.'

'That's all right, I can wait.' I knew the pecking order. But Freddy would have none of this and as he carried on I began to redden.

'Yoo serve 'er missus.' Then, looking at the other customers he continued, ''Er's a good wench 'er is. 'Er 'elped ter start me gooin'.' I made an excuse and left but not before I gave him my address and asked him to deliver an order weekly, which he did on his pushbike. Freddy Jones prospered, bought a horse and cart and delivered door-to-door while his wife ran the shop. I always got choice goods and I never regretted buying my first car.

I went everywhere in that old banger. You didn't need a licence to drive in those days so I never passed a test. I could drive quite well considering. However, I made one mistake. I could drive straight and change gears correctly when turning corners but I couldn't reverse for the life of me. One Friday afternoon I went to draw the workers' wages and came out of the bank to discover that there was a dustcart in front and a motor behind so that I could only get out by reversing first. I sat there for nearly two hours and I dozed off. The next thing I knew I felt a hand on my shoulder and when I opened my eyes I saw a policeman standing by the open car door.

'You all right miss?' he inquired in a fatherly tone of voice.

'Y-yes, why?' I managed to say.

'I've been round the block a couple of times and seein' you still here outside the bank, I wondered...' His voice trailed off.

'I'm all right, thanks, Constable.' Now I could see the road was clear I was anxious to be off. He smiled when I added why I'd been parked for so long. No doubt a policeman today wouldn't have seen the joke or if he did he would still have to book me.

Not long after I'd bought the car, on a hot July day I decided to take Mary for a run and I must admit that I wanted Mum's neighbours to see I had a car and so show off a bit. I parked near the school that we had attended and went to fetch my sister. I found her putting out another tray of doughnuts to cool.

'Bleedin' doughnuts an' flower all over the place!' I heard Bill's voice from inside the house.

'They've 'elped ter keep us gooin',' Mary shouted back.

'An' where's me dinner?' he bawled again.

'In the oven! An' yer can get it yerself, yer big an' ugly enough!' Mary was capable of holding her own with her husband.

When they saw me they stopped quarrelling but Bill turned on me.

'An' what d'yoo want? Mrs High and Mighty!'

'You've got nothin' I want! An' if I did want anything, yer'd be the last one I'd ask,' I snapped back.

At that he stood up, put on his cap and made to go out, but when she saw what he was doing Mary questioned him.

'Well, if yer want ter know, I'm goin' tattin'. I've bought meself an' 'orse an' cart,' he replied triumphantly.

'An' where yer think yer gooin' ter keep it?' Mary sounded scornful.

'I've bought some straw an' I'll keep 'er in the brew' ouse.'

This provoked further argument which was brought to a dramatic halt by the intervention of the nag which it appeared Bill had already installed in the temporary stable. There was a loud clatter in the yard and when we'd dashed out to see what it was we found the tin tray on the bricks and the horse hungrily eating the remains of the doughnuts. In a rage Mary snatched up the tray and hurled it towards the luckless horse and although she missed her aim, the horse could see how the land lay and she turned and trotted down the yard and into the street. She was heading for Kiniver's stables, the same stables Granny had hired the horse from when she moved out of our house years before. Mary guessed where Bill had bought the nag and continued to vent her wrath about the ruined doughnuts on Bill.

'An' 'ow much did yer give for that bloody nag?' she screamed, to the amusement of the inevitable crowd that had gathered to be entertained.

'Two quid,' her husband answered defiantly.

'Two pound?' Mary yelled in disbelief, 'why, 'er's only fit fer the knacker's yard. Yer bring it back 'ere an' I'll throw yer both out.'

And with that she marched back indoors, for all the world the spit of our Mum. Bill turned on his heel and ran after his horse and I made excuses and left them to it. Later, I found out that Kiniver had refused to give the horse back because Bill hadn't paid for a bag of oats he had had and a fierce argument had ensued in the course of which the pair had almost come to blows; it was only settled when a bobby appeared on the scene, threatened to arrest Bill and ordered the horse to be taken to the knacker's yard. Thus ended Bill's foray into the rag and bone trade.

12
All's Well That Ends Well

It was during 1938, while I was waiting for Barnardo's to make up their minds to give me my children back that the fears about war were growing. These were fuelled after Hitler invaded the Sudetenland, and nobody was fooled by Mr Chamberlain when he returned with his scrap of paper and promises of 'peace in our time'. Everybody made jokes about Hitler and Chamberlain's paper but the reality of the situation made itself felt when we saw the young lads joining up and the Territorials parading the streets and strutting about pretending to be grown-ups in their ill-fitting uniforms. The sight of them made me feel sick and I became depressed thinking about life in wartime without my children by me. Then came the ultimatum and we were really at war with Germany.

My old banger eventually gave up the ghost in the spring of 1939 and I had to leave it by the side of the road and catch a bus. It was some time since I'd had to use one and I'd forgotten what it was like to travel home on a bus loaded with workers. The conversation was about air-raid shelters and ration books. One old woman was very agitated.

'Gawd 'elp us all. I remember the larst lot. Me 'usband was gassed.'

'Don't worry ma,' an elderly man reassured her, 'it won't larst long this time. It'll be over be Chris'mas, yow'll see.'

'It's the bloody gover'ment wot causes all these bleedin' wars!' exclaimed another old codger. 'But I don't see any of 'em goin' out ter fight. No! That lot live in the lap o' luxury while the young 'uns get theea 'eads blown away. I done me bit in the last bleedin' lot but they ain't gettin' me this time for the King's bloody shillin' an' two bob a day!'

'I was a conchie in the last war an' I 'ad an 'ell of a time with the neighbours. Called me a traitor they did,' ventured another, more forthright than prudent. 'But thank Gawd, I'm 'ere ter tell the tale now,' he continued.

At this a big burly fellow jumped up from his seat and made for the last speaker.

'Tell wot tales?' he yelled down at the unrepentant conscientious objector. 'It was yower bleedin' sort that stayed at um, werkin' an' gettin' rich while others 'ad ter goo ter the front an' fight fer the likes o' yow.' He getting red in the face.

'Somebody 'ad ter go ter the munitions,' the other said timidly.

'Yus! Young girls an' women who 'ad ter leave young babbies. Werked all hours they did, an' my mother was one of 'em,' put in a third.

I believe that they would have come to blows if the conductor hadn't appeared and pushed them back into their seats. This was typical of the sort of talk there was in the final months of 1939.

Production was going over to war work and I had to let some of my girls go because my work went slack as the demand for the luxury enamelled brooches I was making declined. Soon I had too little work to keep going and I had to look for some kind of war work myself. I was fortunate in spotting an advertisement for a contractor to enamel officers' pips. I had a regular order making these for years, as well as other orders for enamelling Auxiliary Fire Service badges, WVS badges and other enamelled items. I had to take on more workers and things were looking up, at least financially; but I was still depressed about the children. It seemed Barnardo's was determined to prevent me ever seeing them again.

Then one day in November 1939 I arrived home to find a letter marked 'Urgent'. I picked it up and tore it open when I saw the postmark; London. It was to inform me that I was to meet the mid-day train from London the next day and that my children would then be handed over to me. I was so excited I couldn't eat or sleep that night. I kept looking at the clock, imagining that it was going slow and thinking that day would never break. Eventually it was time to get up and I went along to the shop, got together the urgent orders and then when the girls arrived I told them I was giving them the day off and why. I locked up the premises and hurried home to light a fire, warm the beds and tidy everything before going to meet the train.

It had been eight long, worrying years since I'd kissed the children goodbye at Dr Barnardo's in Moseley and the Second World War had just begun, not the most auspicious moment to resume a settled family life. In retrospect it seems likely that Hitler had as much to do with Barnardo's deciding I was a fit person to care for my children as anything else. However, I was not thinking about why they were returning that morning as I nervously prepared the house to receive them. I was more anxious about whether they actually remembered me still. Kathleen was now fourteen years old, Jean was twelve and Mary nearly nine. I knew Mary wouldn't know me because she'd been a mere babe in arms when she left, and she showed no signs of recognition on the few occasions I'd seen her since. She'd been fostered out with Jean for about eight years and we'd had no real contact in the interim. I had seen Kathleen more; she'd been there at the homes when I had visited, but these visits had been few in the last years while I had been so busy building up the business.

So mid-day found me waiting on the windy platform, stamping my feet to keep warm and scanning every train that arrived in case I should miss them. The porters got fed up with me inquiring which was the London train only to receive the same reply: 'It'll be 'ere at two.' Then finally it drew into the station, all steam and swirls of smoke. I surveyed the passengers disgorging from the carriages and for a terrible moment doubted whether they were on the train, but then I saw Kathleen step down from an open carriage door and as I ran along the platform towards her I saw two women, holding Jean and Mary by the hand, follow her out of the carriage.

'Hello, Mom,' Kathleen called out as soon as she'd spotted me. I threw my arms round her and we hugged each other. When they saw this the two stern-faced elderly women came towards us.

'Are you Mrs Flood?' one of them inquired.

'Yes,' I replied.

'Sign here,' the other said curtly, handing me a document. I'd been caught by Barnardo's getting me to sign things before and I wasn't going to put my name to this without reading it carefully. When she saw what I was doing the first woman intervened to say that it was simply to say that I had the children safely. She was anxious that I signed it quickly, she explained, because they had to get back aboard before the train continued on its journey as they had other children with them to take on to other destinations. So I did as she asked and without another word the women returned to their carriage, leaving me alone with the somewhat bewildered children.

Jeannie wasn't sure who I was, and Mary had no idea: that was clear from the puzzled expressions on their faces and their silence. Then Katie told them who I was and I kissed each in turn and we made our way back along the platform to the gates.

They were famished, not having had anything to eat since they had left, so I took them into a nearby cafe where they ate ravenously. They were excited and apprehensive and it wasn't until I got them home that they began to settle down.

I stoked the fire and took their coats and berets and while they sat round the fire, taking in their new home, I laid the table with cakes and other goodies I'd bought specially for them. When they'd eaten their fill I took them upstairs to show them their bedrooms and I was relieved to see they were pleased with what they saw.

We had lots to talk about after such a long time: they about their 'aunties' and me about the firm. When Kathleen heard about this she was excited about starting there herself and this is what she did. I taught her the skills involved, how to check the work for quality, how to make out orders, invoices and statements of accounts. She received a wage and was very happy. This suited me because now I had only to attend to the workshop in the mornings and had the afternoons free to be with the children.

Taking care of Jean and Mary was harder than I had

imagined it would be. They seemed restless and couldn't settle down in their new surroundings. I suppose, looking back, that I was a stranger to them; they had been young when they'd left and although they had been well cared for by their 'aunties', they'd been deprived of a mother's affection. It must have seemed as if I had abandoned them to the not-so-tender mercies of the 'mothers' at Barnardo's; they were too small to grasp the situation and probably wouldn't have understood even if they could. Then, out of the blue, they were brought back and here was I lavishing all the care and attention on them I could, trying to make up for the years we'd been apart. Yes, it must have been extraordinarily difficult for them to adjust, especially for Mary, to whom I was literally a complete stranger. I was trying to buy their love and affection and I realised later that I rushed them in my eagerness to develop a maternal relationship with them. I gave them too much, too soon: that was my big mistake and they saw only the gifts and treats, not the love that prompted the giving of them. In short, I spoiled them.

We moved from the rented house into one I had bought, and it was just as well we did because the house in Albert Road was bombed not long afterwards. We fell into a routine of having tea, closing the blackout curtains, then listening to Radio Luxemburg before heading for the shelter to sleep. The problem was that Mary could not settle to life in a city, having been used only to the countryside, and when she came home one day in tears because she was not being evacuated like the other children in her class I relented and agreed to let her go. I was very upset because I was only just beginning to know her and it hurt that she was so keen to leave me, but she was more affected by the Blitz which was then at its height in Birmingham and I decided reluctantly that it would be for the best if she went. During the time she was evacuated I took Jean and Kathleen to see her and I could see that she was happier living in the country than she had been in bombed-out Birmingham.

But troubles with the girls were not over. Jean began to rebel. One night I heard her crying in bed and when I went to see what was the matter with her she turned on me.

'I hate you! I hate you!' she screamed at me as
helpless beside her bed. In truth I had missed out on
motherhood and I didn't really understand the childr
could do was to ask limply, 'Why?'

'I don't like this town, nor the bombing. I want to
to my auntie's in the country,' she wailed.

'But Jean,' I answered, 'I wanted you home here be
thought we could start a new life and be happy togethe

'No! I don't like it here and one day I'm going t
away!' She spurned my attempts to break down the w
resentment that she'd built between us. I attempted to r
with her and I even promised that I would buy a cottage i
country when the war was over, but she just pulled
bedclothes over her head. I was getting nowhere so I retu
downstairs to make a cup of tea and think. I wondered i
done the right thing to bring them away from the coun
where they'd been happy with the two maiden sisters for eigl
years. Perhaps my ambitions for them were simply a reflection of my own selfish desire to have them with me. With the
war at its height and Jean such an obviously self-willed child I
was concerned lest she should take it into her head to run off
one day while I was at the workshop. I didn't know what to
do for the best so I decided to talk it over with Kathleen, who
was now sixteen. She had a bright idea that I hadn't thought
of: why not let Jean come to work with us where an eye could
be kept on her? I put this to Jean and she jumped at the
chance. I paid her a wage and she settled down there and
really enjoyed it. Now she was happy I began to relax too.

We were still spending every night down the shelters. These
were actually the large cellars under the shops along Soho
Road which had been converted from storerooms and are no
doubt still used for this purpose because many of the buildings are still there. During the war anything of use was con-
scripted into the war effort and these makeshift shelters were
second home to us. Some people were Air Raid Wardens but
there was a need for more to volunteer their services; I dearly
wanted to do so, but what with my business and the children I
couldn't find time to do a regular duty. However, I did the

best thing. I called on all the women who were neighbours
ours, except those who had young babies, and organised
m to knock on people's doors and help the old and infirm
the shelters at the first sound of the sirens. Several of us
ganised ourselves into a patrol and we brought back the
ews that everyone wanted to hear, namely that their houses
were still standing. We were given whistles to blow if we were
in trouble and out we went amidst the falling incendiaries to
keep watch.

One of my companions was a young woman named
Phoebe. She was Black Country born and bred, a rough and
ready sort who swore like a trooper. She had a heart of gold
though and we became friends. Many's the time we patrolled
the streets together and it was during these walks that we
exchanged stories: she had had as rough a time as I had. One
night as we walked along the darkened street we paused to
light fags and she said, 'I wundeer wheea my olt mon is
ternight?'

'Why don't 'e come down the shelter, Phoebe?' I asked.

'Not 'im!' she replied with a laugh. ''E's too busy knockin'
it off with some tart. 'E's an 'orny olt bleeda.'

I cannot say I was shocked exactly; such carryings on were
all too common in my experience but I was curious as to why
such a spirited lass as this should put up with that kind of
treatment.

'If 'e's like that why don't you leave 'im?' I asked.

'Well, Kate, 'e brings 'is money um, that's one good fault
'e's got. But I wouldn't care if 'e dain't drink sa much,' she
replied.

'Does he drink a lot then?'

'Drink a lot?' she repeated with a laugh. ''E soaks 'is bloody
bread in it!'

As I began to laugh she nudged me and said, 'Yo ain't 'eard
nothin' yet. One night I was in bed when 'e cum um drunk, it
musta bin about two in the mornin' an' as soon as 'e got in bed
– just in 'is shirt – 'e lit a fag an' fell asleep. It warnt lung afore
I smelt summat bernin'. It was the flock bed smoulderin'.
With thet I kickt 'im outta bed an' ran fer a bucket o' wata.

Well, when I come back 'e was standin' in 'is short shirt with 'is cock in 'is 'and, pissin' over the bed.' At this we both burst into fits of laughter before I recovered enough to ask, 'What 'appened then?'

''E 'ad the bleedin' sauce ter arsk me ter get back in bed with 'im. "Cum on," 'e said, "it's wet but warm."'

'And did yer?'

'I 'ad ter, there wus nowhere else ter goo, but I did manage ter turn the mattress over an' sleep at the foot.' When I continued to laugh she said in mock seriousness, 'Yo'll larf yer bleedin' 'ead off one day when I got time ter tell yer some of 'is antics!'

Phoebe was a great tonic to me on those blacked-out nights and in later years we remained great friends and neighbours. She was dragged up, one of sixteen children, and her father a miner. In turn I told about my own childhood, little better than hers, about the theft of the pig when we went hop-picking, and about Granny. We amused each other for hours with tales about 'the old days', a habit that the reader can see I have not lost.

There was a spirit of camaraderie in the shelters; we had sing-songs to raise our hearts. There was a young woman named Rose Smith; her father owned the cut-glassware shop above, and each night she and her young man would play banjo and concertina while we sang our hearts out to drown out the sound of the bombing. They were a great bunch of characters; often they would slip across to The Freighted Horse for a nip and return tiddly, but who could blame them for trying to remain merry? None of us knew if we would see tomorrow.

While we were out on patrol one night, Phoebe and I called in to my house to fill flasks with cocoa to take back for the children. Suddenly a series of incendiaries rained down nearby. We dashed out to see what damage had been done but in the confusion I lost sight of my friend. I blew my whistle and a second or two later she appeared, tearing down the street carrying two dustbin lids.

'Put this on yer bleedin' 'ead,' she cried out to me over the din, 'while I get a bucket o' sand.' Being unofficial we had no tin hats like the regular Wardens. We looked like a couple of coolies that night, rushing about with buckets of sand, trying to quench the flames. It was real panic stations and no mistake.

I always left my door open, day and night. You could trust everybody in those days. I would leave a big kettle of boiling water on the stove and several cups, milk, tea and sugar on the table for the Wardens to go in and make themselves a cup of tea. There was also a drop of the hard stuff should any of them prefer that to the weaker brew. On quiet nights when there were no raids I would invite the neighbours in for a sing-song. Somebody would play the piano and I would start the ball rolling with one of my jolly songs or a story and soon I had the nickname 'The Merry Widow'.

During April 1941 we had the worst raids. They lasted from dusk to dawn and although we women did our best, the Wardens almost pushed us down the shelters, saying that it was not fit for us to be out. Then the shelters were really crowded with people from all over. Children would be crying and women weeping and all were praying to the Lord to bring us safely through the night. We sang 'The White Cliffs of Dover' and 'Pack up Your Troubles' to keep up our spirits until the morning when the 'All Clear' sounded and we emerged, blinking, into the cold grey light of dawn to survey the night's destruction. Several of our neighbours had been killed in their cellars. This was the nearest the reality of death had come to us so far but I was soon to discover to my shock the personal horror of the Blitz. A Warden came running up, breathless and asked for me by name. When I told him who I was he informed me that Camden Drive had been bombed and that Mary and Mum had both been killed.

The cold, damp walk to the Drive sticks clear in my memory even now. I prayed that the Warden had been mistaken or that it had been another house that had been hit. Although we'd never seen eye-to-eye, blood is thicker than water after all. I stumbled over bricks and rubble where bombs and incendiaries had destroyed buildings in the streets leading to the Drive. Then I came to the top of the hill and could see at once that my worst fears had been realised. There were dozens of people standing about looking dazed; some were weeping quietly. Parties of rescue workers were digging into the rubble for the bodies of victims. I pushed through the crowd until I found myself prevented from going further by an Air Raid Precaution Warden and a fireman. It was only after I'd explained why I was there that they let me through. When I got to the heap of bricks that had been my childhood home I found that Jack, Frank, Charlie and Liza were already there. I asked Jack if the Warden had been right and he nodded sadly. Frank said there was nothing we could do, which was true, but I wasn't satisfied with their explanation of what had happened. I wanted to know why they hadn't been in the shelter in the basement of Stern and Bell's warehouse. Jack answered that no one had had a chance because the bombs fell before the warning had sounded. A few survivors had been dug out but many had suffered the same fate as Mum and Mary.

I didn't stay long but made my way along the cobbled streets; I was angry that they'd died like rats without a chance. They were like plenty of others who struggled along for years through the Depression in the hope of a better tomorrow and this was it. They'd had a brief glimpse of prosperity when the war industries had taken on labour, and the same war had snuffed them out as if they had never been.

However, I had little time to brood because I had to go to check that my business premises were still intact. When I arrived I found that some of the girls had started work. They pointed out a hole in the roof and when I investigated I found an unexploded incendiary bomb under the slates and plaster that littered the floor. I screamed at them to get out at once. They hadn't noticed it there but now they needed no second bidding to collect their gas masks and evacuate the place post-haste. When we were outside I called to some firemen who were shoring up some nearby buildings. They came as cool as you like and carried the bomb out. Luckily for them it turned out to be a dud.

Mum's and Mary's funeral was a few days later. I followed the coffins and saw them buried in Warstone Lane cemetery nearby. It was another bitter April day and there were crowds of mourners. This was not a private occasion. Dozens were buried that day. The coffins were lined up in rows outside the church, stretching back out through the iron gates into the street. The bell clanged all day long. I did not see what my Mum's and sister's injuries were and I was glad to remember them as they were when I last saw them. In fact I didn't visit the site of our yard again for forty years, and when I did the memories it brought back started me writing.

There is little left to tell of my story. The war dragged on for years after that, but the raids stopped and we were to settle down to an almost normal life; that is, if you don't count the rationing and shortages and news of casualties from the various theatres of war. These were far away, though, and I could take some comfort in having Kathleen and Jean with me, and I was in any case fully occupied with the war effort.

When peace broke out in 1945 I fetched Mary home from Wales and I put her in the workshop with her sisters, thinking she would settle down. She wanted to serve in a fruiterer's so I let her but she hopped about from one thing to another, never staying anywhere long. Eventually she entered nursing and I breathed a sigh of relief. She worked with tubercular patients at Selly Oak hospital for a time but she left and went on the buses! She tried hairdressing and later the Women's Royal Airforce. While she was serving in Singapore she met and married a Scotsman and eventually they settled in the USA and raised four sons there.

Jean has four daughters and four grandchildren herself now. She was a very attractive girl and when she was sixteen had the boys after her like flies round a honey pot. I had to keep my eyes open, especially where the Yanks were concerned. You don't need me to repeat the reputation they had. I dare say it was overdone, but I knew of girls who got more than they bargained for by going out with an American. I had no case to worry though; I knew I could trust my girls to take care of themselves and they didn't let themselves or me down. There were some incidents, however. Once I remember a travelling salesman calling with some samples. Kathleen said he'd been before but I hadn't seen him. I was making out an order and could watch as he walked over to the bench where Jean was working. They exchanged words and I saw Jean shake her head and blush. At this I intervened and asked him what he wanted.

'I only asked her if I could take her out for a ride in the car. May I?' he added.

'No yow may not,' I told him firmly, leaving him in no doubt.

'There'd be no harm,' he insisted smoothly. 'I'd have brought her back safe.'

'Maybe you would and maybe not. But she's scarcely sixteen and you're probably a married man.' I gave him the flea in the ear he deserved and he took his order and left. Later I discovered that he'd given Jean a gold chain and pendant but she'd been too scared to tell me and had flushed it down the toilet.

My son returned safe after the war and he married a Scots girl and they have four children and six grandchildren now. Kathleen is happily married and she and her husband now live with me, so you could say that all in all, despite some sticky patches, I've had a successful life. I have twelve grandchildren and ten great grandchildren. My one regret is that I missed out on Kathleen, John, Jean and Mary's childhood but I can do nothing about that now. I have got lots to be pleased about. I have many dear friends and to cap it all I am an author whose work, I am told, has been enjoyed by many people. My original ambition that my people should not be forgotten has been achieved and now, a week away from my eighty-second birthday, I have only that one nagging regret: the loss of those years half a century ago when my children needed a mother's care and love so much.